Intellectual Growth

ABOUT THE AUTHOR

PANNEER SELVAM is born in Salem - Valappady of Tamil Nadu. He started his career as school teacher in New Delhi in the year 1991. He joins as lecturer in DIET, perundurai of Erode in 2000. Bharathiyar University were gave the Philosophy in Doctorates in Language and Education. He is the seventh diploma holder from National University of Educational Planning and Administration (NUEPA), New Delhi in 2002. In 2005, the Tamil Nadu government was given the 'Excellence Award' for his unrivalled teaching activities and some organization also. He has published more than hundreds of Research Papers and books in the field of Education. At present he is working in the department of Education, Bharathidasan University, Tamil Nadu.

ABOUT THE BOOK

Education is a process of human empowerment for the achievement of better and higher quality of life. It tells man how to think and how to make decisions. Training of a human mind is incomplete without Education. Only through the attainment of Education, Man is enabled to receive information from the external world, to acquaint him with past history and receive all necessary information regarding the present. Education is an important social activity planned and shared by the parents and the society. Education is a process of learning to live the life of a community Education has been defined by different people in different ways. A search for knowledge cannot yield something meaningful if this relation with the existing knowledge has not been examined. A research study is never conducted in a vacuum. Hence an attempt was made, as far as possible, to find out what has already been done. A review of literature gives both thematic as well as methodological direction. Adolescence, usually characterized by the youthful exuberance as its most endearing hallmark is a transition period between childhood and adulthood.

❐

Intellectual Growth

Dr. S.K. Panneer Selvam
Assistant Professor, Department of Education
Bharathidasan University, T.N.,India

AMIGA PRESS INC.

AMIGA PRESS INC.
H.O:- 28-A, Indra Park, St.No-9
Near-Chander Nagar, Krishna Nagar
Delhi: - 110051 (India)
Tel: - 011-22504028, +91-98736-57000
Email: - amigapress@gmail.com
info@amigapress.co.in
amigaeditorial@gmail.com
amigapub@gmail.com

Website: - www.amigapress.co.in

This edition is published by Amiga Press Inc.

ISBN: 978-93-84533-65-6

First Published 2020

Printed and bound in India by Replika Press Pvt. Ltd.

Contents

1. Awareness on Yoga Education 1

Definitions of education; Yoga; Meaning of yoga; Definitions of yoga; Nature of yoga; The aim of yoga; Concept of yoga; Importance of yoga; Stages of yoga; Statement of the problem; Background of the study; Operational definitions of the terms; Higher secondary students; Namakkal district; Objectives of the study; Hypothesis of the study; Scope of the study; Delimitation of the study; Organization of the thesis; Conclusion.

2. Review of Related Literature 14

Review of related literature; Purpose of review literature; Indian studies on yoga; Analogy; Conclusion.

3. Methodology of the Study 28

Overview; Design of the study; Objectives of the study; Hypothesis of the study; Tools used for the study; Preliminary draft of the tool; Pilot study; Reliability and validity; Personal data sheet; Size of the sample; Administering the tool; Scoring key; Statistical measures used in the study Delimitations of the study; Conclusion.

4. Awareness on Yoga Education 34

Analysis and interpretation; Descriptive analysis; Differential analysis; Level of significance; Conclusion.

5. Awareness on Yoga Education **39**
Findings, conclusions and recommendations; The study in retrospect; Methodology in brief; Restatement of the problen; Objectives of the study Major finding of the study; Conclusion of the study; Recommendations;Sugg-estions; Education implication; Discussion; Areas of research for the future; Conclusion.

6. The Problem and its Perspective **43**
Social maturity; The nature of social maturity; Social maturity and adolescents; Characteristics of social maturity; Importance of social maturity; Emotional competence; Definition of competency; Features of competency; Competencies in life situations; Competencies to be developed; Adolescents and emotional behaviour; Emotional competence; Personal competence; Elf management; Relational competence; Relational management:; Self-actualization; Definitions of self-actualization; Maslow's basic principles:; Self actualization; Self actualization needs; Characteristics of self-actualized people:; Statement of the problem; Definitions of technical terms; Operational definition; Need and significance of the study; Objectives of the study; Limitations of the study; Conclusion.

7. Review of Related Literature **68**
Importance of the review of related literature; Studies related to social maturity; Studies related to emotional competence; Studies related to self actualization; Conclusion.

8. Design of the Study and Method of Investion **87**
Statement of the problem; Design and method of the study; Hypotheses of the study; Tools used in the study; Rao's social maturity scale; Emotional competence scale; Self actualization scale; Sambling design; Pilot study; Estabilishing reliability and validity; Validity; Main study; Statistical techniques used in this study; Mean; Standard deviation; 'T' test; F-test; Conclusion.

9. Analysis and Interpretation of Data **97**
Analysis of social maturity, emotional competence and self-actualization scores; Testing of hypotheses; Social maturity; Inference; Emotional competence; Inference; Self-actualization; Inference; Inference; Influence of family income on self actualization; Inference; Correlation between social maturity and emotional competency; Inference; Correlation between the social maturity and self actualization; Inference; Correlation between the emotional competency; Inference; Conclusion.

10. Conclusion **114**
Statement of the problem; Objectives of the study; Hypotheses of the study Sample for the study; Tools used in the study; Limitations of the study;

Major findings of the study; Educational implications; Suggestions for further study; Conclusion.

11. The Problem and its Perspectives **121**
The concept of personal growth; Definitions of personal growth; Characteristic of personal growth; Concept of the coping behavior; Meaning of coping behavior; Definition of coping behavior; Characteristic of coping behavior; Coping mechanism; Harmful coping method; Meaning of socio-economic status; The concept of socio-economic status; Definition of socio-economic status; Definition of stress; Causes of stress on students; Academic stressors; Means of academic stress; Statement of the problem; Operational definitions of the key terms; Objectives of the study; Significance of the study; Delimitations of the study; Conclusion.

12. Review of Literature **134**
Studies related to personal growth;Studies related to coping behavior; Studies related to socio-economic status; Studies on academic stress; Conclusion.

13. Research Design and Methods **148**
Design of the study; Variables selected; Hypotheses of the study; Method of the study; Research tools selected for present study; Descripition and scoring procedure of the tools used in the present study; Personal growth initiative scale; Coping behavior inventory; Socio economic status scale; Academic stress inventory; Pilot study; Establishing reliability and validity of tools used; Sample; Main study; Statistical techniques used; Conclusion.

14. Analysis and Interpretation of the data **158**
The major categorisation of the sample based on the major variable of the study; Inference; Categorisation of the sample based on coping behavior; Inference; Categorisation of the sample based on socio-economic status; Inference; Categorisation of the sample based on academic stress; Inference; Correlaton between socio-economic status and academic stress; Inference; Conclusion.

15. Findings and Summary **180**
Statement of the problem; Objectives of the study; Hypotheses of the studyResearch tools selected for present study; Major findings of the study; Educat-ional implications; Delimitations of the study; Suggestions for the further study; Conclusion.

16. Introduction **188**
Sgsy methodology

17. Review of Literature **214**
Impact of nregs.

18. Research Methodology **219**
Area profile ariyalur district; Nregs; Operational definitions.

19. Statistical Analysis and Findings **229**

20. Discussion **252**
Conclusion.

Bibliography **258**

❐

1

Awareness on Yoga Education

Education is a process and it is a continuous, complex, dynamic and lifelong process. The importance of Education has been realized by everyone and every nation. The root meaning of Education is given as bringing up or leading out or making manifest the inherent potentialities in a pupil. Broadly speaking, education refers to any act or experience that has a formative effect on the personality of an individual. The role of Education is to make growth and development in the individual's life. It includes that all the influence which act upon an individual during his passage from cradle to grave. In other words Education is life and life is Education. It is not giving of facts and detain alone, but it is a man making process.

Education is the process by which people acquire knowledge, skills, habits, values or attitude. It is the chief means of acquiring and teaching the essential knowledge and skills. Education is very closely liked with solving social problems such as improvement in the state of health, population control, and the eradication of poverty, thus constituting a major to a country is socio-economic development, and as such it represents one of the most important in international co-operation.

Knowledge in basic skills, academics, technical, discipline, citizenship Our society says only academic basics are important and that is based on collecting knowledge without understanding its value. the processing of knowledge, using inspiration, visionary ambitions, creativity, risk, ability to bounce back from failure, motivation There is a huge disconnected gap and this is a problem for high school students in particular answer is, all elements in the opening paragraph and more, relate to education and all should be considered. In short, Education is a dynamic in the life of every individual, influencing his physical, mental, social, emotional and ethical development.

Education is an important social activity planned and shared by the parents and the society. Education is a process of learning to live the life of a community Education has been defined by different people in different ways. The meaning of education has been changing according to people, places and times. Some took education to mean the process, others the result, still others the methodology. Since the concept has changed the definitions have also changed. Yet, there are certain definitions, which are all time popular and also acceptable.

A compare hensive definition of education must take into consideration a few factors. The are i) The individual who is to be educated and ii) The society in which education is to take place. Education can be best described as "the nature of personal growth". When Education is considered as the conservation transmission and renewal of entire culture, then it becomes an instrumental by which a community maintains itself.

Education is a process of human empowerment for the achievement of better and higher quality of life. It tells man how to think and how to make decisions. Training of a human mind is incomplete without Education. Only through the attainment of Education, Man is enabled to receive information from the external world, to acquaint him with past history and receive all necessary information regarding the present. Without Education, man is as though in a closed room and with education he finds himself in a room with all its windows open towards outside world.

Developing multimedia Course ware in teaching exercise Physiology for physical Education major – May 2006

DEFINITIONS OF EDUCATION

- "Aristotle" - has defined education as "creation of a sound mind in a sound body"
- "Pestalozzi"- defined education as a "natural harmonious and progressive development of men's innate power's
- "Mahatma Gandhi"- wrote, "by Education, I mean an all round drawing out of the best in child and man body, mind and spirit".
- "Vivekananda"-"Education means the manifestation of divine Perfection already existing in man".

- "John Dewey"-Education is the development of all those capacities in the individual which will enable him to control his environment and fulfil his possibilities.

YOGA

Yoga is one of the gifts of our rich heritage. Dr. Radhakrishnan said, "Yoga is a way of life". It is a system that makes us cultured human beings. The value of yoga is not doubt immeasurable, and now – a – days yogic training is being more and more recognized especially as India's unique contribution to physical Education activities, yoga is a scientific and systematic discophile for a successful organization of all the energies and faculties of internal human being with a view to attaining the highest caustic communion with the cosmic reality of god. Yoga is an ancient practice combining meditation with training the body which originated in India five thousand year ago (vikneskar & kuvalayananda, 1971)

Yoga the science of man based on our ancient wisdom and culture has laid down technology consisting of various psycho physiological processes for dealing with the body – mind complex. It tries to harmonious and physical Benefits of yogasanans: a) The endow cranial system is controlled and regulated and correct quantities of different hormones are secreted from all glands in the body b) Through regular practice, in paired organs can be rejuvenated and carry out their normal functioning, c) systems like circulatory, respiratory, nervous, excretory, glandular, muscles, and bones are coordinated to help one another.

Yogic practices helped to deal with delinquency and criminal behavior and improved academic performance. Yoga was helpful to deal with headache, meditation intake and symptoms of stress perception. Yoga helped to solve the confusion between self-ideal disparity and ideal self. Yoga helped to decrease anxiety level in the gymnastic group. It helped to improve the mental health and emotional maturity of adolescent girls hatha yoga improved and fastened a psychophysical balance. The modern yoga students understand the importance of this ancient tradition, it is effective in reducing stress using breathing exercises and mindful meditation, reducing stress using breathing exercises and mindful meditation, reducing anxiety level and improving mental health, improving mental health and self-concept and reducing stress using breathing exercises and mindful meditation reducing anxiety level and improving mental health, improving mental health and self-concept, and reducing anxiety and improving adjustment. Yoga and meditation enhance self-esteem, self-disclosure, improves emotional intelligence and enhances social adjustment of jail inmates, and helped to decrease depression. So, yogic practices help to improve physical health, reduce anxiety, depression, and stress, and improve mental health, self-concept and emotional maturity of individuals. Yoga is the richest and noblest legacy the ancient Indians have gifted to the world. It is a timeless programmatic science; it is an experimental science; it is an age old science; it is a culture –cum-science; it is the grandest of all sciences; it is the science of the integral man; it is the science of sciences. It is the mother of all sciences. Yoga is the culture of tomorrow.

Yoga is a method of education in the society. It is an art of successful living. It is a way of healthy living at all levels. It is a tool for positive change. It is the remedy for all worldly miseries. It is the science of creativity and personality development. It is a voyage of discovering truth or knowing the reality. It is a utilitarian commodity. Yoga is a total experience of human life. Thus, yoga is as old as civilization. Yoga is as old as mankind. Yoga is creation. Yoga is intimate and ultimate.

Yoga in India has a long history. Its earliest beginnings are lost in the obscuring of ancient Indian history. Yoga is a universal way of life, which in above all castes. Creeds, regions, languages and nations. It is an education that completely provides human beings good health for better living. Yoga is a health providing activity having its influence in all aspects of health, namely physical, mental and spiritual.

Developed in India, yoga is a psychophysical discipline with roots going back about 5,000 years. Today, most yoga practices in the west focuses on the physical postures called "Asanas", breathing exercise called "Pranayama", and meditation. However, there's more to it than that, and the deeper your go the richer and more diverse the tradition becomes. The word "yoga" means union linguistically; it is related to the old English "yoke". Traditionally, the goal of yoga is union with the Absolute, known as Brahman, or with Atman, the true self. These days the focus is often on the more down to – earth benefits of yoga, including improved physical fitness, mental clarity, greater self – understanding, stress control and general well being. Spirituality, however it is a strong underlying, theme to most practices. The beauty of yoga is in its versatility, allowing practitioners to focus on the physical, psychological or spiritual, or a combination of all three. For thousands of years yoga was a secret technique with little or no written material and was practiced by memorization and demonstration from the Guru to the Discipline. Yoga was a special feature of the Dravidian civilization. They mainly really upon the evidence brought forward by the of the Indus civilization. Certain relics like that of mother Goddess, and certain phallic symbols suggest a type of tundra yoga. Certainly yoga must have been much older than the archaeological record, which is the only reliable source we have at present.

Yoga is said to be an integral subjective science. Its division into spiritual, mental and physical cannot be separated from each other. The word yoga is derived from the Sanskrit root "yujir" meaning to 'yoke' or 'union' or 'to join'. Yoga is equanimity and control of the senses and the mind. Yoga is a spiritual technique, a way, a path, a method that has something to offer to everyone, religions and the non- religious, men and women irrespective of age and faith. Yoga is a way to a healthier, happier and harmonious life.

Yoga has a complete message of humanity it has a message for the human body. It has a message for the human mind and it has also a message for the human soul. Will intelligent and capable youths come forth to carry this: message to every individual not only in India, but also in every other part of the world".

Efficiency and performance quotient. Yoga is one of the greatest disciplines in the world and can be practiced at each stage with positive results. It aims at controlling one's physical, mental and spiritual climate. The circulation of blood, the degree of tension in the muscles and in the nerves is all subjected to progressive control (Devi, 1994).

The main aim of yoga is integrating the body mind and thoughts, so as to work for good ends. In our modern life style the human body is easily affected by many diseases, mostly due to our food habits, daily routines, and also because of air and water pollution, etc. through systematic and regular yoga practices our body may be made healthier and its resistance power to fight against the diseases could be enhanced mind gets sharpened, and the concentration and memory power may be developed. Thus, power of mind could be realized for thinking the right good thoughts. Then the good and healthy thoughts can develop in the right direction. Yoga paves the way for an individual to do any action peacefully and perfectly. The main objectives of the yogic practices are making a man from diseases, ignorance, egoism, miseries, the affiliation of old age, fear of survival and so forth. In recent times yoga has become integral part of physical education and sports. Athletes and sportsman are mentally prepared and physically warmed up by yogic techniques to improve their efficiency in their performance in the play ground.

People who start yoga usually find that after a few weeks they feel more robust and energetic, lighter and springier. The postures directly affect the muscles, joints and skin but also the whole organism glands, never, internal organs, bones, circulation and respiration.

Yogic techniques, which aim at physical and mental self – culture, have convincing scientific bares and produce consistent physiological changes. It has been reported that yoga's are capable of achieving remarkable, feats of endurance and controlling their autonomic functions. There is evidence that the practice of yoga improves cardiac – respiratory

MEANING OF YOGA

The word yoga is derived from the Sanskrit root yuj meaning to mind, Join, attach and yoke, to direct and concentrate one's attention in to use and apply. It also means union or communion. It is the true union of our will with the will of God. It thus means the yoking of all the power of body, mind and soul to God, it means the disciplining of the intellect, the mind the emotions, the will, which that yoga presupposes, it means a poise of the soul which enables one to look at life in all it is aspects evenly.

The word yoga is derived from the Sanskrit root 'YUJIR' meaning to 'yoke' (or) 'union' (or) 'to join' a combination of body, mind and thought. In due course of time the body is opting to deteriorate and succumb to diseases. Mind is life, it can be used for good purpose or for bad purposes. It remains warring and gets no peace. By proper and regular yogic practices, the body becomes healthier and increases its resistance power to diseases yoga sharpens the intellect and increases the power of concentration and purifies the soul. Thus the body, mind and the soul gets unified and works for the betterment of a harmonious life.

The Bhagavath Gita also gives other explanations of the term yoga and lays stress up on karma yoga. It is said work alone is your privilege, never the fruits there of Never let the fruits of action be your motive and never case to work. Work in the name of the Lord, abandoning selfish desires. Be not affected by success or failure, this equipoise is called yoga.

Yoga is not for him who gorges too much, not for him who starves himself. It is not for him who sleeps too much, not for him who stays awake. By moderation in eating and in resting, by regulation in working and by regulation in working and by concordance in sleeping and awaking, yoga destroys all pain and sorrow. Yogi stages are practices and followed in life, virtues like mortality, morally sound conduct and good character are developed in man. Be sides there is all round progress in human life, physically intellectually and spiritually and man attains physical fitness and mental equanimity.

DEFINITIONS OF YOGA

- Swami Sivananda- "Yoga is universal in its application leading to an all round development of body, mind and soul."
- Sri Aurobindo - "Yoga is a methodical effort towards self perfection by the development of the potentialities of the individuals."
- Bhagavad Gita - "Yoga is a power of creation."
- Krishnamoorthy- " Yoga is awareness".
- Patanjali- " Yoga is a process of gaining control over the mind", "Clarity of thought is yoga."

- Amarakosa- " Yoga is training in the techniques of Harmony and also a preparation for the total integration of human personality."
- Vyasa Bhashya- "Yoga implies integration of the personality of man as a whole."
- Swami Nithyananda- "Yoga is the ultimate practice for body, mind and being."

NATURE OF YOGA

Yoga is one of the six systems of Hindu philosophy. Unlike so many other philosophies of the world, it is a philosophy that is wholly practical.

Yoga philosophy holds not only the answers to all problems, but also offers a scientific way to transcend his problems and suffering. The philosophy of yoga is caring, sharing and empowering. Yoga philosophy provides knowledge, strength, solace and peace. The purpose of yoga is to overcome ignorance and gain awareness of self. Western traditions of health and healing have tended to separate body and mind. But yoga tradition has a very strong link between the two.

Yoga helps man to have power to cure his disease as well as to control his premature death. Where all the methods of modern medical treatment fail, the yogic treatment succeeds. Hatha yoga has the capacity to replace medical hospitals. Science is partially unified knowledge; yoga is completely unified knowledge.

Yoga has been designed in such a way that it can complete the process of evolution of the personality in every possible direction. That is why yoga has so many paths- Hatha yoga, Karma yoga, Bhakthi yoga, Raja yoga, Jnana yoga, Kundalini yoga and so on. Yoga helps to reach the highest state of Ananda. Ananda means moral, divine and intellectual perfection. Yoga way of life is an experience which cannot be understood intellectually and will only become living knowledge through practice and experience. It leads to super-consciousness.

Yoga thus has transformed this earth the play ground of animal-men into a play ground of godly men. It enhances the practice of any religion. it is a way of life for the followers of all religions. Yoga has become into its own. Thus, yoga enhances spirituality.

THE AIM OF YOGA

According to the Yoga Sutras of Patanjali, the ultimate aim of Yoga is to reach "Kaivalya" (emancipation or ultimate freedom). This is the experience of one's innermost being or "soul" (the purusa). Then one becomes free of chains of cause and effect (Karma) which tie us to continual reincarnation. In Kaivalya one is said to exist in peace and tranquillity, having attained absolute knowledge of the difference between the spiritual which is timeless, unchanging and free of sorrows, and the material which is not.

This is considered desirable as life is analyzed as ultimately full of sorrows and pain even pleasure and joy leave pain and loss when they have gone as nothing in the material world is permanent.

Yoga is therefore a spiritual quest. However, along the path of path of yoga, the aspirant also gains health, happiness, tranquillity and knowledge which are indicators of progress and an encouragement to continue their practice. Buddhism and other Eastern spiritual traditions use many techniques derived from yoga.

CONCEPT OF YOGA

Yoga is one of the world's oldest branches of spiritual inquiry and one of the long – standing, most intense experiments on the human spirit.

The word "yoga" comes from the Sanskrit root "yuj" which means to "yoke" or "To join together". It is a technique to join the body, mind and spirit and to create a feeling of union. Yoga can also be defined as "Mindfulness", or process of directing the attention towards whatever it is we are doing at the moment.

Yoga is a method o training designed to lead to integration or union. It includes physical exercise, but its ultimate goal is the yoking of individual soul to universal spirit. Although yoga today is often taught and practiced as a pursuit for health and fitness in order to accommodate a changing world, the spiritual roots still nourish today's authentic yoga.

Aim of yoga is the attainment of the physical, mental and spiritual health. Yoga is one of the orthodox systems of Indian philosophy, was systematized by Patanjali in his yoga sutra. He advocated the eight – fold path of yoga, popularly Known as "Ashtanga yoga" for all – round development of human personality. They are Yama (restraint), Niyama (Observance of austerity), Asana (Physical Posture), Pranayama (Brething Exercise), Pratyahara (Restraining the Sense Organ), Dharana (contemplation), Dhyana (Meditation) and Samadhi.

IMPORTANCE OF YOGA

The body becomes strong and healthy, excursive fat disappears, the face glows, the eyes are bright and the whole personality radiates a special charm. The whole body is purified and the mind improves in ability to concentrate of the importance are:

- The blood in the different blood vessels is purified through different yoga sanas.
- Yogasanas helps the mind to experience tranquillity .This is progressive intellectual development because of the calm mind.

STAGES OF YOGA

The proper function of the body depends on the several limbs. The absence or the sickness of any one limb affects the health of the whole body. The same principle applies to the study of yoga and its branches. Any inadequacy in the study and the perfection of any the eight steps of yoga will not lead to self – realization.

NEED FOR THE STUDY

Education is the only way to boost yoga awareness. In the long run, Behavior can be modified through the process of Yoga Education. Yoga education would have to aim t producing a health, creating a constituency of yoga-oriented people that is knowledgeable regarding the physical and problem, aware of how to solve these problems and motivated enough to work towards their solution. Such a challenge has to be taken up by educational institutions, and among these, universities and colleges will have to show the leadership.

It is vital to effectively educate man regarding his relationship to the total environment, the relationship which is based on than on superior-subordinate relationship. Hence major goals of yoga education should be to help individuals acquire.

The basic responsibility of the society and government to work for solving yoga problems.

Development of yoga ethics which will motive people to participate in the decision-making process and to demand protection of the yoga so as to advance human welfare and dignity.

Yoga education should aim to provide factual information to students which will lead to the understanding of the intricate system of health balance and man's place in it. Namakkal education district is situated in the coast of Tamil Nadu. It is an educational area. This induced the investigator to make an attempt to study the awareness on yoga among the higher secondary students at Namakkal educational district.

This is an age of science; every human being on the earth is the product of science and technology. Science has made man luxurious by providing comforts of physical life. Due to the materialistic attitude is leading the modern man to the life bondage, miseries, gain, money, reputation and selfishness. Today, we have overstrained ourselves and it may result in body or mind breakdown. In such a condition a person needs timely guidance for diversion of his mind towards creative channel to save himself from disaster of entering the dark world of miseries, frustrations etc. Hence, the need of yoga appears. It can certainly be proved as a big blessing to provide mental, physical and spiritual health and complete well-being. Yoga provides individual with refreshing positive thinking, self-confidence, analytical approach, smooth and calm mental stage with emotional stability and strong will power. Effects of yoga exercises is no doubt vary wide and it influences every activity of an individual.

STATEMENT OF THE PROBLEM

Yoga awareness is of keeping the importance of keeping the health clean and mind relaxation. So the study focuses on the topic entitled "A study higher secondary school students at Namakkal Educational District

BACKGROUND OF THE STUDY

In view of increasing importance of the yoga, students who are the citizens of the nation and will be employed in various walks of life cannot afford to keep themselves from this potential medium. the government has therefore, decided to provide the yoga education by importing profound knowledge and skills developing positive attitude and interest in the yoga.

Today our educational system is knowledge and examination oriented that test only the rote memory of the students. the effective domain such as attitudes is neglected in our teaching. thus the children should also be encouraged to developed positive attitude towards yoga. hence the main outcome of the introduction of yoga is the inculcation of proper attitude towards it. therefore, the present investigation has been undertaken with a view to find out how far the attitude of yoga education developed among higher secondary students.

OPERATIONAL DEFINITIONS OF THE TERMS

Awareness

Paraphrasing Webster's congenital dictionary. Awareness implies vigilance in observing something or experience and alertness in drawing inference from what one observes. Awareness in a personal development sense is a consciousness impact that you are being and the impact that you are having on others. Higher your awareness by imaging a small creature on your shoulder who watches over what you think and what he observes in your ear.

Yoga

Yoga is one of the greatest disciplines in the world and can be practiced at each stage with positive results. It aims at controlling one's physical, mental and spiritual climate. The circulation of blood, the degree of tension in the muscles and in the nerves is all subjected to progressive control (Devi, 1994).

Yoga Awareness

It is a state of being conscious about yoga. It may be defined as to help the individual to gain variety of information and experiences to acquire basic knowledge and understanding of yoga and problems associated with it.

HIGHER SECONDARY STUDENTS

After the completion of the high school level of education, students enter the secondary level. (i.e) in standard XI in higher secondary school. New they attain the adolescence stage as teenagers.

NAMAKKAL DISTRICT

Since Namakkal is a growing busionalized and educational town it is apt for the study.

OBJECTIVES OF THE STUDY

The following objectives were formulated for the present study.

- To find out the yoga awareness of higher secondary school students in Namakkal Educational District.
- To find out the significance difference in the yoga awareness of Boys and girls (gender)
- Locality of the student (Rural & Urban)
- Types of the school (Government & Metric)
- Parent's occupation (Government & Private)
- Subjects. (Arts & science)

HYPOTHESIS OF THE STUDY

- There is no significant difference between boys and girls towards awareness on yoga.
- There is no significant difference between rural boys and girls towards awareness on yoga.
- There is no significant difference between urban boys and girls towards awareness on yoga.
- There is no significant difference between Government school boys and girls towards awareness on yoga.
- There is no significant difference between Matriculation school boys and girls towards awareness on yoga.
- There is no significant difference between Government occupation of male and female parents towards awareness on yoga.
- There is no significant difference between private occupation of male and female parents towards awareness on yoga.

- There is no significant difference between arts group boys and girls towards awareness on yoga.
- There is no significant difference between science group boys and girls towards awareness on yoga.

SCOPE OF THE STUDY

The topic is an investigation of the awareness of yoga among higher secondary students at Namakkal District .this is the survey study. The investigation attempt to know the awareness on yoga among higher secondary school students at Namakkal District.

This study will be of great help for the education particularly for the teacher since teacher since the concept of education has been changing from time to time.

The awareness may different student to student. One can learn and do anything with involvement only when he had a better awareness towards it. In this content investigator attempts to study the awareness on yoga in higher secondary student in various categories

DELIMITATION OF THE STUDY

1. The study has been limited to NamakkaL District only.
2. The study has been restricted to the higher secondary school students only
3. This study has been restricted to the 11th standard students only
4. This study adopted survey method using questionnaires to collect data from respondents
5. A purposive stratified random sample was used to choose the subject to be included in the study
6. This study is focused mainly on the Variables, Gender, Locality, Various subjects, Types of schools, Parents occupations.

The ensuring chapter deals with the data analysis of the study

ORGANIZATION OF THE THESIS

The report of the thesis will be presented according to be following sequences.

The first chapter gives introduction, definition of terms, statement of problem, Hypothesis objectives and Delimitation of the study.

Second chapter deals with the review of related literature which are done in India and abroad related to this problem.

Third chapter gives a detailed account of research procedures and methodology used in this problem.

Fourth chapter deals with the tabulation of analysis and the interpretations of the data in detail.

Fifth chapter describes the findings, conclusion and certain recommendations about the problem.

This is followed by the Bibliography and appendices which consist of the told used for the problem and the related matters.

CONCLUSION

In this chapter the investigator described the statement of the problem taken for the research study, objectives of the study delimitations of the sturdily and need for the study.

In the following chapter, a review of related literature and studies conducted in relevant areas will fol.

❒

2

Review of Related Literature

A good thesis is one that how to replicate or extend the previous work with improvements to reduce bias, eliminate flaws consider pertinent variables, settle unsolved issues to check contradictory or uncertain finding". The aim of this chapter is to record briefly a survey of literature related to the problems under study. It is necessary to enter on any research project. This will help in understanding the various aspects of the problem.

The purpose of this chapter is to record briefly the findings of research studies carried out on various topics that are related to the problem under study. An essential of research project is the review of the related literature In the words of Good,the key to the vast store house of published literature may open doors to sources of significant problems and explanatory hypotheses and provide helpful orientation for definition of the problem, back ground for selection of procedure, and comparative data for interpretation of results. In order to be truly creative and original, one must read extensively and critically as stimulus thinking.

The research worker must be acquainted with up-to-date information about what has been thought and done in the specific area from which he intends to take up a problem of research. A review of related literature gives the scholar an understanding of the previous work that has been done in the area, it enables him to know the means of getting to the frontier in the field of his problems, methods and limitations and it enables him to locate comparative data useful in the interpretation of results.

Review of related literature is an essential step in educational research, in reflective thinking; the second step is the survey of all ready available data that should also be considered as a necessary step which would enable the researcher to base his rational argument for the justification of the study.

REVIEW OF RELATED LITERATURE

A review of related literature is a direction to find out the reality and the beneficial nature and the reliability of a work undertaken, keeping in mind the material that are available in connection with the topic. A review will give the investigator a vivid idea of what he should do and how he should go about his investigation. Clarke, D.H and Clarke, H.H. (1970) gave the importance of review of related literature as that of before completing a plan for a research understanding, the investigator needs to conduct a literature search in the area of the proposed investigations.

The review of related literature is an instrument in the selection of the topic formulation of hypothesis and defective reasoning leading to the problem. It helps to get a clear idea and supports the findings with regard to the problem under study (Tirumalai Swamy1995).The research scholar had come across several books, periodicals, journals, internet and unpublished thesis while searching for relevant facts and findings that are related to this present study. Such of these facts are given below for a better understanding and to justify his study.

The phrase Review of literature consists of two words Review and Literature of a particular are of any discipline which includes theoretical practical and its research studies. The literature in any field forms the foundation upon which all future work will be build. If we fail to build foundations of knowledge provided by the review of literature one work is likely to be shadow and that has already done better by someone else.

A search for knowledge cannot yield something meaningful if this relation with the existing knowledge has not been examined. A research study is never conducted in a vacuum. Hence an attempt was made, as far as possible, to find out what has already been done. A review of literature gives both thematic as well as methodological direction. In a rare case a study may justify accomplishment of a new knowledge without paying attention to what has been done carrier. In an age where we already find vast store of knowledge, it is necessary to examine what has been done before we boast of a new achievement (Barotia and Sharma, 1999). Hence, a brief review of the studies related to the present problem is described in this chapter.

PURPOSE OF REVIEW LITERATURE

The following are the some of the purposes of the review of literature.

- It provides ideas, theories, explanations or hypothesis valuable in formulation the problem.
- To avoid the risk of duplicating some of the studies already undertaken.
- To suggest methods or research methodology appropriate to the problem.
- It widens the horizon of the researcher.
- It suggests valuable basis for hypothesis.
- It helps delimit the problem.
- It helps the investigator not to allow the mistake (or) pit fall which occurred in the previous findings.
- To locate comparative data useful in the interpretation of results.
- It contributes to the investigator for the general scholarship.
- It helps to locate data that can be used in comparative interpretation of results

INDIAN STUDIES ON YOGA

Bhole et al., (1970) – found the yogic exercises significantly improving the vital capacity. It was reported that significant increase in hemoglobin contents of the blood and the lymphycytes after yogic treatment (significance level 5% noted).

Udupa (1971) and others selected twelve subjects and gave Hatha yoga practices for a period of three months and they found that lower level of pulse rate was maintained for three months. It was concluded that physical stress of fast running had increased the pulse rate the difference was not statistically significant.

Pollock (1971) and others conducted a study on effects of waling on body composition and cardiovascular function of middle aged men. In this study sixteen sedentary men were trained four days per week for twenty weeks. The vigor of walking was progressively increased in accordance with the tolerance of each individual by the last week, the men averaged 4.7 miles per hour sub stained improvement occurred in maximum oxygen consumption sub – maximal heart rate and resting diastolic blood pressure and reductions of body weight and present of fat, showing that vigorous waling can be effective as an adult training activity.

Gopal (1973) and others studied the effect of yogasanas and pranayamas on blood pressure, pulse rate and some respiratory function. Two groups of male volunteers 20-33 years in age and having the same average height and weight were studied. The experimental group consisted of 14 subjects in yogasanas and pranayamas for a period of six weeks. The control group consisted of 14 normal untrained subjects, who carried out non-yogic exercise i.e long walk and playing light games. Pre – test and posttest were conducted to both the groups before and after training. The results of both the groups were compared. The trained persons and greater vital capacity, more tidal volume and less respiratory rate than the untrained group. The prescribed standard exercise increased the respiratory rate in both the groups but the increase was less in the trained group who instead exhibited a corresponding increase in total volume.

Gopal (1973) – found a men heart rate about 71 beats per minute for a group which had been trained in yoga for six months for a group which regularly engaged in long walks and light games. Afterwards both groups did 20 jumps and sit-ups. The yoga groups mean heart rate increased to 100 and 7 less than of the light exercises group. A group with at least 6 weeks of certain Hatha yoga practice followed strenuous exercises with 1 minute sitting and then 3 minutes of either sitting, mild exercises or savasana Relaxation. Just after the exercises the heart rate Averaged over 180 and after one minute of sitting it dropped to 130. after 3 more minutes of sitting, it dropped to 17 more beats per minute, a lesser drop than that following 3 minutes of savasan relaxation. This suggests that savasana relaxation facilitates pulse deceleration following exercises.

Gharote (1973) – conducted a study on the effect of yogic training on physical fitness. He employed fliesman basic fitness test. 17 males and 12 females were his subjects and they were given three weeks training in selected yogic exercises. He found significant increases of 7.74 in fitness index in males and 11.75 in females.

Gharote and Ganguly (1973) – observed that nine weeks practice in yogic culture was helpful to improve general physical fitness level of 49 cadet police who were already conditioned to physical activities. But the control group was engaged only in school schedule. The physical fitness of the subjects were judged through (a) Fleishman – basic fitness tess(b) cureton's flexibility test (c) skin-fold and (d) Harvard – step test. The improvement was most significant in flexibility.

Dhanaraj (1974) studied the effect of yoga on selected physiological parameters. The results indicated increases in basal metabolic rate. Tidal volume in basal state. Thyroxine, hemoglobin, vital capacity, chest expansion breath holding time and flexibility after yoga training. He observed decreased in basal heart rate and basal respiratory rate when yogic training was discontinued for six weeks following six weeks treatment, a significant decline in flexibility and breath holding time were noticed.

Nayar (1975) and others investigated the effect of yogic exercise on human physical efficiency. The studies were conducted on 53 cadets of National Defense Academy (NDA) representing there groups, doing routine NDA training, NDA training plus athletics and NDA training plus yogic exercises. Each cadet was assessed both under basal state and during a fixed exercise on bicycle ergometer. The parameters of assessment included ventilation minute volume, the rate of respiration, oxygen consumption, pulse rate, blood pressure, mechanical efficiency and maximum oxygen take capacity. Four additional assessments were made under resting condition, viz vital capacity (VC) maximum breathing capacity (MBC) forced expiratory volume (FEV 10 sec) and breath – holding time. All the three groups showed a significant decreased in pulse rate during exercise. The yogic group in addition recorded a highly significant increase in breath – holding time (from 54 to 106 sec) and VC (from 1.98 to 2.89 L/M2 body surface area). It is also recorded a significant increase in FEV 1.0 sec (from 1.69 to 1.94 liters per M2 body surface area). The remaining two groups (doing routine NDA training and NDA training plus athletics) recorded only significant increase in VC. Ventilation minute volume, rate of respiration, blood pressure, mechanical efficiency, maximum oxygen uptake capacity and MBC remained unaltered in all the three groups.

Ghorate,Ganguly and Moorthy (1976) reported in the study of430 school boys in the age group of 6 to 20 years of yogic training for 3 weeks showed on improvement of 36.8 % in comparison of 20% improvement on minimum muscular fitness.

Gharote (1977) says, health and physical fitness can be maintained only by carefully selected physical activities, which are called exercise. It could be evaluated only in terms of the effects that are obtained in promoting particular factors of physical fitness.

Astrand and Rodhal (1977) brought out the difference between heart rate and pulse rate. Thus heart rate is the number of ventricular beats per minute as compared from records of the electrocardiogram or blood pressure curves. The heart rate can easily be determined by osculation with a stethoscope or by palpitation over the heart, both during rest and exercise. Pulse rate is the frequencies of pressure waves propagated along the peripheral arteries, in normal healthy individuals. But this is not necessary so in patients with arrhythmias in such cases the output of blood by some beats may be too small to give rise to a detectable pulse wave.

Omen (1981) – investigated the comparative effects of isometrics, yogic physical culture and combination training on body composition and physical fitness status of high school boys. ANACOVA revealed that all the three experimental groups showed significant improvement in physical fitness status and significant reduction in percentage of fat (body composition). And when all the groups influenced significantly than that of the other two groups in developing physical fitness status and reducing percentage of body fat.

Karwande (1981) made a study on the comparative effect of yogic and physical exercises on anxiety level and mental fatigue of children. This study was carried with sixty male students from VII and VIII standard. The average age of the subjects was 12 years. The test of anxiety level and mental fatigue were taken as criteria measures for the purpose of the study. The test were taken before and after the experimental period of six weeks. He concluded that anxiety level can be reduced either by training in selected Asanas was superiority to the training in physical exercise for both variables though the difference was not statistically significant.

Thankamma Ommen (1981) compared the isometrics yogic physical culture and combination training on body composition and physical fitness status of high school boys. Result of this study has shown that all the three exercise groups showed a significant increase in toe-touching scores. The inter group differences show that yogic physical culture group is more helpful in developing flexibility than the isomeric and combination groups, and in dynamic flexibility. Comparatively yogic exercises were the best in developing dynamic flexibility.

Ganguly (1981) found that daily one hour training in yigic physical culture for three weeks as per N.F.C progaramme was found to improved cardio-vascular endurance significantly as measured by 20 Harvard step test.

Uppal (1982) in his study, investigate endurance training employing show continou8s running method, which significantly reduces resting systolic and diastolic pressure of forty boys at secondary school. Slow continuous running method significantly lowers systolic blood pressure after exercises of the secondary school level boys, no significant change found out in resting and exercise blood pressures in the case of control groups as it was obviously a reflection of inactivity.

Moorthy (1982) conducted a study on minimum muscular fitness of school children of age group from 6 to 12 yrs and compared the influence of selected yogic exercises and physical exercises on them. In that study, 1000 children (571 boys and 429 girls) from 2nd standard to 11th standard attended at three schools in pune 90 boys and 90 girls who had failed were randomly.

Moorthy (1982) – surveyed the minimum muscular fitness of school children of age group six to eleven years and also compared the influences of selected yogic and physical exercises on them.

Thousand children from second standard to seventh standard at three schools in Pune were selected at random as subjects. Based on their low fitness level, ninety children were selected for experimental purpose. The children were randomly allotted to yogic exercises group, physical exercises group and control group of thirty each. They were undergone their respective treatment for six weeks. Finally he concluded from the results of the study that both the experimental groups significantly improved the minimum muscular fitness after six weeks training when compared to control group. Further, he concluded that yogic exercise group improved significantly the minimum muscular fitness when compared to physical exercise group.

The effect of pranayama a controlled breathing practice, on exercise tests was studied in athletes in two phases, sub-maximal and maximal exercise tests. At the end of phase 1 (one year) both the groups (control and experimental) achieved significantly higher work rate and reduction in oxygen consumption per unit work. There was a significant reduction in blood lactate and an increase P/L ratio in the experimental group, at rest. At the end of phase II (two years), the oxygen consumption per unit work was found to be significantly reduced and the work rate significantly increased in the experimental group. Blood lactate decreased significantly at rest in the experimental group only. Pyruvate and pyruvate – lactate ratio increased significantly in both the group after exercise and at rest in the experimental group. The results in both phases showed that the subjects who practiced pranayama could achieve higher work rates with reduced oxygen consumption per unit work and without increase in blood lactate levels. The blood lactate levels were significantly low at rest (Raju, 1994)

Hoare (1984) Conducted a study and concluded that yoga release energy and helps us to channel it creatively: it breaks physical and mental tension and habits which conditions our response to life and it helps us to live freely with spontaneity and awareness. Yoga is a perfectly balanced physical and mental exercise and towards all efforts that one made toward achieving its knowledge.

Victory Ronrcy (1985) conducted a study of comparative study of the pulse rate and systolic Blood pressure of college sprinters and long distance runners. For the 30 long distance runners were taken as subjects. The long distance runners have a decreased pulse rate than the sprinters. In the systolic blood pressure, there is significance but not much difference between sprinters group and long distance runners.

Makwana (1988) conducted a study to find out the effect of short – term yoga practice on ventilator function tests. For this purpose they used 35 healthy normal male subjects, their age ranging from 20-50 years. The experimental group of 25 subjects underwent 10 weeks of yogic practices 90 minutes daily in the morning. Yoga training limited the exercise i.e surya namaskar, sharirsanchalam, eleven asanas, pranayama and prayer. A control group of

15 subjects were not performing yoga or any other physical exercise. All the subjects were tested as ventilator function in the beginning before starting yoga training and practices and again after a period of 10 weeks of yogic practices.

Mall (1989) – found Sava Sana, a yoga relaxation method to be of great utility in reducing the heart rate, systolic and diastolic pressure of all the four recovery techniques. Nine weeks training in yogic physical culture was helpful to improve general physical fitness level of forty-nine cadet police who were already conditioned to physical activities as against the control group of forty-nine engaged only in school schedule as judged through (a) Fleischer man

Backialakshmi (1990) – evaluated the influence of selected asana and aerobic exercises on selected motor fitness and physiological variables. Ninety boys from Kendra Vidalia, Karaikudi, were divided into three homogeneous groups as control, asana and aerobic exercises group based on their initial performance. Asana and aerobic exercises groups were given treatment for six weeks duration. Finally she came to a conclusion that both the asana and aerobic exercises had significantly improved motor fitness.

Krishnan (1991) – estimated the effect of selected yogic and Bharathiam exercise on physiological variables. Ninety boys between the age group of 13 to 15 years were selected as subjects for this study. The subjects were divided into three groups of 30 each by lot method. Group A was treated as control and group B and C were given yoga asana and Bharathiyam exercises respectively for a period of six weeks. The results indicated that both yogic and Bharathiyam exercises programmers had significantly improved the physiological variables. Further he concluded that yogic training programmed significantly improved the physiological variables than Bharathiam exercise training programmed.

Kirshnan (1991) conducted a study on the effect of exercise and yogic exercises on physiological variables among school boys. In this study 90 students were selected from thirumayam. Three groups were randomly selected of which one served as control group and other two served as experimental groups. With Bharathiyam and yoga Sana exercises, respectively. They were measured for selected physiological variables like pulse rate, breath holding time, cardiovascular efficiency and vital capacity before training as well as immediately after six weeks of training. The significance of the difference among the means of control group, bharathiyam group and yoga Sana group, pre test and post test were determined by 't'-ratio through analysis of variance, Bharathiyam and yogic group significantly improved the pulse rate, breath holding time, cardiovascular efficiency and vital capacity.

Sahay (1992) and others investigated the changes occurring in various biochemical parameters in normal healthy volunteers subject training in Yogic practices pranayama, vajrasana, bhujangasana, shalabhasana, dhanurasana, makarasana, halasana, naukasana, ardha – matsyendrasana, sirshasana and shavasana for a period of three months. the parameters studied included fasting, blood sugar, serum cholesterol, serum triglycerides, serum lactate dehydrogenase, serum creatine – phosphokinase, serum cholinesterase, blood lactate, blood pyruvate and urinary creatine. The subjects were 53 males aged 28 the mean body weight being 58 kg and 20 female's aged 25 the mean body.

Zant and Kusma (1993) studied the effectiveness of a community based exercise and health education programme to improve cardiovascular fitness and body composition on 25 subjects. Subjects participated in a supervised aerobic training programme for 12 weeks. Resting heart rate, blood pressure, weight, body composition and after training. Date was analyzed using ANOVA. Subjects of the exercise session saw significant ($p<0.05$) reductions in systolic blood pressure, resting, resting and heart rate post exercise hand sum of 6 skin fold percent of 6 skin fold percent of 6 skin fold percent of body fat and fat workload. Subjects significantly increased maximal exercise workload. These results indicate that a community based exercise workload. These results indicate that a community based exercise and health education programme results in beneficial changes in fitness and body composition.

A questionnaire was developed in order to estimate the dietary in takes of garlic per person per month and to record three blood pressure readings on each individual. It was given to 101 adult subjects presenting to the family practice centre of a hospital in the city of Karachi, Pakistan. The various demographic parameters including age, sex, marital status and education were recorded. Those subjects found to be overweight with a known history to hypertension, diabetes melhitus, is chaemic heart disease and smoking and on meditations, which affect blood pressure and were excluded from the study to remove the effect of confounding variables on blood pressure. The data were analyzed, an average garlic use of 134 g per month was found, 67% of the subjects used garlic in cooked food while the rest used it either in the raw form or in pickles, 59% thought that dietary use of garlic is healthy. Subjects with blood pressure on the low side were found to consume more garlic in their diets (waris Qidwai 2000)

Madanmohan, Thombre DP, Balakumar. B, Nambinarayanan TK, Thakur S, Krishnamurthy.N, Chandrabose.A, (1993) – studied the effect of yoga training on reaction time, respiratory endurance and muscle strength. There is evidence that the practice of yoga improves physical and mental performance. The present investigation was undertaken to study the effect of yoga training on visual and auditory reaction times, maximum expiratory pressure, maximum aspiratory pressure, 40 mmHg test, breath holding time after expiration, breath holding time after inspiration, and hand grip strength, twenty seven student volunteers were given yoga training for 2 weeks.

There was a significant ($p<0.001$) decrease in visual RT(from 270.0 I 6.20 (SE) to 224.81±5.76ms) as well as auditory RT (from 194.18 ± 6.00 to 157.33 ± 4.85 ms). MEP increased from 92.61 ± 9.04 to 126.46 ± 10.75 mmHg; our results show that yoga practice for 12 weeks results in significant reduction in visual and auditory RTS and significant increase in respiratory pressures, breath holding times and HGS.

Raju PS, Madhavi S, Prasad KV, Reddy MV, Reddy ME, Shahay BK, Murthy KJ (1994) – studied the comparison of efforts of yoga and physical exercise in athletes. The effect of pranayama a controlled breathing practice, on exercise test was studied in athletes in two phase; sub-maximal and maximal exercise tests. At the end of phase I (one year) both the groups (control and experimental) achieved significantly higher work rate and reduction in oxygen consumption per unit work. There was a significant reduction in blood lactate and an increase in P/L ratio in the experimental group at rest. At the end of phase II (two years). The oxygen consumption per unit work was found to be significantly reduced and the work rate significantly increased in the experimental group. Blood locate decreased significantly at rest in the experimental group only. Pyruvate and pyruvate llactate ratio increased significantly in both the groups after exercise and at rest in the experimental group. The result in both phases showed that the subjects who practiced pranayama could achieve higher work rates with reduced oxygen consumption per unit work and without increase in blood lactate levels. The blood lactate levels were significantly low at rest.

Dhanaraj (1995) – administered a study to investigate the effect of yogic and physical exercises on flexibility and cardio-respiratory endurance of Madurai Kamaraj University players. Hundred and fifty men students were selected at random as subjects. They were randomly divided in three groups of fifty each. Experimental group A underwent selected yogic exercises and group B underwent selected physical activities for 12 weeks and the control group C did not engage in any of these programmes. Analysis of covariance revealed that both yogic and physical training groups had shown significant improvement in the flexibility and cardio-respiratory endurance, and when two experimental groups were compared with each other, the yogic training group was more effective than physical training group.

Radhalakshmi (1997) – conducted a study to assess the effect of selected yogic and physical training on physical fitness of school girls in Kerala. To achieve this purpose 90 girls were selected as subjects from Jawahar Navodaya Vidyala, Ernakulam, Kerala state. The age range from 12 to 15 years. They were randomly divided into three groups of thirty subjects each as group A (yogic training group), group B (physical training group), and group C (control group). Yoga and physical training were given to group A and group

B respectively for 8 weeks whereas group C did not participate in any of these training programme. The concept of ANACOVA revealed that even though yogic and physical training had significantly improved the physical fitness, the yogic training group influenced more significantly than the physical training group in developing physical fitness.

Naveen KV, Nagarathna R, Nagendra HR, Telles S (1997) – studied that the yoga breathing through a particular nostril increases spatial memory scores without lateralized effects. Un inostril breathing facilitates the performance on spatial and verbal cognitive tasks, said to be right and left brain functions, respectively. Since hemispheric memory functions are also known to be lateralized, the present study assessed the effects of uninostril breathing on the performance in verbal and spatial memory tests. School children (N=180 whose ages ranged from 10 to 17 years) were randomly assigned to four groups. Each practiced a specific yoga breathing technique: (i) right nostril breathing, (ii) left nostril breathing, (iii) alternate nostril breathing, (iv) breath awareness without manipulation of nostrils. These techniques were practiced for 10 days. Verbal and spatial memory was assessed initially and ofter 10 days. An age – matched control group of 27 were similarly assessed. All 4 trained groups showed a significant increase in spatial test scores at retest, but the control group showed to change. Average increase in spatial memory scores for the trained groups was 84%. It appears yoga breathing increases spatial rather than verbal scores, without a lateralized effect.

Tommijean Thomas, Ph.D, Christopher D.Jori, Ph.D, Benjamin A. Thomas B.A (1998) – assessed the benefits of practicing Iyengor yoga, personality traits, emotional stability, coping and cognitive states among 21 men and 36 women attending an intensive training workshop in celebration of yogacharya Dr. K.K.S. Iyengar's 75th birthday were quantified. It was hypothesized that experienced yoga practitioners would obtain higher scores on the battery of psychological test than normative samples. Statistical Analyses revealed that the coping, stamina and self-control level of the yoga practitioners were significantly elevated and, relative to norms, the mood of the yoga experts was characterized by emotional stability, high energy, exhilaration, and vigorousness with reduced feelings of hostility, tension / anxiety, and apathy. Personal reports indicated that yoga had notable influence on the participants in four areas: (a) physical gains, (b) mental and emotional functioning; (c) personal growth and (d) general life satisfaction. These findings provide support for the proposition that yoga practice is associated with enhanced mental and physical health. Selected for experimental purposes. 30 boys and 30 girls were randomly selected for experimental purposes. 30 boys and 30 girls were randomly allotted for control group. Experimental group I (physical exercises) and Experimental Group (II) (Yogic exercise) were undergoing the treatment for a period of six weeks. He concluded that both experimental groups showed significant improvement after six weeks training when computed to control group. The percentage of improvement was seen much greater in yogic group than in physical exercise group.

Madanmohan, Kaviraja udupa, Ananda Balayogi Bhavanani, Chetan Chinmaya Shatapathy and Ajit sahai (2000) studied the modulation of cardiovascular response to exercise by yoga training. This study reports the effects of yoga training on cardio – vascular response to exercise and the time course of recovery after the exercise. Cardiovascular response to exercise was determined by Harvard test using a platform of 45cm height. The subjects were asked to step up and down the platform at a rate of 30/min for a total duration of 5 min or until fatigue, whichever was earlier. Heart rate (HR) and Blood pressure response to exercise were measured in supine position before exercise and at 1, 2, 3, 4, 5, 7 and 10 minutes after the exercise. Rate-pressure product and double product. Which are indices of work done by the heart were also calculated. Exercise produced a significant increase in HR, systolic pressure, RPP and DOP and a significant decrease in diastolic pressure. After two months of yoga training, exercise induced changes in these parameters were significantly reduced. It is concluded that after yoga training a given level of exercise leads to a milder cardio vascular response, suggesting better exercise tolerance.

Manjunath, Shirley Telles (2001) took twenty girls between 10 and 13 years of age, studying at a residential school they were randomly assigned to 2 groups on group practiced yoga for one hour fifteen minutes per day, 7 days a week, while the other group was given physical training for the same time. Time for planning and for execution and the number of moves required to complete the tower of London task were assessed for both groups at the beginning and end of a month. These three assessments were separately tested in increasingly complex tasks requiring 2 moves, 4 moves and 5 moves. The pre post data were compared using the wilsoxon paired signed Ranks Test. The yoga group showed a significant reduction in planning time for both 2 moves and 4 moves tasks (3.99 and 59.1) execution time in both 4 moves and 5 moves tasks (63.7 and 60.3) and in the number of moves in the 4 moves tasks 120.9 percent). The physical training group showed no change. Hence yoga training for a month reduced the planning and execution time in simple as well as complex tasks (4,5 moves) and facilitated reaching the target with a smaller number of moves in complex tasks (4 moves).

Yogacharya Vishwas Mandlik, (2002) – studied the effect of Jalandhar Bandh on Blood pressure. It is observed that the blood pressure increases during the Kamchatka. It is also warned strictly in all yogic texts to perform all the three Bands have during Kamchatka. The position and the description of the Jalandhar Bandh indicate that there is some relation in between increased blood pressure and Jalandhar Bandh. Jalandhar Bandh created the pressure on the carotidal sinus which in turn reduces the blood pressure.

Hence the Hypothesis is "performing the Jalandhar Bandh in the proper way helps to reduce the Blood pressure".

Gore et al (2003) effects of yoga and Aerobics Training on cardio respiratory functions in obese people" as an outcome of one month programme of weight reduction using yoga practice and Aerobics, female Residential yoga group (FRYG) of 25-40 age range, showed a significant and consistent reduction in systolic blood pressure (SBP) in all the tasting sessions. Their peak expiratory flow Rate (PEFR) also improved in two of the follow up (RU) testing sessions. FRYG of 41-70 age rang reduced their SBP significantly in two of the FU sessions as well as a significant increase in PEFR was recorded. Pulse rate (PR) did not sow significant changes. FMRYG (female Non-Residential yoga group) of 25-40 age range with a normal BP and PR initially, showed a significant reduction in DBP in two of the FU testing sessions, while the increase in their PEFR was not significant. FNRYG of Age 41-70 showed a significant improvement in PEFR in post-test and first FU; yet, reduction in 13p was non-significant statistically. Female Aerobic group (FAG) of age range 25-40 showed no significant reduction in BP and PEFR. However, FAG of age range 41-70 age range did not show significant change in BP and PEFR, however, MAG (Male Aerobic group) of the same age range showed significant reduction in SBP only, in one of the FU testing sessions. Their PEFR showed significant reduction, MAG of age range 25-40 showed non-significant reduction in BP and PEFR.

Mishra et al (2003) cardiac Efficiency of long distance runners and yoga practitioners" cardiac efficiency of 120 male students, in the age range 16 to 17 years from the Aggarsain public school Kurukshetra, Haryana, was tested through Harvard step test. The students were divided in to three equally matched groups viz. long distance running group (Group A), yoga group (Group B) and control Group (Group C). Duration of the experimental period was 6 months which was divided into two sessions of 3 months each. Results of 2x3 factorial ANOVA revealed that yoga practitioners had higher cardiac efficiency those long distance runners.

Govindarajulu (2003) – "Effect of yoga practices on flexibility and cardio Respiratory endurance on high school girls". Sixty (n=60) high school girls (age 12 years) volunteered for a pre-experimental group design, where the practice of selected yoga practice was given as an intervention to the experimental group 'A' (n1=30) for a period of eight weeks. The control group 'B' (N2=30) was not allowed to participate in the experimental treatment. The pre-and post tests were conducted on flexibility and cardio-respiratory endurance. The results of ANOVA revealed that there was in improvement in the flexibility and no significant change was evident in the cardio – respiratory endurance. Thus, short-term yoga is useful in improving.

Moorthy (1983) – estimated the detraining effect of yogic and non-yogic exercises on minimum muscular fitness. For this purpose 90 students were selected at random from six to eleven years of age. The data on minimum muscular fitness were collected after discontinuing the training for both yogic and non-yogic exercises group. The minimum muscular fitness was decreased in non-yogic exercise group. The minimum muscular fitness was decreased in non-yogic exercises group whereas yogic exercises group retained for longer duration. Hence the investigator concluded from the results of the study that yogic exercises are more advantageous than non-yogic exercises in improving and maintaining minimum muscular fitness.

ANALOGY

Out of total 41 studies identified, the investigator found all studies conducted in India. Majority of the studies belonged to survey studies and few of them are experimental studies.

Most of the studies followed random sampling technique in the collection of data and the size of the selected samples range from 60 to 430 samples. In majority of the studies data was collected from the school students. In majority of the studies the questionnaire, opionnaire rating scale developed by the investigator was utilized as a tool. Since all the reviewed studies were related to yoga, yogic exercise, training, practice, yogic culture. Other studies are related to yogasanas, few studies related to body composition and cardiovascular functions, physical functions.

Mean, standard deviation and 't' test where the statistical techniques followed in majority of the study.

CONCLUSION

The investigator collected the studies related to the yoga awareness based on the studies revealed the investigation designed his research, method, sample size, location and variables of the study. The following chapter deals with methodology of the present investigation.

❐

3

Methodology of the Study

OVERVIEW

The Methodology followed in the present study is described in this Chapter. The present study is a Normative Survey Research which aimed to measures the Awareness on Yoga among Higher Secondary Students. The Design of the study construction of the Tool, Pilot Study, Validity and Reliability, Size of the Sample, Selection of the Sample, Administering the Tool among the Students, Scoring Methods, Statistical Techniques utilized etc., have been reported in detailed manner in this present Chapter and ends with the Limitations of the study.

DESIGN OF THE STUDY

Research design is a plan, a structure and a strategy of investigation conceived to obtain answers to various issues in research. The object of research design is to test the research hypotheses. The research design, therefore, is built in the principle of maximization of the results of the study, minimization of variance. A research design however, is not a highly specific plan to be followed without direction. Rather, it is series of guideposts to keep right direction. Thus, research design is the process of planning a research, choosing methods and procedures that can be expected to yield meaningful and most interpretable results.

TABLE. 3.1: Schematic Representation of the Reserarch Design

S. No.	Type	Sources
1.	Nature of the research	Normative Survey Research
2.	Tools Developed	Awareness on Yoga among Higher Secondary Students .
3.	Variables	Higher Secondary Students
4.	Demographic Variables	Students Gender Types of School Locality Parents Occupation Subject
5.	Sampling Technique	Stratified Random Sampling Technique.
6.	Size of the Sample	Students – 150 Boys -73 Girls-77
7.	Statistical Techniques used	Mean, Standard Deviation, 't' test

The present study belongs to Normative Survey Research. The Demographic Variables used are Gender, Type of Schools, Locality, Parents Occupation, Subjects. The Tools use in the Study is Awareness on yoga among Higher Secondary Students at Namakkal District, along with a Personal Data Sheet to know the background of the Students; Random Sampling technique was followed in his study. Data was collected from 150 Students in different locations of Namakkal District. The Statistical Techniques used Mean, S.D and't' Test.

OBJECTIVES OF THE STUDY

The following objectives were formulated for the present study.

1. To find out the yoga awareness of higher secondary school students in Namakkal Educational District.
2. To find out the significance difference in the yoga awareness of
3. Boys and girls (gender)
4. Locality of the student (Rural & Urban)
5. Types of the school (Government & Metric)
6. Parent's occupation (Government & Private)
7. Subjects. (Arts & science)

HYPOTHESIS OF THE STUDY

- There is no significant difference between boys and girls towards awareness on yoga.
- There is no significant difference between rural boys and girls towards awareness on yoga.
- There is no significant difference between urban boys and girls towards awareness on yoga.
- There is no significant difference between Government school boys and girls towards awareness on yoga.
- There is no significant difference between Matriculation school boys and girls towards awareness on yoga.
- There is no significant difference between Government occupation of male and female parents towards awareness on yoga.
- There is no significant difference between private occupation of male and female parents towards awareness on yoga.

TOOLS USED FOR THE STUDY

To access the Factors Influencing the Yoga Education among Higher Secondary Students in Namakkal District with three types of Four Point Rating Scale was developed under the Similar Statements. In the type of tools, with the options such as Strongly Agree, Agree, Disagree and Strongly Disagree were utilized.

PRELIMINARY DRAFT OF THE TOOL

The investigator being a Higher Secondary Students was going on to write appropriate statements related to the objectives of the study.

Awareness on Yoga among Higher Secondary Students in Namakkal District. The steps on the different issues based on the experience of Teachers and other aspects the investigator refine the written statements in all the three Opionnairres. After the corrections, the Opionnairres had 50 Statements only. Then it was administered as a Pilot Study.

PILOT STUDY

The above Opionnaires was neatly typed and administered among the 40 Students, their respective our College Staffs and our College B.Ed Students in the time of Pilot Study the two Opinonnaire had 50 statements for students. After completion of the pilot study, gathered valuable suggestions, corrections and deleting of some statements were taken by the investigator and refine the Opionnaires.

Finally the tool was consists of 50 statements, the above the tools were used to a study on finding the Awareness on Yoga Education among Higher Secondary Students.

TABLE. 3.2: Students Opionnaire: Factors Influencing

S. No	Students		Total
	Positive Items	**Negative Items**	
1.	1,2,4,6,8,10,12,13,14,17,18,20,22,24,26,28,30,32,34,35,36,40,41,43,45,47,4849,50.	3,5,7,9,11,16,19,21,23,25,27,29,31,33,37,38,39,42,44,46.	
	30	20	50

The above table 3.2 shows the student opionnairre to access the influencing factor for the students awareness of special education this tool consists of 4 point scale with 30 positive and 20 negative statements.

RELIABILITY AND VALIDITY

Reliability applies to a measure when similar results are obtained over time and across situations. It should be noted that reliability is a necessary condition for algidity, but a reliable instrument may not be valid. A reliable but invalid instrument will yield consistently may not be valid. A reliable but invalid instrument will yield consistently inaccurate results.

The one type of opionnairre was to access the awareness on Yoga Education among Higher Secondary students, Teachers and their students as said about in the pilot study and also discuss with the Senior Lecturers working in the Kasthooribha Gandhi College of Education Numskull for their valid suggestions. A few modifications where down in the wordings and options for a few statements utilized in the Opionnairre

For validating the preliminary draft of the Opionnairres, it was administered the Students, The investigator used the Test and Retest method, the test 't' value found in the Opionnairres such as 0.05, accordingly all the influencing factors. Then the tool was accepted as the valid tool for administering in the study.

PERSONAL DATA SHEET

To know the background of the Students, The investigator used personal data sheets along with the Developed Questionnaires. It asked for details of Gender, type of School, Locality, Parents Occupation and Subjected. The students were asked to fill in all the particulars given in the personal data sheets. A specimen copy of the personal data sheet and opionnaire used in this study is given in the Appendix – I Tamil version was used for this study.

SIZE OF THE SAMPLE

There are so many School in Namakkal district among that the investigator select the Two School in random sampling method the name of the Schools as follows.

N.S.A.U G. Hr. Sec. School at Namakkal
Trinity Matriculation Hr. Sec. School at Namakkal
From the above areas the investigator has taken from this study.

TABLE. 3.3: List of Boys and Girls samples

S.No	Category	Students
1.	Boys	73
2.	Girls	77
Total		150

The present study is done by Normative Survey Method. The Stratified Random Sampling Technique is followed. The size of the sampling was 150 Students only.

ADMINISTERING THE TOOL

The opinnaires were administered separately among the 150 students, 73 Boys Students and 77 girls Students of the following Sampling Schools in Namakkal district. The name of the Sampling Schools in Namakkal District following

TABLE. 3.4: Name of the Sampling Schools in Namakkal District from Which the Samples are collected

S.No	Name of the School	District
1.	N.S. Arumuga udaiyar Government Hr. Sec. School at Namakkal	Namakkal District
2.	Trinity Matriculation Hr. Sec. School at Namakkal	

The above table 3.4 shows the name and the district of the 2 Schools from which the samples are collected.

SCORING KEY

The Opinonnairre consists of 30 Positive Statements and 20 Negative Statements. The Negative questions were scored as 1/2/3/4 and positive questions were scored as 4/3/2/1. They are Strongly Agree, Agree, Disagree and Strongly Disagree. The total maximum scores for the Tools were 150 and the total minimum scores to the same are 50 respectively.

STATISTICAL MEASURES USED IN THE STUDY

After scoring the filled in Opinionnarrie, a Master Table was prepared by plotting the scores. Different Statistical Measures such as Mean, Standard Deviation and't' test to find out the Significant Relationship between Mean Average Scores were used in the present study for finding out the influence of the problems.

DELIMITATIONS OF THE STUDY

Broadly speaking, any study is impossible without limitation. Research studies is general will have delimitation due to many factors .This study too has some delimitations. It is the responsibility to the researches to see that the study is contacted with maximum care in ordered to be reliable.

However, the following delimitations were unavoidable in the present study,

1. The study has been limited to Namakkal District only.
2. The study has been restricted to the Higher Secondary Students only.
3. The study has been restricted to the XI th Std Student Only.
4. This study adopted survey method using questionnaires to collect data from respondents.
5. A purposive stratified random sample was used to choose the subject to be included in the study.
6. This study is focused mainly on the Variables, Gender, Locality, Various Subjects, Types of Schools and Parents Occupations.
7. The ensuring chapter deals with the data analysis of the study.

CONCLUSION

This chapter deals with methodology of the present investigation as enumerated This it gives brief details about selection of sample, pilot study, administration of tool on the study, data collection and statistical technique use in this study, In the following described the detailed methodology of the study in the chapter analysis and interpretation of the data for the present study is next chapter.

❐

4

Analysis and Interpretation

Any research work could be meaningful when the data were analyzed and interpreted properly. Therefore the researcher has given much important to this part. The data collected from the sample analyzed and interpreted in the following heads.

a. Descriptive analysis
b. Differential analysis

DESCRIPTIVE ANALYSIS

It includes comparison of measures of central tendency such as the mean and the measures of variability such as standard deviation. The calculated values are used to describe the properties of the different sub-samples.

One hundred and fifty students from Namakkal District constituted the sample. He variable studied in the present judgment was with reference to some selected variables like gender, locality, types of schools, parent's occupation, student's subjects.

After the data was collected, it was classified as the above mentioned variables.

DIFFERENTIAL ANALYSIS

It contains the determinations of the statistical significance of the difference between references to selected variables. It contains't 'test. A 't' test is a numerical procedure that takes into account the difference between the means of the sample present in the scores. Thus the 't' test is a technique to find out whether the difference the mean performance is significant or not.

LEVEL OF SIGNIFICANCE

Experimenters and research workers choose several arbitrary standards for their convenience. These arbitrary standards are called level of significance. Most commonly used level of significance is 0.01 and 0.05 level. for the present investigation, the researcher has used 0.05 level as significance to analyze the existence of various hypotheses.

TABLE. 4.1: Significant Difference between Boys and Girls Towards Awareness on Yoga

S. No.	Variables	N	Mean	Standard deviation	't' Value	Significant Level of 0. 05
1	Boys	77	71.31	5.68	2.13*	1. 97
2	Girls	73	74.03	8.11		

*- Significant **- Significant

In order to study the significant of the difference, the 't' value is calculated. it is 2.13 at 0.05 level and it is represented in table 4.1.the 't' value is higher than the table value. Hence it is concluded that, there is significant difference exists between boys and girls higher secondary school students in their yoga awareness. Thus, the framed hypothesis is rejected.

TABLE. 4.2: Significant Difference between Rural Boys and Rural Girls Towards Awareness on Yoga

S. No.	Variables	N	Mean	Standard deviation	't' Value	Significant Level of 0. 05
1	Rural Boys	31	70.41	5.648	2.956*	1. 97
2	Rural Girls	36	74.52	5.738		

*- Significant **- Significant

In order to study the significant of the difference, the 't ' value is calculated. it is 2.956 at 0.05 level and it is represented in table 4.2.the 't' value is higher than the table value. hence it is concluded that, there is significant difference exists between boys andgirls higher secondary school students in their yoga awareness. Thus, the framed hypothesis is rejected.

TABLE. 4.3: Significant Difference between Urban Boys and Urban Girls towards Awareness on Yoga

S. No.	Variables	N	Mean	Standard deviation	't' Value	Significant Level of 0. 05
1.	Urban Boys	46	71.91	4.159	1.518**	1. 97
2	Urban Girls	37	73.94	7.23		

*- Significant **- Significant

In order to study the significant of the difference, the 't' value is calculated. it is 1.518 at 0.05 level and it is represented in table 4.3.the 't' value is lower than the table value. Hence it is concluded that, there is significant difference exists between boys and girls higher secondary school students in their yoga awareness. Thus, the framed hypothesis is accepted.

TABLE. 4.4: Significant Difference between Government School Boys and Girls towards Awareness on Yoga

S. No.	Variables	N	Mean	Standard deviation	't' Value	Significant Level of 0. 05
1	Gov.Boys	34	71.82	5.949	0.158**	1. 97
2	Gov.Girls	34	72.26	7.68		

*- Significant **- Significant

In order to study the significant of the difference, the 't' value is calculated. it is 0.158 at 0.05 level and it is represented in table 4.4.the 't' value is lower than the table value. hence it is concluded that, there is significant difference exists between boys and girls higher secondary school students in their yoga awareness. Thus, the framed hypothesis is accepted.

TABLE. 4.5: Significant Difference between Metric School Boys and Girls towards Awareness on Yoga

S. No.	Variables	N	Mean	Standard deviation	't' Value	Significant Level of 0. 05
1	Mat.Boys	43	70.67	5.53	2.54*	1. 97
2	Mat.Girls	39	74.02	6.32		

*- Significant **- Significant

In order to study the significant of the difference, the ' t ' value is calculated. it is 2.54 at 0.05 level and it is represented in table 4.5.the ' t ' value is higher than the table value. Hence it is concluded that, there is significant difference exists between boys and girls higher secondary school students in their yoga awareness. Thus, the framed hypothesis is rejected.

TABLE. 4.6: Significant Difference between Government Occupation of Boys and Girls Parents towards Awareness on Yoga

S. No.	Variables	N	Mean	Standard deviation	't' Value	Significant Level of 0. 05
1	Boys	31	70.90	6.19	1.97**	1. 97
2	Girls	34	74.02	6.618		

*- Significant **- Significant

In order to study the significant of the difference, the 't' value is calculated. it is 1.97 at 0.05 level and it is represented in table 4.6.the 't' value is lower than the table value. Hence it is concluded that, there is significant difference exists between boys and girls higher secondary school students in their yoga awareness. Thus, the framed hypothesis is accepted.

TABLE. 4.7: Significant Difference between Private Occupation of Boys and Girls Parents towards Awareness on Yoga

S. No.	Variables	N	Mean	Standard deviation	't' Value	Significant Level of 0. 05
1	Boys	46	71.47	5.312	2.332*	1. 97
2	Girls	45	74.11	5.516		

*- Significant **- Significant

In order to study the significant of the difference, the 't' value is calculated. it is 2.332 at 0.05 level and it is represented in table 4.7.the 't' value is higher than the table value. Hence it is concluded that, there is significant difference exists between boys and girls higher secondary school students in their yoga awareness. Thus, the framed hypothesis is rejected

TABLE. 4.8: Significant Difference between Arts Group Boys and Girls towards Awareness on Yoga

S. No.	Variables	N	Mean	Standard deviation	't' Value	Significant Level of 0. 05
1	Arts Boys	42	71.33	6.23	1.914**	1. 97
2	Arts Girls	35	74.14	6.57		

*- Significant **- Significant

In order to study the significant of the difference, the' t ' value is calculated. it is 1.914 at 0.05 level and it is represented in table 4.8.the ' t ' value is lower than the table value. Hence it is concluded that, there is significant difference exists between boys and girls higher secondary school students in their yoga awareness. Thus, the framed hypothesis is accepted

TABLE. 4.9: Significant Difference between Science Group Boys and Girls towards Awareness on Yoga

S. No.	Variables	N	Mean	Standard deviation	't' Value	Significant Level of 0. 05
1	Science Boys	35	71.42	4.87	2.064*	1. 97
2	Science Girls	38	74.18	6.528		

*- Significant **- Significant

In order to study the significant of the difference, the 't' value is calculated. it is 2.064 at 0.05 level and it is represented in table 4.9.the 't' value is higher than the table value. Hence it is concluded that, there is significant difference exists between boys and girls higher secondary school students in their yoga awareness. Thus, the framed hypothesis is rejected.

CONCLUSION

Data analysis is ultimately necessary for any research. The obtained data was subjected to necessary statistical compotation the results these analyzed in terms of the corresponding table value are interpreted accordingly; his findings were calculated without any researchers bias which serves as a recommendation for further study.

❐

5

Findings, Conclusions and Recommendations

In this chapter an attempt had been made to consolidate all the findings of the present study, the investigator also made some recommendation, which include the relevant area for this research and lastly the conclusion. The findings are based on the result collected from the opinioner.

THE STUDY IN RETROSPECT

The aim of the present investigation was to find out the awareness on yoga among higher secondary student at Namakkal District.

METHODOLOGY IN BRIEF

For the present study normative survey method was adopted. For the sample of the study, 150 students of Namakkal District were contacted. The tool used for the collection of data is yoga awareness scale

RESTATEMENT OF THE PROBLEN

The problem under the study is entitled as awareness on yoga among higher secondary students at Namakkal district.

OBJECTIVES OF THE STUDY

The following objectives were formulated for the present study.

- To find out the yoga awareness of higher secondary school students in Namakkal Educational District.
- To find out the significance difference in the yoga awareness of
- Boys and girls (gender)
- Locality of the student (Rural & Urban)
- Types of the school (Government & Metric)
- Parent's occupation (Government & Private)
- Subjects. (Arts & science)

MAJOR FINDING OF THE STUDY

The following are the major findings of the present study.

1. Awareness on yoga among Higher secondary students is Dependent of their Gender.
2. Awareness on yoga among higher secondary students is Dependent of their rural area & Independent of their urban area
3. Awareness on yoga among higher secondary students is Independent of their Government School & Dependent of their Matriculation School
4. Awareness on yoga among higher secondary students is Independent of their parental occupation at government sector & Dependent of their private sector.
5. Awareness on yoga among higher secondary students is Independent to Arts group students & Dependent to science group students.

CONCLUSION OF THE STUDY

The present study concludes that the students adopt themselves to the changing word.

1. Yoga reducing the problem of unhappiness, restlessness, emotional-imbalance & hyperactivity towards school students.
2. Yoga is simply a means of maintaining health & well- being in an increasingly stressful society
3. Yoga aims at bringing the different bodily functions into perfect co-ordination so that they were for the goad of the whole body
4. Practice of yoga help to develop awareness regarding the interrelationship among the emotional mental & physical levels
5. The specialty of the yogic process is that the faculties get sharpened in have with the spiritual process of man.

6. Finally, yoga should be included in the school curriculum as a compulsory subject for the harmonious development of all students (body, mind & soul)

So the present study focused on Awareness on yoga among Higher Secondary students at Namakkal District.

RECOMMENDATIONS

The following recommendations are made;

1. Similar study can be conducted on wider samples.
2. A similar study may be undertaken by selecting different Districts of the same state.
3. A similar study may be conducted even in High school student.
4. A similar study may be conducted in various colleges and teacher training institutions.
5. Need of orientation program towards yoga, among teachers of different Group

SUGGESTIONS

1. Proper yoga study, training
2. Higher secondary students need proper counseling and guidance from the yoga teachers to create self - interest and motivation for better academic performance.
3. Parent's should show satisfaction with their child's past and present performance in their academic.

EDUCATION IMPLICATION

The findings of the present investigation, are important for improving the awareness program of yoga, the following are the major recommendation that have been made from this study, the teach problem of discouraging attitude towards awareness programme.

The result of the study shows that the Awareness on yoga is high in general.

Hence yoga must be introduced as a part of curriculum in school education.

Proper orientation and refresher training must be provided periodically to the yoga teachers.

The pray of yoga is very important in School hours.

DISCUSSION

From the collected data the investigator found that this study reduces blood pressure and stress in their life activity. The investigator study on Awareness on yoga higher secondary schools students. The investigator study on various level schools children's and their Awareness programmed towards yoga. The investigation have no similar results has compare to collected review.

AREAS OF RESEARCH FOR THE FUTURE

Research is a chain activity their purpose of any research in education is 10 find solutions for problems related to teachers students, learning etc. But investigation on one problem always leaves many related research questions that can be investigated by other researchers: some of the areas for research in the future may be as follows,

- The present study can be repeated with wide sample.
- A similar study can be conducted on the professional college.
- A study can be conducted to find out the demographic and motivational variables associated with yoga activities.
- A similar study can be conducted on the high school students
- The present study could be undertaken at various states in India
- A study can be conducted on the primary, secondary and higher secondary school teachers,
- Development of CA , package on the awareness on yoga,
- A critical study on evolving strategies promoting the awareness on yoga among the arts and science college students.

CONCLUSION

The present study made on awareness of yoga among students the findings of the present study reveal that awareness among gender subjects locality types of school parents occupation with respect to the questionnaire.

❐

6

The Problem and its Perspective

Adolescence, usually characterized by the youthful exuberance as its most endearing hallmark is a transition period between childhood and adulthood. Its distinctiveness is reflected in rapid, physical, psychological, emotional, and behavioral changes and developments that take place during this period. The suddenness of the changes and developments quite often results in anxieties and causes confusion and unrest among adolescents. Since these changes and developments are primarily related to sexual development which has traditionally been a taboo, adolescents do not have access to accurate information through authentic sources like family or educational institutions. More importantly, they do not get any opportunity to equip themselves with the needed coping skills, the lack of which makes them vulnerable to risky behavior.

Besides, being a phase of physical maturity, adolescence is a period of progress towards mental, intellectual and emotional maturity. Since the adolescents lack proper understanding of the implications of this period and relevance of the socio-cultural influences, they start distancing themselves from the adult world. The suddenness and rapid race with which the changes take place in the body and mind of adolescents and other influences generate a number of problems and special needs which adolescents find difficult to understand on their own. So far, there is no authentic source readily available to them through which they can get scientific knowledge regarding the changes and developments in them, they fall back upon the peer-group that it is ill-informed which provide wrong information. They develop misconceptions resulting in awkward and undesirable behavior.

It is necessary for the adolescents to behave in a right manner and establish themselves and cooperate at home and outside. The need authentic knowledge that help them understand the process of growing up. They have to be well equipped to cope with the problems which they confront during the transitional phase. They need guidance and independence simultaneously to explore life for them in order to attain a level of maturity required to make responsible and correct decisions.

Adolescents and Physical Health

Physical health of the children must be good for the success and efficiency in all fields of life. The teachers should regard this aspect of development as very important and pay much attention. Good school and teachers should see that children have proper physical growth and motor development. The teachers should provide for adolescents growth in the school through useful activities and adapting its programs to individual variations and gaps. To ensure this regular medical and health examination should be conducted under expert medical supervision.

Teachers should realize that physical growth and motor development have an important effect on the behavior of the adolescent learners. They should know there are individual differences in this area. These individual differences should be understood, respected and provided for terms of suitable programs. Class room and curricular activities which involve physical strength, motor speed accuracy and co-ordination of bodily parts should be adapted to variations in physical and motor development. Varied sports and games suitable for all types of learners should be provided in daily school functioning. Practical information concerning physical growth, personal hygiene, food habits etc, should be imparted to adolescents in an interesting manner.

The play activities, craftwork and other manual work in a school are very valuable for the optimum physical growth and motor development. They should form integral part of the curriculum. The growth of motor behavior as reported in various research finding, point out to the specific development task at various age levels. This knowledge can help the teacher is setting his/her expectations for the learners and in framing the programs in accordance with their needs. This may also serve as safeguard against the possibilities of their developing irrational worries and anxieties regarding abrupt development taking place in their bodies.

Some of the useful manual activities are woodwork, spinning, weaving, book-binding, gardening, tailoring and the like. If these activities are introduced as group projects, these will help not only motor development but make the acquisition of knowledge and information practical and real and would promote a spirit of co-operation among adolescents.

Adolescence and Social Growth

Adolescents are the period of increased social relationship and contact. The school should therefore, provide adequate and ample opportunities leading to the social growth of the adolescents. It should aim at creating such a conductive as would develop satisfying social relations.

Group loyalty becomes pronounced during this period. Family pride and loyalty are also well-marked. Co-operation reaches its peak. Adolescents are a period of strong friendship or hostility. The Adolescents needs proper education on how to develop healthy and desirable relations with their classmates. When he is denied the peer status, he is frustrated. He exhibits a strong desire to reform others and is critical of social injustice in the community. Teacher should try to encourage among adolescent's group compatibility, kindness, sympathy, fair play, courtesy, politenesses, dependability, self confidence, co-operation, leadership and cheerfulness.

Teacher can inspire them to participate in co-operative activities without conflict. He can also guide adolescents to take responsibilities. With the expert guidance of the teacher, students must realize how to accept different roles in accordance with the demands of different situations. It depends on the efficiency of the teacher how he guides them to put group benefits before selfish gains.

Adolescence and Emotional Stability

Emphasizing the importance of emotions in life, it is written that emotions are basic, primeval forces of great power and influence designed by nature to enable the organism to cope with circumstances which demand the utmost effort for success or to add colour and spice to once living. People's emotions control their behaviour. Adolescence is marked by heightened emotionality. Emotions like love, anger, hate, jealousy, fear, worry and joy etc, all reach its peak. At no stage the child is so restless and emotionally perturbed as in adolescence. He is too sensitive and moody. The adolescent lives on intensely emotional life, in which one can see once more the rhythm of positive and negative phases of behavior in his constant alternation between intense excitement and deep depression. This is why the period is often stated as a period of stress and strain. Sometimes he is hilarious but on other occasion he is depressed. He may develop morbid fears and inferiority complex.

If the teacher is aware about all these upheavals of adolescents, he can guide accordingly. Developing proper emotions and controlling them is very essential objective of education during adolescence. Meeting social demands as well as to eliminate the damaging effects of emotions on attitudes, habits, behavior and physical well being, control of emotions is essential. Control does not mean repression but it means learning to approach a social situation with rational attitude and repression of those emotions which are socially unacceptable. The class-room teacher can play an important role to reduce pressures that interfere with adolescent's emotional development.

Proper training- A teacher can use devices and methods to control fears of inadequacy in various situations by developing competencies and skills, thus developing self-confidence.

Development of resistance-A teacher should help the adolescents to examine themselves in finding the causes of failure and frustrations thus developing in them the resistance to frustrations.

Proper understanding- As the adolescent is beset by problems of divided loyalties accentuate by the lack of adult privileges and responsibilities, he is very sensitive and does not welcome any criticism. It becomes the utmost duty of the teacher to understand the adolescents and change the attitude towards him, try to provide him the proper environment for the expression of pent up feeling and can suggest the same for parents at home.

Fair treatment, sympathy, co-operation, and freedom of action within a reasonable limit should be given to adolescents and no unnecessary restriction should be imposed. A variety of interests should be developed to avoid frustration.

Teach the adolescents to relax by providing opportunities for hobbies, cultural activities, catharsis through play, free discussion, drama etc.

Suggesting the parents not to over protect the child can be an effective way of handling the emotion of youth.

- **Verbalization of Feelings:** Adolescents should be trained to express their feelings. As the verbalization of pent up emotional feelings release mental tension and as emotions are put into words, they become diffused, less intense and manageable. The teacher must develop a clear recognition of the desirability of achieving free and constructive expression of emotions which will result in progress towards desired goal.
- **Health:** Poor health of the children may cause irritable behaviour like worry anxiety, fear etc. Hence the health of children should be properly looked after,. Moreover, teachers can guide them that should study when they are not tired lest it should result in negative learning and feeling of inadequacy.

- **Picnic and Tours:** The teacher can organize picnics, excursions and tours to provide them opportunities to understand each other and to come closer. This may resolve many problems.

Moral Development and Education

One of the causes of increasing restlessness, indiscipline, dishonesty and aimlessness among the youth of India is that there is no proper provision of religious and moral education in our system of education. Ours is a secular state and therefore, the doubts are expressed in the provision of religious instructions inside the schools. But it is a false fear standing on erroneous grounds. Actually the roots and the goals of the all religions are one and the same; the essence of all the religions is morality. Parents, social workers and administrators should join their hands in creating suitable atmosphere and offering opportunities of practicing moral qualities. The emphasis should be shifted from rituals to ideals.

Teachers may organize morning assembly in the school, celebrate festivals and national days, undertake visit to backward and slum areas and render some sort of service to the people living in such areas.

Camps, social service programmes, games, community and school are very effective in the moral development of the learners.

Teachers may guide the adolescents by urging them that their moral duty is to be sincere to the institution, community and nation. They can be involved in activities such as campus cleaning, adult literacy campaigns etc.

Intellectual Development and Education

The dramatic physical and psychological changes that occur in adolescence may tend to obscure the fact that impressive changes in cognitive development are taking place at the same time. Indeed it is correct to say that adolescence is the period during which the capacity to acquire and utilize knowledge reaches its pack efficiency. They become curious to know what others think about them.

Here the teachers can play a very important role. Effective development can take place if teachers provide a variety of rich and concrete experiences and challenging activities for the learners. The home and school surround the adolescents with problematic situations. In the process of solving problems and meeting difficulties the adolescents develop their power of thinking and reasoning. Hence, it is the duty of the teachers to avoid too much advice or lecture, over emphasis on text book and cramming but encourage the use of discussion and socialized teaching.

For intellectual growth nothing can beat a good library. Adolescents by nature are adventurous and inquisitive. They can quench this thirst of theirs by reading stories of great explorations and inventions. The adolescents are always eager to express both orally and in writing. Literary societies and school magazines can satisfy this urge.

The adolescents, if not fully occupied, would become a devil's workshop by creating trouble for themselves and for others. Therefore, to utilize their leisure time profitably certain hobbies should be introduced in schools.

Provision for vocational education – There is a strong desire of achieving independence in adolescents. What occupation should they choose, how they can earn their livelihood are some questions, the answers to which they try to seek. Here arises the need of proper vocational guidance and vocational education for them. There is a strong need to provide job-oriented and vocation based practical education to the adolescents, otherwise there is a danger, that they may turn into anti social behaviourists.

SOCIAL MATURITY

Definitions of Social Maturity

"Maturity is the blossoming of man's character in to a unified totality. It discerns the process that contributes to the psychological and physical growth and well being of man" - Nazareth , N. Pia and Marie. Ewaples(1978)

"An adolescent who gets along with and work well with others. He ought to develop self reliance in matters of taste and he ought to develop tolerance of human differences" - Abraham spending (1967)

"Social maturity is the degree of social participation as measured by child's activities, attitudes and play interests. It is related to physical growth and maturity and to mental ability" Henry e. garrett. (1968)

THE NATURE OF SOCIAL MATURITY

As stated above, the maturity of a person is influenced by various social factors. Some of the important factors are as follows:

i. Concept of Dependence – Independence

Dependence –independence –patterns of behavior s are acquired in the course of day-to-day interaction. An individual is required to modify his behavior in terms of asserting his independence and seeking success in the socio-cultural context. Age variations are important with reference to dependence- independence.

ii. Self-Control

Self-control, as part of social maturity, is necessary for decision making and facing the consequences. Too many impositions on students result in developing either a rebellious or subservient attitude. Acquiring self-control is partly maturational and partly learnt behavior. The students studying in a secondary school understands that the society does not expect him to regress to childhood behavior at this age. He tries to come up to the expectations of the society and this he achieves by controlling his behavior.

iii. Stress

Stress is a part of everybody's life and everybody has to overcome stress. Every time there is a stress situation, a mature individual mobilizes the available sources and utilizes them to the best of his ability to overcome the stress. Stress situations help individuals learn to put forth their very best to resolve stress. Students have to learn to cope with stress and competition in the course of development in the course of development but this stress should not hamper the process of their adjustment.

iv. Social Maturation

Socially mature people are aware of their roles. During the process of social growth students learn to live up to the expectations of the society in which they live. In every society the male and female roles are different. Individuals who voltaic these expectations and do not take the appropriate roles are the sign of socially mature person.

v. Ability to size up a social situation

Another component of social maturity is to size up a social situation and reaction for it appropriately. A mature student is able to perceive a hint in social situation and accordingly modify his behavior. He understands his mother's behavior by absorbing her facial expression or change in her tone. He will understand that she does not approve his actions. He can amend his behaviour accordingly. This ability increases as the student matures and this is desired for social adjustment.

SOCIAL MATURITY AND ADOLESCENTS

Social maturity is a term commonly used in two ways with reference to the behavior that conforms to the standards and expectations of the adults secondly, with reference to the behavior that is appropriate to the age of the individual under observation. Thus, the social maturation permits more detailed perception of the social environment which helps adolescents to influence the social circumstances and develop stable patterns of social behavior. If an individual is slow to adopt these patterns of social behavior, he is judged as being retarded in social development. So it is necessary for adolescents to acquire more matured pattern of behavior to be accepted by society and to be socially matured. It has been found that the highly chosen pupil participated more frequently in social skills than the poorly accepted pupils. Amongst the other social skills that are significantly related to social maturity are sensitivity to the social needs of companion, inclination and social skill to satisfy their needs and certain personality traits such as positive social aggressiveness, friendliness etc. are congruent with social sensitivity and compliance. All these further lead to satisfactory interpersonal adjustment, whereas, unpopular adolescents lack such psychological adjustments because they are socially insensitive or maladjusted.

High social maturity will also help the adolescents to overcome their depressive symptomatology. The adolescents need to be identified with their depression level and can be helped to overcome depression problems with the social support so that they can lead a happy and successful life in the present and in the future.

CHARACTERISTICS OF SOCIAL MATURITY

Social maturity is the final expected outcome of social development and socialization. Certain characteristics of social maturity are as follows:

A social mature person has a sense of his proper place and role as a member of the social group. He is willing and able to orient himself in the various activities and customs of the group.

He is able to assume a reasonable amount of responsibility to adjust himself to the inevitable limitations and restrictions of the community life. He can be original and yet conform to the broad pattern of his social environment. He evaluates social problems not from a purely selfish point of view but has regard to the rights and opinions of others. Accepts responsibility for his actions, does not indulge in self-pitying.

A socially mature person is relatively free from devastating emotions and is able to control his emotions in socially acceptable behavior. He has a realistic level of aspiration and has a sound moral and social code that saves him from conflicts and feelings of guilt.

He has many friends and contributes to social welfare. He has a realistic self-concept, being conscious of his assets and limitations. He is relatively secure and so open to new experiences which contribute to his continuous development.

In short, co-operation, pleasing manners, consideration for others, positive and optimistic outlook on life and emotional maturity are signs of socially matured individual.

Social maturity is evidenced in the capacity of the individual friendships that meet the needs of others as well as his own. Vatsysyan (1990) states "A mature individual from the social stand point is one who co-operates with all those with whom he comes into contact and contradicts them only when such a course of action becomes inevitable. He is never ill-mannered choosing instead to appear very well mannered, considerate and friendly to all " consequently has a large circle of friends. An adult, who has attended that stage has required by the standpoint, evinces great interest in art, study, games etc.

A socially matured person studies the works of greatest authors and takes interest in games and forms of recreation suitable to his station in life. His activities and conduct are scrupulously in conformity with his age and sex. He has the power of independent decision and judgment. He gives every evidence of being well balanced adjusted with himself and his behavior towards other individuals.

Elizabeth B.Hurlock (1959) says, "The socially mature individual has a sense of his proper place and role as a member of a group. He is willing and able to orient himself in the various activities with others and customs of the group, to make the proportionate contribution to the work to be done, to take a suitable part in the social exchange to assume a reasonable amount of responsibility and to adjust himself to the inevitable limitations and restrictions of community life without waste of energy or loss of satisfaction". He can be original and yet conform to the broad pattern of the cultural environment.

Taneja R.P. (1989) says, "Social maturity refers to degree of growth in social and vocational abilities". The socially mature individual mature individual treats the members of his family as friends. In this role he shows the affection, loyalty, consideration and respect for all family members. As a citizen the socially mature person accepts his obligations and performs them faithfully. He makes good adjustments to all types of people without prejudice based on their religion, race or skin colour.

The matured accepts his friends as they are and does not criticize or to change them as a socially immature person does. He is loyal to them and feels a sense of responsibility towards them when they need his help. Although social life may add greatly to his happiness, the mature person is self-sufficient enough that he can be happy when circumstances make it possible for him to be with his family, friends or acquaintances.

The mature individual can be found to possess the trait of good humor and pleasantness. The important point is that he keeps himself alive, with vigorous interests that make him interesting to be with. The mature individual possess a feeling of social concern and gets very involved in situations that call for obedience to social norms too. The person equipped with the human sensitivities that make for maturity will usually have powerful concern with social problems and ways of alleviating them. For all his social –mindedness, for all his savoring of human relationships, the maturing individual is not dependent on always having company.

The mature person knows that he has to go on choosing alternatives, that each alternative costs him something, and there are things he will never be able to do and experience. He also knows that there are things he will never be able to do again, that he can never recapture his youth or relive his first encounters with certain experiences. He knows that his integrity is continually threatened by practical demands, by reductive temptations, by concessions and compromises, by conflicting values, and can only be preserved at the cost of some psychic strain. He knows that the only real rewards in life come with continued growth, and that there is no room in the one material life he has for major regrets. The individual who has approached maturity can know that he has loved, had done his work has made his mark on people.

IMPORTANCE OF SOCIAL MATURITY

Social maturity has been defined as an indication of willingness and ability to orient oneself in the various activities and customs of the group, to make a proportionate contribution to the work to be done, to take a suitable part in the social exchange, to assume a reasonable amount of responsibility and to adjust oneself to the inevitable limitations and restrictions of community life without waste of energy or loss of satisfaction.

Personal social needs of the adolescent stem from growth characteristics of the adolescent period and from the kind of society in which he lives and to which he is expected to adjust and contribute.

Social Maturity

Social maturity is the degree to which an individual has acquired the social and socialized behaviors that are usual and expected for his age and his status or the social behavior characteristics of the typical adult member of a society.

EMOTIONAL COMPETENCE

Competency

The capacity, skill, or ability to do something correctly or efficiently, or the scope of a person's or a group's ability or knowledge. In linguistics, this term introduced by the US linguist and philosopher Noam Chomsky to denote a person's unconscious knowledge of grammatical rules of a language, especially those of transformational grammar. Competency is the ability to perform a function skillfully and effectively.

DEFINITION OF COMPETENCY

In attempt to define competence in terms of performance criteria, we must bear in mind that their achievement is part of the process of becoming effective in a particular context. Many factors will determine how effective a person is in any role. Some are definable as performance criteria, while others relate to environmental and contextual pressures, or interpersonal skills and relationships, working in terms of confidence and adaptability.

FEATURES OF COMPETENCY

- Competencies to be demonstrated by the students are derived from explicit conceptions teacher's role and are publically stated in such a manner that the students learned behaviours are related to specified competencies.
- Criteria are to be employed in assessing competencies that are stated in terms of expected levels of mastery under specified conditions.
- Assessment of competency depends on students performance as the primary source of evidence and strives for objectivity.
- Student's rate of progress is determined by demonstrated competencies rather than time or course completion.
- Instructional programme is intended to facilitate the development of specified competencies.

COMPETENCIES IN LIFE SITUATIONS

Competencies are simply a way of stating very explicitly what a profession believes to be essential for effective practice related to that specific profession alone. The competencies, thus, identify categories of activities that generalist social workers are expected to master. The specific activities that comprise each competency are many, and will be used at different times and in different ways depending on the specifies of each practice situation.

In one situation the person seeking help may need a great deal of information in order to function more effectively. In another case the person may have the necessary information but many need to be linked with others so that they can collectively use the information most effectively.

COMPETENCIES TO BE DEVELOPED

Competence in the use of any methodology involves being able to choose intelligently with the knowledge, experience and skill to make chosen methods work effectively. This can only be acquired by experience developed among the Higher Secondary Students follows:

1. Competence to understand the right process of learning, including, learning by doing, learning to be, learning to do and learning to become.
2. Competence to devise dynamic methods in the day-to-day situations based on the needs and interests of children
3. Competence to organize the classroom in such a manner that different kinds of activities may be organized in it so that children may receive required guidance from teacher.

4. Competence to become an example of qualities he/she wants to develop among his/her students, realizing that example is superior to more instruction and preaching.
5. Competence in regard to language, delivery of speech and other method of communication.
6. Competence in regard to the contents of the subject that he/she is supposed to teach.
7. Competence to engage children in a meaningful manner so that children may develop capacity to ask questions and may be inspired to find out the answers by themselves.
8. Competence to innovative so as to create proper environment in the classroom to enable children to develop wider horizons of perceptions.
9. Competence to develop among students a scientific temper, which is often confined to cultivation of various attitudes, includes objective observation, experimentation and consideration of every point of view relevant to the enquiry in a logical manner.

ADOLESCENTS AND EMOTIONAL BEHAVIOUR

Behaviour was defined by Watson as on action, which can be seen and observed in an objective way. This means behaviour is the way in which an individual carries out his activities. Behaviour of an individual is influenced by the internal body environment as well as external environment around him.

Adolescent behaviour has been studied from very early times. Plato characterized the adolescents to be argumentative and easily excitable while Aristotle described them as impulsive, prone to excess and exaggeration and lacking self-restraint. The period of adolescents in the life of an individual is characterized as problematic and has been studied for a long time.

Adolescents are characterized by

1. Anxiety
2. Mood swings
3. Confusion/Indccision
4. lethargy
5. Argumentation
6. Anger/irritability
7. Experimentation.

This behaviour is normal behaviour pattern in adolescents.

Anxiety- It is an uneasy mental state concerning impending or anticipated ill. According to Hurlock, anxiety is marked by apprehension, uneasiness and fore boding from which the individual cannot escape; it is accompanied by a feeling of helplessness because the anxious person feels blocked and unable to find a solution to the problem at hand.

Mood Swings- The adolescents are characterized as moody. Sometimes they feel pleasant and on the other times they are depressed. This is due to their disturbed physiological condition because of effect of hormones.

Confusion/Indecision-Erickson characterizes the adolescents with identity vs confusion crisis. The physical and intellectual changes during adolescents disrupt their sense of continuity and personal wholeness. They pay great attention on how other people view them. Their choice are usually supported by the reactions of parents and other people. They are not able to make decisions and keep changing their roles. So they are said to be in a state of confusion/ indecision.

Lethargy-Adolescents tend not to eat properly and rapid pace of their growth makes them undernourished. As a result they become weak and lethargic.

Argumentation-Adolescents are greatly influenced by peers and they enjoy doing things with their group. Since they are growing up they want to take decision themselves and want to do things their way, while adults (parents and teachers) want them to behave like mature individuals. This leads to arguments between them.

Anger/irritability-In adolescents, thwarting of desires, interruption of activities in progress, constant fault finding, teasing, lecturing, or making unfavorable comparisons with other children lead to anger. Older children when fail to realize their goals, they become angry at themselves or at the people they believe have stood in their way.

Experimentation-Adolescents show risk taking behaviour. They want to try doing different things. They are greatly influenced by their peer group. They want to be viewed as adults and tend to indulge in, alcoholism and even drug abuse.

EMOTIONAL COMPETENCE

Emotional competence is what results and enhances our personal, relational and professional performance, and what ultimately helps us attain an overall increase in our quality of life. According to Daniel Goleman, Emotional Competence is a learned ability grounded in Emotional Intelligence. Emotional Intelligence influences our potential for learning the practical emotional competencies, and developing the emotional literacy necessary for quality of life, life satisfaction, and overall happiness.

Emotional competence emerging with the huge impact in our society. It is the crucial factor determining the academic performance of adolescents at school and their interpersonal relationship at home. Adolescents face many challenges in everyday life, so based on Golemans research (1998) in order to be a well rounded functioning individual, a person must possess skills to excel in life, such as to plan, motivate, manage feeling and handle relationship. By approaching life tasks armed with emotional competence skills.

PERSONAL COMPETENCE

Self Awareness

Emotional Self Awareness

People who are emotionally Self Aware know which emotion they are experiencing at any given moment. They recognize the relationship between their own thoughts and feelings and are cognizant of their beliefs, values and goals.

Accurate Self-Evaluation

People who accurately evaluate themselves are aware of their strengths, but also recognize and accept their weaknesses. They are open to ongoing growth and development by learning from their mistakes and experiences, are introspective, and open to constructive feedback and new possibilities.

Self Confidence/Self Esteem:

These types of people are self-assured and know their self-worth. They present themselves and their views authentically and powerfully. They respectfully stand up for their views/truths even when doing so is unpopular. They make decisions and follow up with appropriate action. They are open and respectful of others' opinions even in face of disagreement.

ELF MANAGEMENT

Self Control/ Management

These types of people do well regulating and managing their reactions/ impulsive feelings/ distressing emotions. They stay collected, centered, focused and positive even in emotionally challenging situations and under pressure.

Trustworthiness and Conscientiousness

These types of people are ethical and are ready to confront unethical behavior in others. They are consistently reliable in their commitments, accountable for their responsibilities, and keep their promises. Such individuals are straightforward and authentic in their communication, own their imperfections and the mistakes they make, are planned and organized with their objectives, and stand up strongly for their values and principles in every aspect of their lives.

Innovative and Adaptable

These types of people are original in their ideas and open to new solutions. They risk thinking outside the box and are comfortable staying within what is familiar and acceptable. They handle multiple responsibilities simultaneously. They manage changing circumstances effectively, and are adaptable and flexible in how they manage changing priorities and circumstances. They are grounded in the present-"the here & now" - but also recognize the past as a valuable resource for information.

Motivation and Growth Orientation

These types of people are inwardly motivated to grow and achieve desired goals despite challenges and difficulties. These people always adhere to ethical standards and principles, and constantly look to gain new knowledge and opportunities that are compatible with their vision and that will improve their overall conduct.

Commitment/Integrity

These types of people are purposeful and intentional in their pursuit of their personal and common vision. At the same time, these people strongly adhere to ethical values, principles and standards of conduct.

Intentionality/Initiative and Positivism

These types of people seek opportunities that go beyond what is required/ expected. They enroll, motivate and support others in the pursuit of a vision, despite set-backs and challenges. They are motivated by what is possible rather than by fear of failure. They face obstacles and set-backs realistically, and move forward from breakdowns or setbacks by intentionally looking for what is possible, rather than looking for who is to blame.

RELATIONAL COMPETENCE

Relational Awareness

Empathy

These types of people are sensitive and understanding of others. They listen effectively and respectfully and are attentive to others' emotional cues, feelings, needs and perspectives.

Supporting Others

These types of people support others to grow and thrive by focusing on their strengths and reinforcing their positive aspects rather than focusing on the negatives. They acknowledge and appreciate others for their contribution and conduct. They seek to develop and enhance relationships. They value diversity and differences, viewing them as possibilities.

Build Partnerships/Connections

These types of people are "connectors." They are friendly and outgoing and promote cooperation and collaboration. They seek and cultivate relationships that are mutually satisfying and valuable, and they promote harmonious interactions among people.

RELATIONAL MANAGEMENT:

Positive Impact on Others

These types of people are able to help people see the big picture and influence them in seeking out desired positive outcomes while adhering to ethical values and principles.

Conflict Resolution and Communication

These types of people effectively focus on identifying positive solutions rather than staying stuck on who is "right" or who is "wrong." They are open to dialogue and discussion and are authentic and effective in communication. They are empathetic and manage their emotions appropriately. They are straightforward and open to feedback, respectful listeners, and take responsibility for contributing to both the creation of a breakdown, as well as to arriving at an optimal resolution of any such breakdown.

Collaboration and Connection

These types of people participate in creating and attaining life visions. They are compassionate and considerate of others' needs and preferences, but remember to honor their own feelings as well. They are emotionally open and appropriate. They seek optimal solutions and are amenable to changing that which is not positively impacting themselves or others.

Instrumental in Managing Positive Change

These types of people are oriented toward identifying the positive aspects of a person or a situation. They build on strengths and avoid blaming, judging, criticizing and pointing a finger. They take the initiative in identifying the change necessary toward the achievement of positive/desired outcomes.

SELF-ACTUALIZATION

Concept of Self-Actualization

Self –actualization is not the end of growth... not the path to maturity; but the path of maturity. Self-actualization involves the harmonization of psychic forces (such as the digestion of memory as storytelling which frees the individual from the limitations of the 'ego-life and allows them to live-in the spiritual realm of human existence i.e. the realm e unfolding of human 'of ego transcendence of being self actualization is a function of unfolding of human values of living' – the social values' or morals of morality – the moral faculty for accurate evaluation of the social environment and lead to effective decision making and successful adaptation i.e. depends on motivation by the metaneeds ie metamotivation is functional by the metaneeds i.e. 'metamotivation.' Metamotivation is functional in the process of self-actualisation as mature growth and development of 'moral consciousiness' or 'conscience'. Development of conscience or 'character'-the human 'soul' depends creativity and productivity or 'work'.

DEFINITIONS OF SELF-ACTUALIZATION

Maslow loosely defined self actualization as the full use and exploitation of talents, capacities, potentialities,etc."(motivation and personality)" self actualization is not a static. It is an ongoing process in which one's capacities are fully ,creatively and joyfully utilized "I think of the self-actualizing man not as an ordinary man with something added ,but rather as the ordinary man with nothing taken away.

MASLOW'S BASIC PRINCIPLES:

The normal personality is characterized by unity, integration, consistency, and coherence. Organization is the natural state, and disorganization is pathological.

- The organism can be analyzed by differentiating its parts, but no part can be studied in isolation. The whole functions according to laws that cannot be found in the parts.
- The organism has one sovereign drive, that of Self-Actualization, people strive continuously to realize their inherent potential by whatever avenues are open to them.
- The influence of the external environment on normal development is minimal. The organism's potential, is followed to unfold by an appropriate environment, will produce a healthy, integrated personality.

- The comprehensive study of one person is more useful than the extensive investigation, in many people, of an isolated psychological functions.
- The salvation of the human being is not to be found in either behaviorism or in psychoanalysis, (which deals with only the darker, meaner half of the individual). We must deal with the questions of value, individuality, consciousness, purpose, ethics and the higher reaches of human nature.
- Man is Basically not Evil.
- Psychopathology generally results from the denial, frustration or twisting of our essential nature.
- Therapy's of any sort, is a means of restoring a person to the path of Self-Actualization and development along the lines dictated by their inner nature.
- When the four basic needs have been satisfied the growth need of Self-Actualization need arises: A new discontent and restlessness will develop unless the individual is doing what the individually is fitted for. A musician must make music, an artist must paint, a poet must write-in short, what people can be they must be.

SELF ACTUALIZATION

Self-actualization means experiencing fully, vividly, selflessly, with full concentration and total absorption. It means experiencing without the self-consciousness of the adolescent. At this moment of experiencing, the person is wholly and fully human. This is a self-actualizing moment. This is a moment when the self is actualizing itself. As individuals, everyone experience such moments occasionally. As counselors, teacher can help the students to experience them more often. One can encourage them to become totally absorbed in something and to forget their poses and defenses and their shyness - to go at it "whole hog." From the outside, one can see that this can be a very sweet moment. In those youngsters who are trying to be very tough and cynical and sophisticated, one can see the recovery of some of the guilelessness of childhood: some of the innocence and sweetness of the face can come back as they devote themselves fully into the experiencing of it. The key word for this is "selflessly," and the youngsters suffer from too little selflessness and too much self-consciousness and self-awareness.

SELF ACTUALIZATION NEEDS

Self actualization means to fulfill ones individual nature in all its aspects.

One who is talented in one specific area uneasy, if that talent not nurtured and utilized. He wants to attain perfection in the area.

The high level of functioning occurs, when a person is self actualized people can be motivated towards self actualized.

People can be motivated towards self actualization only when the lower order needs are satisfied.

Based on the theoretical framework of the above variable, an attempt had been made by the investigator to find the relationship between them.

Self-actualization needs involve morality, creativity, spontaneity, problem solving, realizing personal potential, self-fulfillment, seeking personal growth, peak experiences, tolerance (lack of prejudice), acceptance of facts, willingness to be wrong and adjust according with new information encountered.

Abraham Maslow Describes this as

- Need to become more and more of what a human being is.
- Need to become everything that a person is capable of becoming.

For example: Some people have strong need to be an ideal parent. Some people have needs that require being expressed athletically, or in painting, or in inventions, etc. The needs often involve higher learning and ever greater development in specialized skills for actualizing our best potentials to produce the best possible results.

CHARACTERISTICS OF SELF-ACTUALIZED PEOPLE:

i. Perception of Reality

These individuals tend to have a "superior relationship with reality" and are "generally unthreatened and unfrightened by the unknown." In fact, "They accept it, are comfortable with it, and, often are even more attracted by it than by the known. They not only tolerate the ambiguous and unstructured--they like it."

ii. Acceptance

"Even the normal member of our culture feels unnecessarily guilty or ashamed about too many things and has anxiety in too many situations. Healthy individuals find it possible to accept themselves and their own nature without chagrin or complaint or, for that matter, without even thinking about the matter that much."

iii. Spontaneity

The behavior of the self-actualizing individual is "marked by simplicity and naturalness, and by lack of artificiality or straining for effect."

iv. Problem Centering

Self-actualizers customarily have some "mission in life."

Solitude: Self-actualizing individuals "positively like solitude and privacy to a definitely greater degree than the average person."

v. Autonomy

"They have become strong enough to be independent of the good opinion of other people, or even of their affection. The honors, the status, the rewards, the popularity, the prestige, and the love they can bestow must have become less important than self-development and inner growth."

vi. Fresh Appreciation

"Self-actualizing people have the wonderful capacity to appreciate again and again, freshly and naively, the basic goods of life, with awe, pleasure, wonder and even ecstasy, however stale these experiences may have become to others."

viii. Peak Experiences

It's been called "flow" or "being in the zone." Whatever people want to call it, self-actualizers tend to experience it more often than average.

ix. Human Kinship

"Self-actualizing people have a deep feeling of identification, sympathy, and affection for human beings in general. They feel kinship and connection, as if all people were members of a single family." "Self-actualizing individuals have a genuine desire to help the human race."

x. Humility and Respect

All of Maslow's subjects "may be said to be democratic people in the deepest sense...they can be friendly with anyone of suitable character, regardless of class, education, political belief, race or color. As a matter of fact it often seems as if they are not aware of these differences, which are for the average person so obvious and so important."

xi. Interpersonal Relationships

"Self-actualizing people have these especially deep ties with rather few individuals. Their circle of friends is rather small. The ones that they love profoundly are few in number."

xii. Ethics

"They do right and do not do wrong. Needless to say, their notions of right and wrong and of good and evil are often not the conventional ones."

xiii. Means and Ends

"They are fixed on ends rather than on means, and means are quite definitely subordinated to these ends."

xiv. Humor

"They do not consider funny what the average person considers to be funny. Thus they do not laugh at hostile humor (making people laugh by hurting someone) or superiority humor (laughing at someone else's inferiority) or authority-rebellion humor (the unfunny, Oedipal, or smutty joke)."

xv. Creativity

"This is a universal characteristic of all the people studied or observed. There is no exception."

xvi. Resistance to Enculturation

"Of all of them it may be said that in a certain profound and meaningful sense they resist enculturation and maintain a certain inner detachment from the culture in which they are immersed."

xvii. Imperfections: Actualizes

"Show many of the lesser human failings. They too are equipped with silly, wasteful, or thoughtless habits. They can be boring, stubborn, irritating. They are by no means free from a rather superficial vanity, pride, partiality to their own productions, family, friends, and children. Temper outbursts are not rare."

xviii. Values

"A firm foundation for a value system is automatically furnished to self-actualizers by their philosophic acceptance of the nature of self, of human nature, of much of social life, and of nature and physical reality."

STATEMENT OF THE PROBLEM

The present study entitled as "Relationship of Emotional Competence and Social Maturity with reference to Self Actualization of Higher Secondary Students".

DEFINITIONS OF TECHNICAL TERMS

Social Maturity

Social development means social maturity. It means the level of a person who is socially mature. His relations with other human beings his dealing with others and the way takes interest in others. Thus social maturity means attaining maturity in social relationships that is to establish good relations with family, neighbours, friends, playmates, class-fellows, teachers and other members of the society for making and keeping friends. A person having a quality of friendliness and adjustable nature is considered to be a socially matured person.

Emotional Competence

Emotional competence is an understanding of one's own and other's emotions, the tendency to display emotion in a situation socially and culturally appropriate manner, and the ability to inhibit or modulate experiences and express emotion. Emotionality derived behavior is needed to achieve goals in a socially acceptable manner.

Self -Actualization

At each point there is a progression choice and a regression choice. There may be a movement towards defense, towards safety, toward being afraid; but over on the other side, there is the growth choice. To make the growth choice instead of the fear choice may times during the day is to move towards self-actualization. Self actualization is an ongoing process; it means making each of the many single choices whether to lie or to be honest, whether to steal or not to steal at a particular point, and it means make each of these choices as a growth choice. This is movement toward self-actualization.

OPERATIONAL DEFINITION

Social maturity

According to the view of the investigator the term social maturity refers to the overall score obtained by the higher secondary students on rao's social maturity scale (1986)

Emotional Competence

It is a learned capability based on Emotional Competence intelligence, which determines one's potential for learning the practical skills. In the investigation it is assessed by the scores obtained by the students using Emotional Competence scale standardized by Dr.Latha in the year 2002.

Self Actualization

According to the view of the investigator the term of Self Actualization refers to the overall score obtained by the higher secondary students on John Korte's (2007) scale.

NEED AND SIGNIFICANCE OF THE STUDY

Social maturity can only be found through self-knowledge and self-control, based on the objectives existence of a science of human nature. In order to protect socially supported beliefs and conventions, society employs a complex system of prohibitions, backed up by ostracism and punishment. Society sets up a system of socially convenient belief for truth and conventional patterns of behavior for what are right. The individual who chooses to live outside this system has a twofold task, to make his peace with society at an adaptive level and to maintain always his own independent standards of what a high quality life is all about. To accomplish this end he must be able to see what is compulsive or obsessive in himself, working to reduce or eliminate these influences in his life without losing track of the wisdom and strength he already has.

Social maturity is the final expected outcome of social development. The socially matured person knows his role as a member of the social group. The person will organize himself socially and will take part in various activities and customs of the group. A person with high social maturity will know the responsibilities and will be able to adjust himself in the society as he would have good creativity so as to solve the problems of the students. So it is significant to study the social maturity and creativity of the secondary grade students, as it is essential for the classroom learning and effective interaction.

Social maturity has to do with how well people understand the nature of the social world they live within. Social maturity is what enables us to function as healthy adults. A high degree of Social maturity has something to do with a high degree of social skill. Adolescents are by definition, Socially immature, and nobody wants them to stay that the way as they grow in to adults. In fact, a great deal of difficulty involved in helping adolescents finds their way to become mature adults. It includes the development of social skills, psychomotor skills, self care, and social development. Any types of diseases can interfere with these skills.

This study on social maturity will help the researcher to find out the level of Social maturity among higher secondary students and thereby behavior can be categorized. This will enable the parents teacher to deal effectively with their school age children and help them to become mature adult.

Students emotions are important because their thought, feeling and mood affect their subsequent motivated behavior and learning. A study of understanding their emotional competency is undertaken to help them define their emotional needs. The development of emotional competency along with educational and personal progress is of utmost importance in adolescence (Daniel Goleman 1995). Our individual and self centered society is looking for a different perspective to access achievement and success. Underlying this perspective it is important to acknowledge the benefits of recognizing emotional competence among students and understanding how it may impact their well being.

A self actualization individual is not only an artist to himself, but great asset to the society also. Self actualization means to fulfill one's individual nature in all its aspects. One who is talented in one specific area feels uneasy if that talent is not nurtured and utilized. He wants to attain perfection in that area. The highest level of functioning occurs when a person is self actualized people can be motivated towards Self actualization only when the lower order needs are satisfied.

So there is an inherent relation between Social maturity, Emotional Competence and Self Actualization of individuals and an attempt has been made to study the same. Every human being should have the knowledge of good social relationship. Therefore Social Maturity, Emotional Competence and Self-Actualization are very essential and plays a significant role in Higher secondary school students which influences the life of student in their career.

OBJECTIVES OF THE STUDY

1. To find out the level of Social Maturity among higher secondary students.
2. To find out the level of Emotional Competence among higher secondary students.
3. To find out the level of Self Actualization among higher secondary students.
4. To find out the significant difference in Social Maturity among higher secondary students in relation to Gender.
5. To find out the significant difference in Social Maturity among higher secondary students in relation to Number of Siblings.
6. To find out the significant difference in Social Maturity among higher secondary students in relation to Type of Family.
7. To find out the significant difference in Social Maturity among higher secondary students in relation to Type of Management.
8. To find out the significant difference in Social Maturity among higher secondary students in relation to Family Income.
9. To find out the significant difference in Emotional Competency among higher secondary students in relation to Gender.
10. To find out the significant difference in Emotional Competency among higher secondary students in relation to Number of Siblings
11. To find out the significant difference in Emotional Competency among higher secondary students in relation to Type of Family.

12. To find out the significant difference in Emotional Competency among higher secondary students in relation to Type of Management.
13. To find out the significant difference in Emotional Competency among higher secondary students in relation to Family Income.
14. To find out the significant difference in Self Actualization among higher secondary students in relation to Gender
15. To find out the significant difference in Self Actualization among higher secondary students in relation to Number of Siblings.
16. To find out the significant difference in Self Actualization among higher secondary students in relation to Type of Family.
17. To find out the significant difference Self Actualization among higher secondary students in relation to Type of Management.
18. To find out the significant difference in Self Actualization among higher secondary students in relation to Family Income.
19. To find out whether there is significant correlation between Social Maturity and Emotional Competency of higher secondary students.
20. To find out whether there is significant correlation between Social Maturity and Self Actualization of higher secondary students.
21. To find out whether there is significant correlation between Emotional Competency and Self -Actualization of higher secondary students.

LIMITATIONS OF THE STUDY

The present study had been restricted to the following limitations.

- The study has been restricted only to the Higher secondary students.
- It includes a sample size of 600 Higher secondary students.
- The sample has been chosen from Chennai only.

CONCLUSION

The nature of the present study has been discussed briefly in this chapter bringing out the significance of the study, objectives of the study etc. The terms operationally defined in this study have been reviewed theoretically from the related literature available, which gives a broader perspective in the light of which appropriate hypothesis could be framed and tested. A detailed discussion of the related literature follows in the next chapter.

❒

7

Review of Related Literature

The investigator feels that the study of related literature helps in acquiring information about the studies done in the field, protects against unnecessary duplication, guides in carrying out the investigation successfully and makes him familiar with the steps. In the context of identification of a problem for research, the purpose of systematic reading is beneficial to discover the major issues and the research methodologist related to the chosen area. Opinion articles, theoretical discussions and reviews of research give a theoretical grounding to the research study.

Comprehensive sources such as the Encyclopedia of Educational Research, Dissertation Abstracts International, The Hand book of Research, Survey of Educational Research and similar publications are goldmines which could assist the investigator to develop insight into the problem. It helps to formulate hypotheses for the study, to develop a proper research design for the study and facilitate to interpret the research findings in the light of what has already been reported and recorded. In the following pages, a review is made on the studies conducted in India and abroad related to the present study.

IMPORTANCE OF THE REVIEW OF RELATED LITERATURE

Review of related literature is an important pre-requisite for actual planning and execution of any research work. `We should not neglect a particular things because it is of past and should not accept a new one because of its newness. It is only with the reference to old that a new thing can be learned. It is necessary to connect previous knowledge with the new idea to be grasped. It means that to learn a new thing our previous knowledge must be brought to the forefront. It is imperative for a review of previous studies on the subject before embarking upon making a fresh study. In this chapter an attempt has been made to take cognizance of studies, which has relevance to present problem. Sometimes the studies reviewed could not be classified into the areas concerned. The review was intended to provide a background to the study that followed and it was thought that such an attempt would be of great help for the formation of hypothesis.

To widen the understanding of the chosen topic, it is essential to retrace the existing literature on parental encouragement and study involvement. And the review of the literature is done under the following caption:

- Studies related to social maturity
- Studies related to emotional competence
- Studies related to self actualization

STUDIES RELATED TO SOCIAL MATURITY

Kathuria, M. (1974) has investigated some personality determinants of vocational maturity and career inductiveness and the sample consists of 1000 female undergraduates in arts and science course at two women colleges and two women colleges at Ajmer in Rajasthan State, the sample was in the age range of 16 to 21 years. Vocational development inventory by critics. This inventory was prepared by the investigator and it had a reliability index of 0.73. This scale was termed as vocational maturity scale. The major findings were informal experience related to higher scores on the vocational maturity scale and lower scores on the vocational indecision scale.

Ghosh, S (1975) conducted a study on the social maturity of preschool age Bengalee children of Calcutta city belonging to different social-economic groups. His findings were to construct a scale for to appraisal of social maturity. To certify the value of social quotient in predicting the intelligence quotient. To apply the scale for appraisal of social maturity of normal longitudinal study and different clinical groups.

Kale S.V. and Danke, B. D. (1976) has conducted a developmental norm project (5 ½ to 11 years).The study indicating relationship between the independent variables, viz. scores in Mathematics, language and social maturity tests; between the dependent variable and independent variable, between dependent and intervening variable the cognitive development and between independent and intervening variables.

Vora, J.I (1980) in his research works on social maturity of B.Ed., students in Gujarat. The sample size was 855 student teachers from Gujarat University, South Gujarat University and M.S University. Some of the major findings were i) The male students were superior to the female students in their social maturity ii) Age had no relation with social maturity iii) The arts students were socially mature than Science students. iv)The higher socio- economic status had better social maturity.

Savaluk Thongngamkhom (1983) made a study on social maturity and psycho-socio-adjustment factors of B.Ed college students of Thailand. The sample of 922 students from North central region of Thailand was taken in to consideration and the self constructed social maturity tool was tested. The major finding were 1) Students from low socio economic status had more social maturity 2) The students having dominant personality were more socially natured 3) The students having good social adjustment were more socially matured.

Puranik S.D., (1985) has studied the relationship of social maturity of pupils with organizational climate and teacher's morale in the primary schools of Bangalore city. The sample consists of 70 schools 2634 students and 712 teachers. The major findings were, in the development and unaided students and urban location of schools were found to be the most conductive factors. No effect of morale of teachers of both sexes was noticed on the development of social maturity of male 9(or) female students (or) on the students of both sexes even under the influence of organizational climates, school organizations and localities.

Pattramon Jumpangern (1986) conducted a study on socially maturity of higher secondary school students of Western region of Thailand. The sample of 669 was tested by self constructed questionnaire consist of 60 students. The major finding were 1) The higher secondary students coming from urban areas were more socially matured than rural students 2)students having dominance personality traits were more socially matured 3)The students having good leadership traits were more socially matured.

Asthana, Anju(1989) made a study on social maturity among school going chidren in the city of Lucknow. The sample of 450 children studying in Grade I through v were selected randomly. The self constructed questionnaire was used for social maturity. Some of the major findings were i) Social maturity increase with increased in grade level, the growth rate being highest in the first school year ii) Gender did not present a consistent picture of its association with social maturity at different grade levels iii) Girls were found to be more mature socially than boys.

Malin A.J. (1990) conducted a study on the relationship of social maturity with classroom climate and academic achievement. The sample consisted of 1200 students of classes VIII and IX. The tools used were Edward's Social Maturity Scale and achievement test. It is found that students studying in classes IX have higher maturity as compared students of class VIII.

Sarojamma, Y. H. (1990) in his study on reading ability and social maturity of VII Std students, collected, sample of 1,000 students of Kannada medium. The tools used were social maturity scale by Sathyanarayana and Sudha. Some of the major findings were i)There was significant difference in the reading ability and social maturity ii) There was significant difference in the reading ability and students having high and low social maturity.

Mulia R.D. (1991) made a comparative study of the social maturity of higher secondary students. The sample was 350 students from arts stream and science stream. The social maturity inventory constructed by J.I. Vora was used. Some of the major findings were i)There was no significant difference in social maturity among students of the three streams and between the two sexes ii) The interaction effect among streams and gender on social maturity was not significant.

Bhushan, A (1994) conducted a study on social maturity across sex and family vocations. The sample considered of 200 student teachers from two colleges, equality divided between two sexes. Major variables used were sex values and family vocations. The tools used for data collections were the form D value of survey. The study highlights male and female uniformly assigned highest importance to social maturity. Both male and female from service and non-service class had politeness as s sub division on their maturity.

Baues Ann Leslie (1995), investigated on self esteem, social maturity and pattern of social choice. The sample chosen for the study was rural main strain sixth students. Control group (N=9) treatment group 1 (N=30) high school students and treatment group 2 (N=25) adult group leaders. The sample was tested sociometric pattern of choice. COMPSOC tread well and saxton. Some of the major finding were 1)In social maturity some significant difference were found for gender. 2) There was significant relationship between self esteem and social maturity.

Flymin Xavier, J., (2003) attempted a study on social maturity and academic achievement among higher secondary school students. The sample of 300 were taken from government, government aided and private higher secondary schools in Trivandrum. The sample was tested by Rao's Social maturity scale. Some of the major findings were i) Gender has no influence on social maturity iii) Social maturity and academic achievement are positively correlated.

Mani, M., (2004) did his study on social maturity and adherence to school regulation of higher secondary students. Taken the sample of 300 higher secondary school students studying in 5 different schools in Chennai. Rao's social maturity scale was used for administration. Some of the major findings were i) Gender has significant bearing on social maturity and adherence to school regulations iii) There is significant relationship social maturity and academic achievement.

Saravanan, K., (2005) attempted a research on social maturity and self concept among higher secondary school students. The sample of 249 boys and girl who studied XI STD in various schools in Chennai was taken. Rao's social maturity scale was used for administration. Some of the major findings were i) Social maturity is found to be moderate. ii) Gender has no influence on social maturity iii) Type of school had no significant difference on social maturity.

Thiagu. S (2005) Conducted a study on creating and social maturity of secondary grade teacher trainees. The tools used in the study were verbal test of creative thinking prepared and standardized by Bager mehdi (1973) and measure the social maturity of the secondary grade teacher trainees the social maturity scale designed and standardized by nalini and rao was used. The sampling technique used was stratified random sampling. The study was conducted among 225 secondary grade teacher trainees drawn from different training institutes. The mean scores obtained for the men and women teacher trainees for flexibility level of creativity shows that female members scores higher than the male teacher trainees and it is statistically and thus the empirical hypothesis is retained. I was found that a significant difference occurred in the originally level of men and women teacher trainee. Significant different found between teacher trainees studying in government and government aided secondary grade training institutes. On their Social adequacy, personal adequacy interpersonal and social maturity.

Surjit Singh and Dr.Praveen Thukrall (2010), Conducted a study on social maturity and academic achievement of high school students. The study aimed at studying the relationships of social maturity with academic achievement of high school students and also to see the regional and gender differences on the basis of their social maturity. The study was conducted over a sample of 400 (200 boys and 200 girls) high school students studying in Xth class in 8 different schools (4 urban and rural) affiliated to CBSE New Delhi. Dr.Nalini Rao`s social maturity scale was used to measure social maturity and the aggregate score of the selected students in the board examinations was taken to their level academic achievement. The results reported that there exists significant relationship between social maturity and academic achievement of high school students. No significant differences were observed between boys and girls as well as rural and urban high school students on the basis of their social maturity.

Lee and Sang Kill and Yi (2011) conducted a study on family systems as predictors of career attitude maturity for Korean high school students. This study Examined the relationships between family systems and high school students career development family adaptability and family cohesion were considered as indicators of family function, and career attitude maturity was conceptualized as a representative factor explaining adolescents career development. A total of 634 high school students participated in this study Overall, the results showed that family adaptability and family cohesion were both significant predictors of tenth graders career attitude maturity. The effects parents educational backgrounds on career attitude maturity were negligible. How ever the relationships were inconsistent across gender. For female students, family cohesion was a more influential predictor of career attitude maturity then family adaptability, while the opposite pattern was observed for the male students.

STUDIES RELATED TO EMOTIONAL COMPETENCE

Megrew and scott (1989), investigated the relation between adaptive and maladaptive behaviour and other important human competence constructs in the context of a model of personal competence. It was concluded that adoptive and maladaptive behaviours were distinct dimensions separate from, but related to, the dimensions of intelligence and physical competence. Support was also found for portions of Green span's model of personal competence which defines personal competence as a combination of the broad abilities of practical intelligence (adaptive behaviour) emotional competence (maladaptive behaviour), conceptual intelligence, physical competence and social intelligence.

Rajendran and Kaliappan (1990), examined the efficacy of a six month behavioural programme in managing emotional competence level and improving academic performance in higher secondary students (boys) who reported high stress associated with personal inadequacy, fear of failure, and interpersonal difficulties. Programme components included training in relaxation, study skills, assertiveness and effective communication. Post-test results revealed, increased personal adequacy reduced fear of failure and improved interpersonal relations teachers and parents. Overall changes in stress levels led to improved academic performance.

Schechtman (1990), proposed a classroom intervention programme based on value clarification theory, designed to enhance the therapeutic atmosphere. This holistic intervention took into account cognition, emotion, and behaviour.

The programme was oriented towards helping the individual over a period of time to become a constructive member of the society.

Palmer and Paisley (1991), presented student assistance programmes structured for intervention with adolescents. These programmes were designed to help students and their families with problems that affect their personal lives and academic performance. Henriksen (1991) described the implementation of a peer-helping programme for the Canadian ninth graders. The programme was designed to train selected students in basic helping skills and to promote their self-confidence, communication skills, problem-solving and decision-making abilities. Helping tasks included tutoring and designing Instructional materials. Results showed that the programme had a positive effect on both the helpers and the school.

Training programmes involving problem-solving skills have been found to improve academic performance (Larson, 1984; Kanchana, 1986) in her study found that study skills training significantly increased the performance of the ninth standard students belonging to low soco-economic status. Many studies have focused on the several correlates of academic performance. Pintrich and DeGroot (1990) examined the relationship among the motivational orientation, self-regulated learning and academic performance of the seventh graders. Self-efficacy and intrinsic value were positively related to cognitive engagement and performance self-regulation. Self-efficacy and test-anxiety emerged as predictors of performance. Intrinsic motivation was found to be enhanced by better conductive environment that highlighted self-determination.

Garner. W (1996) conducted study the purpose of which was to evaluate whether emotional understanding continues to impact children's social competence once they reach middle childhood. Thirty nine low-income third and fourth graders were administered three emotional knowledge tasks: a) emotional roll talking b) knowledge of affective attributions and c) knowledge of emotional display rules. The children also reported on the quality of their peer relations and teachers provided ratings of the children's pro-social behavior. Results revealed that children's attribution of aggression and denial were positively related to their reports of negative peer interactions. Children's pre-social behavior was positively predicted by emotional roll-taking ability and knowledge of pro-social display rules. These findings underscored by importance of emotional knowledge for children's social functioning across early and middle childhood.

Friedman Sara R, Rapport Lisa J (2003), evaluated social and emotional competence using self-report and behavioral measures in adults with attention-defect hyperactivity disorder (ADHD) and controls. Adults with ADHD viewed themselves competent but more sensitive toward violations of social norms than controls. Films depicting emotional interactions were used to assess linguistic properties of free recall and perceived emotional intensity. Although adults with ADHD used more words to describe the scenes, they used fewer emotion- related words, despite rating the emotions depicted as more intense than did controls. In contrast, no group differences for words depicting social or cognitive processes were observed. Overall, adults with ADHD appear more aware of their problems in social versus emotional skills. Findings may have implications for improving the psychological functioning of these adults.

Sarah W. Blackstone, David P. Wilkins (2006), explored the importance of Emotional competence in children with complex communication needs. Research has shown that children with significant language impairments lag behind their typically developing peers in communicative and emotional competence. The research also explores the importance of emotional competence in children with complex communication needs.

Alison L. Miller, Sarah E. Fine, (2007), examined relations between three facts of emotional competence: emotion knowledge, level of negative emotion expression and emotion regulation of low income pre scholars (N=60) and their associations with indicators of classroom adjustment. Emotion knowledge was positively related to positive emotion regulation but was not related to negative expression or negative deregulation. Negative emotion expression was associated with aggression and social skills after covering verbal ability, age and emotion knowledge and negative emotion expression. Positive emotion regulation was related negatively to anxiety and positively to social skills covering all other variables in the model. Results were discussed with regard to using the emotional competence domain to understand how emotion processing relates to early childhood adjustment.

Alysia Y. Blandon, Susan D. Calkins (2007), examined the longitudinal associations between maternal parenting behavior and toddler risk with children's emotional and social competence were examined during the transition to kindergarten, in a sample of 253 children. Toddler risk was characterized by early externalizing behavior and poor emotion regulation skills. The interaction among maternal parenting behavior and toddler risk. There were some significant interactions, although the pattern of results was not consistent across all competence outcomes. Maternal parenting behavior was not directly associated with children's emotional and social competence. In some instances, maternal control has differential implications for children's emotional and social competency depended upon the child's level of early risk and maternal positive parenting.

Lynn R. Offer man, James R. Bailey (2007), studied the relative contributions of emotional competence and cognitive ability to individual and team performance, team- member attitude and leadership perceptions were examined. Focusing on emotional competencies, it was predicted that, although both cognitive ability would account for more variance on individual's tasks, whereas emotional competence would account for more variance in team performance and attitudes and to both leader emergence and effectiveness. Using a sample of undergraduate business majors who completed tasks alone and as members of teams, the results generally supported the hypotheses

Begeer Etal. (2008), studied emotional competence in children with autism: Diagnostic criteria and empirical evidence. The researchers reported four aspects of emotional competence that are important to children's daily social functioning (expression, perception, responding, and understanding), differentiated between mentally retarded and normally intelligent children and adolescents with and without ASD in natural and structured contexts. On various accounts, the emotional impairments of children with ASD that are found in scientific studies

Castejon, Juan Luis (2008), studied on differences in the Socio-Emotional competence profile in University students from different Disciplinary Area. The main objective of this paper is to establish a profile of socio-emotional competencies characteristic of a sample of students from each of the big academic areas in higher education; legal sciences, social sciences, education, humanities, science and technology, and health. An additional objective was to analyse differences between the fields. Method; The study was carried out on a large sample (N=608) of university students from 14 different programs at the university of Alicante (Spain). Assessment was taken using different measures in emotional intelligence, such as TMMS and EQ-i. Result; results of the one way analysis of variance among the different scientific fields revealed that significant differences appear in practically all aspects in Emotional Intelligence, expect for the stress management variable. Discussion: Based on these results, implications are drawn for developing generic socio-emotional competencies in the framework of the European Space for higher education.

Katja Petrowski, (2008), studied children's social-emotional competence development. The social-emotional competence of 65 Asian-American and Latin-American children was observed at the beginning and the end of their kindergarten year. Initially, significant differences existed among these ethnic groups in respect to moral reasoning. Furthermore, the male children showed more deregulated aggression but the female children implemented more moral reasoning than their male counterparts. These ethnic specificities did not disappear over the course of the year. In addition, a significant change in avoidance strategies as well as expressed emotions in the narrative took place over the course of one year. Ethnic specificity in social-emotional competence does exist independent of gender at the beginning as well as well as at the end of the kindergarten year in a multi-ethnic kindergarten classroom. Reported on the quality of their peer relations and teachers provided ratings of the children's pro-social behavior. Results revealed that children's attribution of aggression and denial were positively related to their reports of negative peer interactions. Children's pro-social behaviour was positively predicated by emotional roll-taking ability and knowledge of pro-social display rules. These findings underscored by importance of emotional knowledge for children's social functioning across early and middle childhood.

Shari L. Kidwell, Lisa D. Hinkle (2008), examined attachment in association with preschooler's emotional functioning among 54 predominantly low-income families living in Appalachia. Attachment was assessed t age 4 years using the Strange Situation (Blehar, Water, & Wall, 1978) and classified with the PAA (Crittenden, 2004). Emotional competence was measured via an interview about children's memories for six emotions, rated in terms of both emotion understanding and regulation. Parent-teachers and self-reports of children's internalizing and externalizing symptoms were also completed. Questionnaires and interviews assessed socioeconomic risk and parental symptoms and negative childhood experiences. Children's PAA strategies were significantly associated with risks, emotion regulation and understanding, and symptoms. Children using highly coercive strategies showed the greatest difficulties. Emotion regulation and understanding also were associated with parent- and teacher-report of symptoms. These findings suggest that intervention efforts with at-risk youngsters should target only attachment security, but also emotional competence skills.

Danielle M. Hessler and Lynn Fainsilber Katz (2009), examined associations between emotional competence (i.e., awareness, regulation, comfort with expression) and adolescent risky behavior. Children from a longitudinal study participated at age 9 and 16 (N=88). Semi-structured interviews were conducted with children about their emotional experiences and coded for areas of emotional competence. Associations were examined for the emotions of sadness and anger concurrently during adolescence, and longitudinally from middle childhood to adolescence. Results suggested that children with poor emotional awareness and regulation had a higher likelihood of using hard drugs. Findings suggest that children's emotional competence may serve as a useful point of intervention to decrease risky behavior in adolescence.

Kumar (2009), conducted a study on mental health and emotional competence of prospective teachers of Himachal Pradesh in relation to their gender, stream and social category and found that male and female prospective teachers of science and arts streams belonging to open and reserved categories differed significantly in their "Adequate Depth of Feeling", "Adequate Expression and Control of Feeling", "Ability to Function with Emotions", "Ability to cope with problem Emotions" and "Encouragement of Positive Emotions" Component of emotional competence. Prospective teachers of science and arts streams belonging to open and reserved categories differed significantly in their total emotional competence.

Marion. E. Young (2009), Studied the aspects of emotional competence that protect people from stress, anxiety, and depression, and help to promote positive affect. A total of 163 university students completed a two wave study that involved measuring emotional competence and emotional well-being at 1-year intervals. As expected, Time 1 measures of emotional competence predicted Time 2 measures of well-being, after controlling for Time 1 measures of well-being. Specifically, ineffective problem orientation predicated increases in anxiety and stress, and decreases in positive affect. Difficulty identifying and describing emotions predicated increases in anxiety and decreases in positive affect. Finally, an aspect of difficulty managing emotions (i.e. rumination) predicated decreases in positive affect. Each emotional competence variable predicated unique variance after controlling for other significant variables.

Patricia and Mark (2009), studied classroom teacher, social and emotional competence in relation to student and classroom out comes. The researchers proposed a model of the pro social classroom that highlights the importance of teachers" social and emotional competence (SEC) and well–being in the development and maintenance of supportive teacher–student relationships, effective classroom management and successful social and emotional learning programme implementation. This model proposes that these factors contribute to creating a classroom climate that is more conducive to learning and that promotes positive developmental outcomes among students. Furthermore, this article reviews current research suggesting a relationship between SEC and teacher burnout and reviews intervention efforts to support teachers" SEC through stress reduction and mindfulness programms. Finally, the authors propose a research agenda to address the potential efficacy of intervention

Colle, L.and Del Giudice, M. (2011), investigated the relationship between patterns of attachment and emotional competence at the beginning of middle childhood in a sample of 122 seven-year-olds. Anew battery of tasks was developed in order to assess two facets of emotional competence (emotion recognition and knowledge)of regulation strategies). Attachment was related to the choice of emotion regulation strategies in hypothetical situations.

Holeyannavar, P.G., Itagi, S.K.(2011), studied emotional competence and stressors of 105 primary school teachers was conducted in Dharwad in

2009. Emotional competence was assessed using EC-scale and stressors by stress inventory for teachers (SIT). Results revealed that majority of the teachers (89.5%) showed average to competent levels in emotional competence, followed by 6.7 and 3.8% in incompetent and highly competent levels respectively. Most of them (64.7%) indicated average to high levels of stress and 35.2% with low stress. Age and work experience showed positive and highly significant relationship with the emotional competence of teachers. The stress of teachers showed negative and highly significant relationship with age and work experience. Negative and highly significant relationship was observed between the stressors and emotional competence of the teachers. Thus the study concluded that increase in the emotional competence reduced the stressors of the primary school teachers significantly.

Naveen.k (2011), examined "the emotional competence level of teacher educators". This study aimed at finding the emotional competence level of teacher educators working in B.Ed. colleges with respect to their gender, experience, educational level and marital status. The study was carried out on a sample of 150 teacher educators of district Sonepat and Panipat of Haryana State. The results revealed that teacher educators have an average level of emotional competence and there is no significant difference in the level of emotional competence of teacher educators with respect to their gender, experience, educational level and marital status

Prema. S (2011), Studied Emotional competence family environment, self concept, adolescents in relation to academic achievement. The tools used in the study were personal data sheet constructed by the investigator. Emotional competence scale (latha 2002) family environment scale (bhata and chadha 1993) self concept questionnaires (Dr.Rajkumar sarawat 1981) The data was collected from 300 students. The finding of the study indicate a significant correlation between the academic achievement and emotional competence of adolescence students. The ability of adolescent students to manage their emotion and behaviour is an important prerequisite for academic success. It is also inferred from the present study that the family environment also contributes to a larger extent in enhancing the emotional competence of adolescent students. This could be utilized to study way of decreasing conflict and improve cohesion and caring within families. So as to contribute to emotional competence of adolescent students. Emotional Competence the soft skill could contribute to better interpersonal relationship social skill and improvement in the handling of one's disruptive emotions. So an awareness could be created among parents and teachers to train their works in attaining high Emotional Competence.

Rana (2011) found that level of emotional competence and other variables i.e. sex, stream, family type and type of school did not interact significantly with respect to their combined influence on aggression among senior secondary school students.

Wang and Et all (2011), studied the development and validation of the widener emotional learning scale (WELS), a self-report measure, for assessing students social and emotional competence in higher education. Conceptual specification, item development, psychometric properties, and factor structure of the instrument are reported in the article. The resulting instrument consists of 33 items with 5 subscales; Awareness of Emotions in self and others, Tolerance of difference or Conflict, Interpersonal Relationship Skills, Flexibility in Perspective-Taking Behavior, and Self-Management Skills. A cross-validation study of the WELS with the Bar-On emotional Quotient Inventory (Bar-On EQ-i) provides evidence that, although the WELS assesses some aspects of social and emotional competence also associated also assessed by the Bar-On EQ-I, it makes a unique contribution in assessing flexibility in perspective taking and behavior. Across-validation study of the WELS WITH THE Mayer- Salovey-Caruso Emotional Intelligence Test (MSCEIT) indicates that, in general, The WELS assesses different aspects in emotional competence than the MSCEIT, in a manner that is consistent with the differences in the theoretical approaches underlying the two instruments.

Bagheri (2012) investigated the emotional competence and self-esteem in students of performing arts and students of other fields of art. The results showed that there was significant difference between performing artists and non-performing artists in emotional competence. Emotional competence level of performing artists was significantly higher than the non-performing artists.

Bakshi (2012) conducted a study on emotional competence of adolescents in relation to cognitive and non-cognitive variables and found a positive correlation of emotional competence with intelligence, creativity, academic achievement, family environment and mental health.

Katna (2012) found no significant difference in the emotional competence of senior secondary school students in relation to their gender, stream, locality, type of school and social category.

Kumar (2012) found that secondary school students having competent, average and incompetent level of emotional competence possessed the same level of aggressive behaviour. Also the emotional competence level and gender, stream, and institution type did not interact significantly with regard to their combined influence on aggression among students.

Sunil kumar (2012), studied on "Emotional competence of senior secondary school teachers in relation to their age, gender, type of school & locality "In developing society, a teacher has assumed a greater responsibility to bring out good citizens who could carry out the profession in a dignified and productive manner. To support the work of the organization teachers must have not only technical management skill but also skill in managing emotions, there as well as those of other individuals in the organization. Emotional competent teacher exhibits a high regard for colleagues and subordinates, an understanding of basic motivations as well as basic justice, as willingness to correct faculty situations, and a willingness to take positive, quick, and aggressive action when indicated. In this context the investigators conducted a study of Emotional Competence of 200 senior secondary school teachers. The major objectives of the study were to compare the Emotional Competence of male and female, rural and urban teachers. The Emotional Competence Scale (ECS) by H.C. Sharma and R. Bharadwaj was used to assess the effectiveness of teachers. Mean, S.D and‘t’ test were used to analyze the data. The results indicated that no significant difference was found in Emotional Competence of teachers on the basis of gender whereas a significant difference has been found in Emotional Competence of teachers on the basis of their age and type of school.

Sharma Ritu (2013), examined “A Study of Emotional Competence of Visually Impaired Adolescents” The study was conducted on Visually Impaired Adolescents to know their emotional competence. For the purpose, Scale of Emotional Competence (Sharma H.C. and Bhardwaj, R.) was administered to a sample of 18 visually impaired adolescents (12 boys and 6 girls). Results showed that both genders possess average level of emotional competence. It was seen that only in one component of emotional competence (encouragement of positive emotions) females scored than males.

Sharma and Suman Lata (2013), studied on “Comparative Study of Emotional Competence among students in relation to their Gender and Type of Institute” The major objective of the investigation was to compare the emotional competence among students studying in K.V (KendriyaVidyalaya) and Non K.V schools. It was hypothesized that no significant difference of emotional competence among students studying in K.V and non K.V schools. For verification of the hypothesis, the data was collected by administering ‘Emotional competence scale’ on 200 students of Ludhiana district of Punjab by adopting convenient sampling technique. Mean, SD and t-ratio was used for analyzing data. The finding of the present study revealed that emotional competence of K.V students significantly differ from non K.V students. There is no significant difference in emotional competence of Non KV boys and Non KV girl students of Ludhiana Dist. Another finding of present indicates that gender does not affect emotional competence.

STUDIES RELATED TO SELF ACTUALIZATION

An investigation was made by Beneff, Christene. K. (1991), on staff development in light of Moslow's theory, described the teacher's change process in an organ staff development program, examination faculty development within the framework of Maslow's theory says people are motivated to satisfy physiological safety, security, social self esteem and self-actualization needs programs. Evaluations demonstrated the interdependence of the cognitive and affective realism of professional growth.

Desai Hemant-K (1991), investigated on: self help as an adjust to psychotherapy issues of awareness, motivation and self actualization. The nature of the process involved in the phenomena of psychological change and self development as related to the concept of self help and mutual aid are examined in this paper. Awareness, motivation and self actualization are seen as part so a fundamental process of growth and development. It was suggested that a parallel to the personal growth and developments may be found in the cross roots social philosophy of the self help movement. Two aspects of the self-help movement were examined in detail an analysis of the literature on the subject and a discussion of the various functions of mutual groups. The concept of self help was seen an ides revenant to coping with a rapidly changing environment. The paper was organized into four parts. The first part defined awareness and examined paradigms of eastern and western cultures. The second part examines motivating and mutual aid as a catalyst. The third part on self actualization and discussed social help as self help with affection to the relation between professionals and mutual aid groups and the social complications of the movement towards self help. The fourth part, a conclusion briefly reviewed the paradigm shift that the human services field has been undergoing, using the phrase "paradigm lost and paradigm gained" to sum up the movements away from depersonalized professionalism and towards mutual self help and group process.

Penningtion Martha-c (1992), studied on motivating English languages teachers through job enrichment .Language culture and curriculum Hackman's (1987) job characteristics model of work motivation was described and applied to English language teaching with concrete recommendations made on the basis of Hack man's action principles for job design. The approach results in teacher opportunities for long term growth, career advancement increased self-actualization and development.

Bynum Lourise-L; Seaman, Michael –A (1993), studied on motivations of third age students in learning in retirement institutes. A profile of 452 older adults enrolled in learning in retirements institutes showed they had relatively high economic status and extensive educational backgrounds. They were motivated by self-actualization, perceived cognitive gaps, intellectual curiosity and social contact. An intellectual stimulating curriculum was a pivotal factor in predicating program success and appeal.

The study of Low Guat tin; Marican Mukhthar (1993), was about selected factors and characteristics of self motivation and to innovative dominant factors and features of motivation among 90 Singapore elementary school teachers. Through item analysis, the following factors remerged as underlying motivation, esteem, self- actualization, security autonomy belonging achievement orientation professional challenges and task identity

Benally Herbert John (1994), made an investigation on about journal of Navajo education. He described Navajo philosophy and implications for teaching and learning. He explained four branches of knowing that provide a framework for conceptualizing teaching content as well as interrelationship with in the framework providing opportunities experiences based instruction that enabled students to attain knowledge in ways that spirituality reverences self actualization and happiness.

Lewis John. D (1995), under took a study on self actualization and self concept of 368 intellectually gifted students in grades 4 through 12 were investigated, using the Relation of Self by Youth (ROSY) the Maslowian scale and the Piers Harris children's self-concept scale. It was found that the mean for high school students was higher than for the elementary or junior high students and men for girls was higher than boys.

Brennan, Thomas P. and Piechowski. Michael M. (1997), conducted a Case Studies of Self-Actualization". In this Case studies of self-actualizing people according to the ideas of A. Maslow and the criteria of K.Dabrowski are presented. To find people meeting the criteria of Level 4 of the Dabrowski theory, a pool of 21 subjects was established by nomination. All subjects were given the Definition – Response Instrument to assess levels of emotional development. One man and three women were selected for study based on their levels of functioning. A life history was obtained from each subject. Interviews were the richest source of material. As result, there of the four subjects were found to be self-actualizing. They displayed a commonality possessed by self-actualizers, kindness and simplicity in responding to problem basic to humanity. It was possible to assess the degree of self-actualization with the interviews techniques developed. The interview guide, life history questions and definitions of the dynamisms of self-actualization are included in appendices. (SLD).

Partkin, Kay; Gaa, John; Swank, Paul; Liberman, Dov (1998), conducted study "Psychosocial Development and Self-Actualization across Age Groups : Middle-Aged and Senior Adults Compared Developmentally." In their study they examined the research question whether there is significant differences in psychosocial development and self-actualization exist between adult cohort groups whose childhood development occurred under very different social, economic and technological circumstances. Sample taken for the study comprises of 113 white middle-aged and elderly adults from similar socioeconomic settings. Subjects completed the Measures of Psychosocial Development (MPD) (G.Hawle. 1998) and the Personal Orientation Inventory (POI) (E.Shostrom, 1966), a measure of self-actualization. The only generational difference found for the MPD results was for industry versus University Faculty's Perceived Barriers to Effective Online Instruction." Researchers conducting this qualitative descriptive study explored the attitudes, experiences, teaching practices and perceived barriers to effective online instruction for university faculty. Data collected in a manner that Participants (n=101) were emailed an invitation to participate in the online, open-ended survey research through distance learning list serves within the United States. Faculty from two-and four year universities, nonprofit and for profit institutions, and who had taught online a minimum of two semsters were included in the sample. Data were coded for common themes, and five major catergories emerged Administrative and Institutional Support, Student Readiness, Instructor Readiness, Technical Support, and Academic Integrity, Implications for practice as well as suggestion for enhancing the "Self actualization" of online faculty will be discussed.

Parthiban. M (2008), Conducted study on Investigation in to Adjustment Behaviour of college students in relation their self actualization. The tools used in the study were Adjustment inventory prepare by huge M.Bells (1960) self actualization scale constructed John korte. In this study, a sample 238 students studying in the colleges in tamilnadu during the academic year 2007-2008 were chosen, using staratified random sampling technique. It is clear that there is significant difference between the meen scores of self actualization, adjustment behaviour and the various dimensions of adjustment with respect of course of study of college students. It is also clear that engineering students have high selfa-ctualization has legal study students. Teacher trainees have significantly higher adjustment than engineering and legal study students more over medicos have lesser home adjustment than students with all other branches of study. They have lesser healthy adjustment than students studying in arts and science law and education college. In the case of self assertion teacher trainees are significantly higher than medicos significantly higher than medicon, engineering and legal study students medicos have less emotional adjustment and friendliness than arts and science students. Legal study students and teacher trainees. It is also proved that teacher trainees have higher masculinity than the other four groups of students.

Croft, Gillian; Boyer, Wanda; Hett. Geoffrey (2009), in their article "Self-Actualization: The Heart and Soul of a Potentia-Based Life Skills Program for a Child with Multiple Disabilities" says that although every child with disabilities any may come to self-actualization by different means and measurement it is, nevertheless, and important goal. The child with disabilities may be guided toward her goal of self-actualization by being encouraged to find her individual strengths and capacities and by being assisted to successfully interact with her environment. This article explores the use of the scientific method of support the development of a potential-based program that has nurtured self-actualization and the joy of learning for a child with multiple disabilities and chronic illness.

Schruimpf, Michael; Hickman, Philip: Wedlock, Dave (2009), conducted research on "A" Problem Based Learning Project Investigating the Underlying Dimension of Professional Learning Communities in Public Primary and Secondary Schools in the State of Missouri. In their study they provide a quantitative approach to analyzing college students levels of self actualization. Specifically, it addresses the distinction between students from non-rural and rural home towns relative to their level of self-actualization Students from five public state schools in one Midwestern state were surveyed. Self-actualization plays a key role in creating and developing the holistic concept of student Development. These concepts may assist in explaining needs, goals and developmental challenges of college students. Throughout the college years, students may ask themselves many questions, one in particulars "Who am I" Striving for self-actualization assists in answering this question. Development changes, at a crucial time in a student's identity occur in all types of students. Regardless of their background. In their study they focused on the development of students from the freshman to senior year. Development not related to physical characteristics, but to maturity, social interaction skills and the capability to better understand the self, is also known as sefl-actualization. Also, in their study they investigated how a student's hometown played a role in his or her self-actualization. It can be suggested that whether a student comes from a metropolitan or non-metropolitan area is a significant factor in whether or not a student dropped out, transferred or remained at the same institution. At the same time, adjusting to college, once on campus has shown to be affected by a student's hometown. Findings on hometowns and students levels to self-actualization revealed that there is no difference between students from rural and non-rural hometowns on self-actualization. Results did suggest difference for gender, year in school and race on self-actualization. The need for further research is addressed.

Stulter, Susan Lee (2011), in her article gifted girls passion for fiction. The quest for meaning, growth, and Self Actualization illuminate the nature of the relationship that very able girls have with fiction, this is an interpretive account of the meaning that reading fiction holds for verbally gifted preadolescent girls. Ethnographic field methods were used to uncover the essences of the reading experience in the context of their daily lives. Data sources included the researchers field notes the girls taped book discussions, parent interviews and the girls reading journals. Major findings were that the girls read and make meaning in an and around three interconnected areas of intelligence and intensity. intellectual, imaginational, and emotional. As they read fiction, the girls engage in a process of determined growth in each of these domains of human awareness. The girls challenge themselves with difficult literature, critical and empathic thinking, and problem finding. As the girls read and meaning, they are involved in constructing their lives purpose. They are youthful Self-actualization.

CONCLUSION

The review of related literature gave the researcher an understanding of the research methodology, which refers to the way the study, is to be conducted. The review of related research work has enabled the investigator to formulate relevant hypotheses for the present study and to know about the tools and instruments, which proved to be useful and promising in the previous studies. Further, based on this review suitable methodology and a well planned strategy for the present investigation could be adopted.

❐

8

Design of the Study and Method of Investion

Research is the systematic process of collecting and analyzing information to increase our understanding of the phenomenon under study.

The present chapter highlights an overall picture of the design of the study in the form of hypotheses to be tested, the research tools used for the data collection, nature and selection of the sample, reliability and validity of the tools a brief description of the procedures adopted for the data collection, scoring and statistical techniques to be employee for the further analysis of the data. Educational researchers generally use methods such as survey research, experimental research, historical research, ethnographic research and comparative research. In this study research is carried out using survey method.

STATEMENT OF THE PROBLEM

The present study is entitled as "Relationship of Social Maturity and Emotional Competence with reference to Self- Actualization of Higher Secondary students".

DESIGN AND METHOD OF THE STUDY

Choosing a design for a study basically involves selecting the most appropriate techniques to solve the particular problem under investigation (Anderson, Durston and Poole, 1970).

The normative survey method is employed to describe or interpret what exist at present. The survey method gathers data form a relatively large number of cases at a particular time. It is not concerned with the statistics that result when data are abstracted from a number of individual cases.

HYPOTHESES OF THE STUDY

In the present study, the following hypotheses are formulated based on the objectives of the study.

- The level of Social Maturity among higher secondary students is moderate in nature.
- The level of Emotional Competence among higher secondary students is moderate in nature.
- The level Self Actualization among higher secondary students is moderate in nature.
- There is no significant difference in Social Maturity among higher secondary students in relation to Gender.
- There is no significant difference in Social Maturity among higher secondary students in relation to Number of Siblings.
- There is no significant difference in Social Maturity among higher secondary students in relation to Type of Family.
- There is no significant difference in Social Maturity among higher secondary students in relation to Type of Management.
- There is no significant difference in Social Maturity among higher secondary students in relation to Family Income.
- There is no significant difference in Emotional Competency among higher secondary students in relation to Gender.
- There is no significant difference in Emotional Competency among higher secondary students in relation to Number of Siblings.
- There is no significant difference in Emotional Competency among higher secondary students in relation to Type of Family.
- There is no significant difference in Emotional Competency among higher secondary students in relation to Type of Management.
- There is no significant difference in Emotional Competency among higher secondary students in relation to family income.
- There is no significant difference in Self Actualization among higher secondary students in relation to Gender.

- There is no significant difference in Self Actualization among higher secondary students in relation to Number of Siblings.
- There is no significant difference in Self Actualization among higher secondary students in relation to Type of Family.
- There is no significant difference Self Actualization among higher secondary students in relation to Type of Management.
- There is no significant difference in Self Actualization among higher secondary students in relation to Family Income.
- There is no significant correlation between Social Maturity and Emotional Competency of higher secondary students.
- There is no significant correlation between Social Maturity and Self Actualization of higher secondary students.
- There is no significant correlation between Emotional Competency and Self Actualization of higher secondary students.

TOOLS USED IN THE STUDY

The following tools were used for the present study

1. Rao's Social Maturity Scale (1986).
2. Emotional Competence Scale (Latha 2002).
3. John Korte's Self Actualization Scale (2007).

RAO'S SOCIAL MATURITY SCALE

Description

The maturity outcomes of school going population can best be estimated in the light of paucity of such essential increasing instruments. The social maturity scale was developed by Nalini Rao, Department of Education, Bangalore University. The framework for the integrated conceptual virtues of social maturity was adopted from the psycho-social structure formulated by Green Berger et al. The final form or the questionnaire (see Appendix – A) consists of 90 items known as "Rao's Social Maturity Scale (RSMS) (1986)

Administration

The social maturity scales were administered to the respondents in groups in the regular classroom situation. This instructions provided on the first page of the scale booklet is self explanatory. Reading of the instructions by the examiner to the group however ensures better conditions for responding to the items of the scale. The answers were recorded by the respondents on the scale protocol.

The time required completing the scales items are between 45 minutes and one hour classifications sought by the student regarding any item is to be handle by the examiner through encouraging the respondent in deciding for himself rather than by any suggestions.

Scoring

The final form of the questionnaire (see- Appendix A) consists of 90 items. Each item was accorded a four point response spread the intervals of which were labeled 'Strongly Agree' 'Agree' 'Disagree' and 'Strongly Disagree'. The successive response intervals were subsequently scored 4, 3, 2 and 1 with the high score representation mature response. There was no right or wrong answers. The answers are checked against the key and point is given for each item ticked as per the key. The total points obtained give a measure of social maturity scale.

TABLE. 8.1: Showing Scoring Key of the Questionnaire According to the Nature of Items.

Nature of Items	Strongly Agree	Agree	Disagree	Strongly Disagree
Positive 17, 21, 24, 26, 36, 39, 41, 42, 50, 51, 52, 54, 56, 57, 59, 63, 74, 77, 89, 90	4	3	2	1
Negative 1, 2, 3 ,4, 5, 6, 7 ,8, 9, 10, 11, 12, 13, 14, 15, 16, 18, 19, 20, 22, 23, 25, 27, 28, 29, 30, 31, 32, 33, 34, 35, 37, 38 ,40,43, 44, 45, 46, 47, 48, 49, 53, 55, 58, 60, 61, 62, 64, 65, 66, 67, 68, 69, 70, 71, 72, 73, 75, 76, 78, 79, 80, 81, 82, 83, 84, 85, 86, 87,88	1	2	3	4

EMOTIONAL COMPETENCE SCALE

Description

Emotional competence scale was constructed by Latha 2002. This questionnaire consisted of 45 items out of which 37 items measure Emotional Competence. There are 8 items which measure the tendency to be lie fake good.

Administration

The higher secondary school students were instructed that the test consisted 45 questions concerning Emotional Competence. After each question there were four columns "Always" "Sometimes" "Rarely" "Never". If they agree with the question, they were asked to put a tick in the respective choice. They were asked to answer all the question.

Scoring

The scoring to the response given by the respondent should be like the following.

TABLE. 8.2: Scoring the key for Emotional Competence Scale

Response Option	Scoring Procedure
Always	4
Sometimes	3
Rarely	2
Never	1

Item numbers 1,5, 11,13,18,19,20,22,27,31,39,41,44 and 45 are reverse scored while all the other items are scored directly. Range of scored is from 37 to 148. Interpretation of the scores would be as follows.

37 to 74 - Low
75 to 112 - Moderate
113 to 148 - High

The higher the score the higher the Emotional Competence of the subject. If the individual obtained maximum score of 32 on the lie scale (Item No's 6,17,21,26,29,35,39 and 42) it is considered as invalid for analysis and hence omitted.

SELF ACTUALIZATION SCALE

Description

The self actualization scale (2007) constructed and standardize by John Korte was used in this study. It consists of 15 statements. In this scale, options were given strongly agree, agree, somewhat agree and somewhat disagree, strongly disagree.

Administration

The following instructions were given to the students. "This is not a test."Try to understand how you feel about yourself actualization. There are 15 statements. You read each item and record your opinion as you think appropriate by putting (X) against one of the 5 categories viz. Strongly agree, agree, somewhat agree and somewhat disagree; strongly disagree for each of the items. The most appropriate response for each item is the one with you concur as you think it appropriate to you. Be frank ad record your responses accordingly for all the items, don't omit any item, be as fast you can and complete the questionnaire. Try to finish the scale within 20 minutes."

Scoring

Scoring key was done based on the following table.

TABLE. 8.3: Showing the Scoring for Self Actualization Scale

Showing the scoring key for self actualization scale nature of items	Items Numbers	Strongly Agree	Agree	Some what Agree	Some what Disagree	Strongly Disagree
Negative	1, 3, 4, 7, 10, 12,15	1	2	3	4	5
Positive	2, 5, 6, 8, 9, 11, 13, 14	5	4	3	2	1

SAMBLING DESIGN

i. Sample

Owing to the feasibility and viability of the study the research was carried out in Chennai city. Higher Secondary School Students belonging to Government school, Aided School and Private School were selected for the study.

b. Sampling Technique

Stratified random procedure was adopted to select the sample.

c. Sample size

A sample of 600 students was included for the prospective analysis in the present study, which included 200 students are from Government higher secondary school, 200 students are from Government Aided school and 200 students from Private school.

TABLE. 3.04: Showing the Sample taken by the Investigator

S. No	Name and place of the school	No. of students
1	St.Gabriel's Higher secondary school students.	200
2	St.Mary's Matriculation Girls Higher secondary school students	200
3	Dr.Ambedkar Government Higher Secondary School Students	200

PILOT STUDY

A Pilot study was carried out to know the suitability of the time required for the administration of the test and to establish the reliability and validity of the tools. The test was administered to a group of higher secondary school students. From among those selected for the sample of the present study, the reliability and validity of the questionnaire were determined as described below.

ESTABILISHING RELIABILITY AND VALIDITY

Reliability

The reliability of a test may be defined as the degree of consistency with which the test measures what it does measures. A test score is called reliable when we have reasons to believe it to be stable and trustworthy. The reliability of the different tools used for the present study was established as follows.

Reliability of Social Maturity scale

In this investigation, odd-even method was utilized to find out the reliability. It was administered to a group of 50 students from Higher secondary school. Caution was taken to see that none of the items provided diverse meaning when transformed. By computing the correlation co-efficient, reliability was calculated and found as 0.76.

Reliability of Emotional Competence scale

Reliability of emotional competence scale was found to be 0.72 (Cronbach Alpha Method)

Reliability of Self Actualization scale

Test-rested method was used in establishing the reliability of the scale. Karl Person product moments 'r' is worked out for these two sets of scores and it was found to be 0.75 which is the reliability co-efficient

VALIDITY

Validity means the ability to produce finding that are in agreement with conceptual or theoretical values. It refers to the success of the scale in measuring what it meant to measure. A test is valid, when it measures, truly and accurately the ability or quality one wants measure. Thus, validity means truthfulness of the test

Validity of Social Maturity scale

The questionnaire was shown to teacher educators, Psychologists, teachers, educationalist and students to have their opinion on the content validity of the questionnaire, from their response, it was found that the test has very high content validity. Beside the index of validity has been taken as a measure of validity. In this case, it works out to be 0.87 and hence the scale has considered having high criterion validity.

Validity of Emotional Competence scale

Intrinsic Validity of emotional competence scale was found to be 0.85

Validity of Self Actualization scale

The square root of reliability could also to be taken as a measure of validity and this worked to be 0.866 and hence self actualization scale had been considered to have high validity

MAIN STUDY

The validated tools were used for the Main Study to collect the necessary data through survey method using the questionnaire and scale. The study was carried out among Higher Secondary School students in Chennai, Tamil Nadu. In this investigation, the main purpose is to study, relationship of Social Maturity and Emotional Competence with reference to Self- Actualization of Higher Secondary students.

STATISTICAL TECHNIQUES USED IN THIS STUDY

Suitable descriptive and inferential statistical techniques were used in the interpretation of the data to draw out a more meaningful picture of results from the collected data. In the present study the following statistical measures were used.

- Mean
- Standard deviation
- Critical ratio
- AVOVA
- Correlation

MEAN

$$\text{Mean (x)} = A + \frac{\sum fd}{\sum f} \times i$$

Where,

A = Assumed mean

f = frequency

d = deviation from the assumed mean

i = Class interval

STANDARD DEVIATION

Standard Deviation, $SD\ (\sigma) = \sqrt{\frac{\sum fd^2}{N} - \left[\frac{\sum fd}{N}\right]^2} \times i$

Where,

f = Frequency

d = Deviation from the assumed mean

I = Class interval

N = Total frequency

'T' TEST

To continue the significance of difference between means of various measures test is used: 't' ratio is calculated from the relation.

$$\text{T-ratio} = \frac{M_1 \sim M_2}{\sqrt{\frac{\sigma_1^2}{N_1} + \frac{\sigma_1^2}{N_2}}} = \frac{M_1 \sim M_2}{S \in D}$$

Where,

$M_1\ M_2$= Means of the groups

SED = Standard Error Deviation

F-TEST

F- ratio = Variance between the group / Variance within the group Correlation term

$$C = \frac{\sum x_1 + \sum x_2 + \sum x_3}{N}$$

$$BSS = \left(\sum x_1\right)^2 / W_1 + \left(\sum x_2\right)^2 / W_2 + \left(\sum x_3\right)^2 W_3 - C$$

$$TSS = \sum x_1^2 + \sum x_2^2 + \sum x_3^2 - C$$

WSS= TSS - BSS

Where,

x_1, x_2, x_3, are score in different group

C = correction Terms

TSS = Total Sum of Squares

BSS = Between Sum of Squares

WSS= Within Sum of Squares

e. CO-EFFICIENT OF CORRELATION (R)

$$r = \frac{N\sum x\sum y-\sum x\sum y}{\sqrt{(N\sum x^2-(\sum x^2))(N\sum y^2-(\sum y)^2}}$$

x, y – Variables,

N- Total strength.

CONCLUSION

Adopting the methods and the procedures discussed earlier in this chapter tests were administered and marked. This chapter outlined the design of the study, the procedure followed and the nature of the sample. It describes the hypotheses to be tested, selection of tools, and the method of administration and scoring procedures. The obtained data were then analyzed using appropriate statistical techniques. The next chapter presents the analysis and interpretation of the data collected in the light of the hypothesis formulated.

❒

9

Analysis and Interpretation of Data

Research consists of systematic observation and description of the characteristics of properties. The purpose of the research is to discover relationship, which starts with the description of the measures of the variables and goes on to the higher levels of statistical analysis. The data collected was carefully edited systematically concluded.

Thus, in the present study the data collected with regard to the Social maturity, Emotional competence and Self-Actualization among Higher secondary school students in Chennai were analyzed with reference to the objectives and hypotheses of the study. The data have been subjected to the following statistical analysis namely descriptive, differential and correlation. The results of the statistical analysis have been summarized and tabulated.

ANALYSIS OF SOCIAL MATURITY, EMOTIONAL COMPETENCE AND SELF-ACTUALIZATION SCORES

Social Maturity, Emotional Competence and Self-Actualization scores of the entire sample have been analyzed and details are presented below.

TESTING OF HYPOTHESES

SOCIAL MATURITY

Hypothesis 1

The level of Social maturity among higher secondary students is moderate in nature.

TABLE. 9.01: Showing the Level of Distribution and Percentage of Higher Secondary Students on Social Maturity.

Variable	Range	Level	Frequency	Percentage
Social Maturity	209 and below	Low	150	25.0
	210 to 232	Moderate	290	48.3
	233 and above	High	160	26.7
		Total	**600**	**100.0**

INFERENCE

From the above table, it is clear that majority of the higher secondary students fall in the moderate level in their Social Maturity. Hence, the hypothesis 1 is accepted.

EMOTIONAL COMPETENCE

Hypothesis 2

The level of Emotional Competence among higher secondary students is moderate in nature.

TABLE. 9.02: Showing the Level of Ddistribution and Percentage of Higher Secondary Students on Emotional Competence.

Variable	Range	Level	Frequency	Percentage
Emotional Competence.	117and below	Low	158	26.3
	118 to 134	Moderate	280	46.7
	135 and above	High	162	27.0
		Total	**600**	**100.0**

INFERENCE

From the above table, it is clear that majority of the higher secondary students fall in the moderate level in their Emotional Competence. Hence, the hypotheses 2 are accepted.

SELF-ACTUALIZATION

Hypothesis 3

The level of self actualization among higher secondary students is moderate in nature.

TABLE. 9.3: Showing the Level of Distribution and Percentage of Higher Secondary Students on Self Actualization.

Variable	Range	Level	Frequency	Percentage
Self actualization	39 and below	Low	6	1.0
	40 to 45	Moderate	424	70.7
	46 and above	High	170	28.3
		Total	**600**	**100.0**

INFERENCE

From the above table, it is clear that majority of the higher secondary students fall in the moderate level in their self actualization. Hence, the hypotheses 3 are accepted.

DIFFERENTIAL ANALYSIS OF SOCIAL MATURITY

Hypothesis - 4

There is no significant difference in Social Maturity of higher secondary students based on Gender.

TABLE.9.4: Showing the Significant Difference between the mean Scores of Social Maturity of Higher Secondary Students with Regard to Gender.

Variable	Gender	N	Mean	SD	't' Value	L.S
Social Maturity	Boys	353	218.42	19.505	4.322	0.01
	Girls	247	224.91	15.921		

INFERENCE

From the above table, it is clear that the obtained C. R value (4.322) is greater than the table value (2.58) at 0.01 level. Therefore there is significant difference between the mean scores of Social Maturity among Higher Secondary Students with regard to Gender at (0.01) level.

Taking the mean score into consideration, it is seen from the above table that Girl's score Higher than boy's in Social Maturity.

Hence the hypothesis – 4 stating that " There is no significant difference between the mean scores of Social Maturity among Higher Secondary Students with regard to Gender" is rejected.

INFLUENCE OF SIBLING ON SOCIAL MATURITY

Hypothesis-5

There is no significant difference in Social Maturity of higher secondary students based on Number of Sibling.

TABLE. 9.5: ANOVA Showing the Significant Difference between the Mean Scores of Social Maturity of Higher Secondary Students with Regard to Siblings.

Variable		Sum of Squares	DF	Mean Squares	F Value	L.S
Social Maturity	**Between Groups**	12.970	2	6.485	0.019	NS
	Within groups	202385.80	597	339.005		
	Total	202398.77	599			

INFERENCE

From the above table, it is clear that the obtained 'F' value (0.019) is lower than the table value (3.01) at 0.05 level. Therefore there is no significant difference between the mean scores of Social Maturity among Higher Secondary Students with regard to Number of Siblings.

Hence the hypothesis – 5 stating that " There is no significant differnce between the mean scores of Social Maturity among Higher Secondary Students with regard to " Siblings" is accepted.

INFLUENCE OF TYPE OF FAMILY ON SOCIAL MATURITY

Hypothesis-6

There is no significant difference in social maturity of higher secondary students based on Type of Family.

TABLE.9.6: Showing the Significant Difference between the mean Score of Social Maturity of Higher Secondary Students with Regard to Type of Family.

Variable	Type of family	N	Mean	SD	't' Value	L.S
Social Maturity.	Nuclear	416	222.13	18.181	2.087	0.05
	Joint	184	218.74	18.666		

INFERENCE

From the above table, it is clear that the obtained C. R value (2.087) is lower than the table value (2.58) at 0.05 level. Therefore there is significant difference between the mean scores of Social Maturity among Higher Secondary School Students regards to Type of Family at 0.05 level.

Hence the hypothesis – 6 stating that "There is no significant differnce between the mean scores of Social Maturity among Higher Secondary Students with regard to "Type of Family" is rejected.

INFLUENCE OF TYPE OF MANAGEMENT ON SOCIAL MATURITY

Hypothesis-7

There is no significant difference in Social Maturity of higher secondary students based on Type of Management.

TABLE.9.7: ANOVA Showing the Significance of the Difference between the mean Scores of Social Maturity of the Students Studying at the Higher Secondary with Respect to Type of Management.

Variable		Sum of Squares	DF	Mean Squares	F Value	L.S
Social Maturity	**Between Groups**	8947.423	2	4473.712	13.806	0.01
	Within groups	193451.35	597	324.039		
	Total	**202398.77**	**599**			

INFERENCE

From the table, it is clear that the obtained 'F' value (13.806) is greater than the table value (4.65) at 0.01 level. Therefore there is significant difference between the mean scores of Social Maturity among Higher Secondary Students with regard to Type of Management.

So further analysis has to be done to find the significance of the difference between the groups.

TABLE.9.7 (A): 9 Showing the Mean, S.D and C.R value for Social Maturity of Higher Secondary Students based on Type of Management

Variable	Type of Management	F	Mean	Std Deviation	C.R Value	L.S
Social Maturity	Govt Vs Govt Aided	200	216.80	16.206	1.862	NS
		200	220.33	21.364		
	Govt Aided Vs Private	200	220.33	21.364	3.098	0.01
		200	226.16	15.907		
	Private Vs Govt	200	226.16	15.907	5.832	0.01
		200	216.80	16.206		

INFERENCE

From the above table following inference have been made.

In the first case, the calculated value (1.862) is lower than the table value (1.96) at 0.05 level of significance, shows that there is no significant difference between students studying in Government and Government Aided higher secondary schools with regard to Social Maturity.

In the second case, the calculated value (3.098) is higher than the table value (2.58) at (0.01) level of significance, shows that there is significant difference between students studying in Government Aided and Private of higher secondary school with regard to Social Maturity at 0.01 level.

In the third case, the calculated value (5.832) is greater than the expected table value (2.58) at 0.01 level of significance, shows that there is significant difference between students studying in Private and Govt higher secondary with regard to Social Maturity at 0.01 level.

Hence the hypothesis – 7 stating that " There is no significant difference between the mean scores of Social Maturity among Higher Secondary Students with regard to " Type of management" is partially verified.

INFLUENCE OF FAMILY INCOME ON SOCIAL MATURITY

Hypothesis-8

There is no significant difference in Social Maturity of higher secondary students based on family income.

TABLE. 9.8: Showing the Significant Difference between the mean Score of Social Maturity of Higher Secondary Students with Regard to Family Income.

Variable		Sum of Squares	DF	Mean Squares	F Value	L.S
Social Maturity	Between Groups	5300.644	2	2650.322	8.028	0.01
	Within groups	197098.13	597	330.148		
	Total	**202398.77**	**599**			

INFERENCE

From the table, it is clear that the obtained 'F' value (8.028) is greater than the table value (4.65) at 0.01 level. Therefore there is significant difference between the mean scores of Social Maturity among Higher Secondary Students with regard to Family Income at 0.01 level.

So further analysis has been done and results are presented in the following table.

TABLE. 9.8 (A): Showing the Mean, S.D and C.R value for Social Maturity of Higher Secondary School Students based on Family Income

Variable	Family Monthly Income	F	Mean	Std Deviation	C.R Value	L.S
Social Maturity	Below 20000	242	218.25	18.460	1.799	NS
	Vs Between 20000 to 50000	234	221.28	18.283		
	Between 20000 to 50000 Vs	234	221.28	18.283	2.505	0.05
	Above 50000	124	226.28	17.365		
	Above 50000	124	226.28	17.365	4.018	0.01
	Vs Below 20000	242	218.25	18.460		

INFERENCE

From the above table following inference have been made.

In the first case, the calculated value (1.799) is lower than table value (1.96) at 0.05 level of significance, shows that there is no significant difference in social maturity of higher secondary students with family income below 20000 Rupees and Between 20000 to 50000 Rupees.

In the second case, the calculated value (2.505) is lower than the table value (2.58) at 0.05 level of significance, shows that there is significant difference in social maturity of higher secondary students with family income between Rupees 20000 to 50000 and Above Rupees 50000.

In the third case, the calculated value (4.018) is greater than the expected table value (2.58) at 0.01 level of significance, shows that there is significant difference in social maturity of higher secondary students with family income Above 50000 and below 20000 Rupees.

Hence the hypothesis – 8 stating that " There is no significant differnce between the mean scores of Social Maturity among Higher Secondary Students with regard to " Type of family income" is partially verified.

DIFFERENTIAL ANALYSIS OF EMOTIONAL COMPETENCY

Influence of Gender on Emotional Competency

Hypothesis-9

There is no significant difference in Emotional Competency of higher secondary students based on Gender.

TABLE. 9.9: Showing the Significant Difference between the mean Scores of Emotional Competency of Higher Secondary Students with Regard to Gender.

Variable	Gender	N	Mean	SD	't' Value	L.S
Emotional Competency	Boys	353	127.29	15.501	0.772	NS
	Girls	247	126.34	13.876		

INFERENCE

From the above table, it is clear that the obtained C. R value (0.772) is lower than the table value (1.96) at 0.05 level of Significance. Therefore there is no significant difference between the mean scores of Emotional Competency among Higher Secondary School with regard to Gender.

Taking the mean score in to consideration, it is seen from the above table that boys score higher than girls in Emotional Competence.

Hence the hypothesis – 9 stating that "There is no significant difference between the mean scores of Emotional Competency among Higher Secondary Students with regard to Gender" is accepted.

INFLUENCE OF SIBLING ON EMOTIONAL COMPETENCY

Hypothesis-10

There is no significant difference in Emotional Competency of higher secondary students based on Number of Siblings.

TABLE. 9.10: ANOVA Showing the Significant Difference between the mean Scores of Emotional Competency of Higher Secondary Students with Regard to Number of Siblings.

Variable		Sum of Squares	DF	Mean Squares	F Value	L.S
Emotional Competency	Between Groups	1073.110	2	536.555	2.445	NS
	Within groups	130998.89	597	219.429		
	Total	132072.00	599			

INFERENCE

From the table, it is clear that the obtained 'F' value (2.445) is lower than the table value (3.01) 0.05 level. Therefore there is no significant difference between the mean scores of Emotional Competency among Higher Secondary Students with regard to Siblings.

Hence the hypothesis – 10 stating that " There is no significant difference between the mean scores of Emotional Competency among Higher Secondary Students with regard to Number of Siblings" is accepted.

INFLUENCE OF TYPE OF FAMILY ON EMOTIONAL COMPETENCY

Hypothesis-11

There is no significant difference in Emotional Competency of higher secondary students based on Type of Family.

TABLE. 9.11: Showing the Significant Difference between the mean Scores of Emotional Competency of Higher Secondary Students with Regard to Type of Family.

Variable	Type of family	N	Mean	SD	't' Value	L.S
Emotional Competency	Nuclear	416	127.49	15.011	1.472	NS
	Joint	184	125.56	14.425		

INFERENCE

From the above table, it is clear that the obtained C. R value (1.472) is lower than the table value (1.96) at 0.05 level. Therefore there is no significant difference between the mean scores of Emotional Competency among Higher Secondary Students with regards to Type of Family.

Hence the hypothesis – 11 stating that "There is no significant difference between the mean scores of Emotional Competency among Higher Secondary Students with regard to Type of Family" is accepted.

INFLUENCE OF TYPE OF MANAGEMENT ON EMOTIONAL COMPETENCY

Hypothesis-12

There is no significant difference in Emotional Competence of higher secondary students based on Type of Management.

TABLE. 9.12: ANOVA Showing the Significance of the Difference between the mean Scores of Emotional Competence of the Students Studying at the Higher Secondary School with Respect to Type of Management.

Variable		Sum of Squares	DF	Mean Squares	F Value	L.S
Type of Management.	Between Groups	371.290	2	185.645	15.130	0.01
	Within groups	125700.71	597	210.554		
	Total	132072.00	599			

INFERENCE

From the above table, it is clear that the obtained 'F' value (15.130) is greater than the table value (4.65) at 0.01 level. Therefore there is significant difference between the mean scores of Emotional Competence among Higher Secondary Students with regard to Type of Management.

So further analysis has been done and results are presented in the following table.

TABLE. 9.12 (A): Showing the Mean, S.D and C.R value for Emotional Competence of Higher Secondary Students based on Type of Management

Variable	Type of Management	F	Mean	Std Deviation	C.R Value	L.S
Emotional Competence	Govt Vs Govt Aided	200	122.42	14.239	5.191	0.01
		200	130.06	15.202		
	Govt Aided Vs Private	200	130.06	15.202	1.253	NS
		200	128.23	14.065		
	Private Vs Govt	200	128.23	14.065	4.105	0.01
		200	122.42	14.239		

INFERENCE

From the above table the following inference have been made.

In the first case, the calculated value (5.191) is greater than table value (2.58) at 0.01 level of significance, shows that there is significant difference between students studying in Government and private Aided of higher secondary with regard to Emotional Competence at 0.01 level.

In the second case, the calculated value (1.253) is lower than the table value (1.96) at 0.05 level of significance, shows that there is no significant difference between students studying in Government Aided and Private of higher secondary with regard to Emotional Competence.

In the third case, the calculated value (4.105) is greater than the expected table value (2.58) at 0.01 level of significance, shows that there is significant difference between students studying in Private and Government higher secondary with regard to Emotional Competence at 0.01 level.

Hence the hypothesis – 12 stating that " There is no significant difference between the mean scores of Social Maturity among Higher Secondary Students with regard to " Type of Management" is partially verified.

INFLUENCE OF FAMILY INCOME ON EMOTIONAL COMPETENCY

Hypothesis-13

There is no significant difference in Emotional Competence of higher secondary students based on Family Income.

TABLE.9.13: Showing the Significant Difference between the mean Scores of Emotional Competence of Higher Secondary Students with Regard to Family Income.

Variable		Sum of Squares	DF	Mean Squares	F Value	L.S
Emotional Competence	Between Groups	2852.834	2	1426.417	6.590	0.01
	Within groups	129219.17	597	216.448		
	Total	132072.00	599			

INFERENCE

From the above table, it is clear that the obtained 'F' value (6.590) is greater than the table value (4.65) at 0.01 level. Therefore there is significant difference between the mean scores of Emotional Competence among Higher Secondary Students with regard to Family Income at 0.01 level.

So further analysis has been done and results are presented in the following table.

TABLE. 9.13 (A): Showing the Mean, S.D and C.R Value for Emotional Competence of Higher Secondary Students based on family Monthly Income

Variable	Family Monthly Income	F	Mean	Std Deviation	C.R Value	L.O.S
Emotional Competence	Below 20000 Vs Between 20000 to 50000	242	124.31	16.150	2.840	0.01
		234	128.23	13.835		
	Between 20000 to 50000 Vs Above 50000	234	128.23	13.835	0.813	NS
		124	129.46	13.301		
	Above 50000 Vs Below 20000	124	129.46	13.301	3.061	0.01
		242	124.31	16.150		

INFERENCE

From the above table the following inference have been made.

In the first case, the calculated value (2.840) is higher than table value (2.58) at 0.01 level of significance, shows that there is significant difference in Emotional Competence of higher secondary students with family income below 20000 rupees and Between 20000 to 50000 rupees.

In the second case, the calculated value (0.813) is lower than the table value (1.96) at 0.05 level of significance , shows that there is no significant difference in Emotional Competence of higher secondary students with family income between 20000 to 50000 Rupees and Above 50000 Rupees'.

In the third case, the calculated value (3.061) is greater than the expected table value (2.58) at 0.01 level of significance, shows that there is significant difference in Emotional Competence of higher secondary students with family income Above 50000 Rupees and below 20000 Rupees at 0.01 level

Hence the hypothesis – 13 stating that " There is no significant difference between the mean scores of Social Maturity among Higher Secondary Students with regard to " Type of family income" is partially verified.

DIFFERENTIAL ANALYSIS OF SELF ACTUALIZATION

Influence of Gender on Self Actualization

Hypothesis-14

There is no significant difference in Self Actualization of higher secondary students based on Gender.

TABLE. 9.14: Showing the Significant Difference between the mean Scores of Self Actualization of Higher Secondary Students with Regard to Gender.

Variable	Gender	N	Mean	SD	't' Value	L.S
Self Actualization	Boys	353	41.92	5.967	1.051	NS
	Girls	247	42.46	6.681		

INFERENCE

From the above table, it is clear that the obtained C. R value (1.051) is lower than the table value (1.96) at 0.05 level. Therefore there is no significant difference between the mean scores of Self Actualization among Higher Secondary School Students with regard to Gender.

Taking the mean score in to consideration, it is seen from the above table that girls score higher than boys in Self Actualization.

Hence the hypothesis – 14 stating that " There is no significant difference between the mean scores of Self Actualization among Higher Secondary Students with regard to Gender" is accepted.

INFLUENCE OF SIBLINGS ON SELF ACTUALIZATION

Hypothesis-15

There is no significant difference in Self-Actualization of higher secondary students based on Number of Siblings.

TABLE. 9.15: ANOVA Showing the Significant Difference between the mean Score of Self-Actualization of Higher Secondary Students with Regard to Number of Siblings.

Variable		Sum of Squares	DF	Mean Squares	F Value	L.S
Self Actualization	Between Groups	6.982	2	3.491	0.089	NS
	Within groups	23547.258	597	39.443		
	Total	23554.240	599			

INFERENCE

From the table, it is clear that the obtained 'F' value (0.089) is lower than the table value (3.01) at 0.05 level. Therefore there is no significant difference between the mean scores of Self Actualization among Higher Secondary Students with regard to Number of Siblings.

Hence the hypothesis – 15 stating that " There is no significant difference between the mean scores of Self Actualization among Higher Secondary Students with regard to Number of Siblings" is accepted.

INFLUENCE OF TYPE OF FAMILY ON SELF ACTUALIZATION

Hypothesis-16

There is no significant difference in Self Actualization of higher secondary students based on Type of Family.

TABLE.9.16: Showing the Significant Difference between the mean Score of Social Maturity of Higher Secondary Students with Regard to Type of Family.

Variable	Type of family	N	Mean	SD	't' Value	L.S
Self-Actualization	Nuclear	416	2.2740	0.4727	0.055	NS
	Joint	184	2.2717	0.4581		

INFERENCE

From the above table, it is clear that the obtained C. R value (0.055) is lower than the table value (1.96) at 0.05 level. Therefore there is no significant difference between the mean scores of Self Actualization among Higher Secondary Students with regard to Type of Family.

Hence the hypothesis – 16 stating that " There is no significant difference between the mean scores of Self Actualization among Higher Secondary Students with regard to Type of Family" is accepted.

INFLUENCE OF TYPE OF MANAGEMENT OF SELF ACTUALIZATION

Hypothesis-17

There is no significant difference in Self Actualization of higher secondary students based on Type of Management.

TABLE.9.17: ANOVA showing the Significance of the Difference between the mean Scores of Self Actualization of the Students Studying at the Higher Secondary with Respect to Type of Management.

Variable		Sum of Squares	DF	Mean Squares	F Value	L.S
Self Actualization	Between Groups	407.730	2	203.865	5.258	0.01
	Within Groups	23146.510	597	38.771		
	Total	23554.240	599			

INFERENCE

From the above table, it is clear that the obtained 'F' value (5.258) is greater than the table value (4.65) at 0.01 level. Therefore there is significant difference between the mean scores of Self Actualization among Higher Secondary Students with regard to Type of Management at 0.01 level.

So further analysis has been done and results are presented in the following table.

TABLE.9.17 (A): Showing the Mean, S.D and C.R Value for Self Actualization of Higher Secondary Students based on Type of Management

Variable	Type of Management	F	Mean	Std Deviation	C.R Value	L.O.S
Self Actualization	Govt Vs Govt Aided	200	42.69	5.382	2.903	0.01
		200	40.98	6.361		
	Govt Aided Vs Private	200	40.98	6.361	2.701	0.01
		200	42.76	6.848		
	Private Vs Govt	200	42.76	6.848	0.122	NS
		200	42.69	5.382		

INFERENCE

From the above table the following inference have been made.

In the first case, the calculated value (2.903) is greater than the table value (2.58) at 0.01 level of significance, shows that there is significant difference between students studying in Govt and Government Aided of higher secondary with regard to Self Actualization at 0.01 level.

In the second case, the calculated value (2.701) is greater than the table value (2.58) at 0.01 level of significance, shows that there is significant difference between students studying in Government Aided and Private of higher secondary with regard to Self Actualization at 0.01level.

In the third case, the calculated value (0.122) is lower than the expected table value (1.96) at 0.05 level of significance, shows that there is no significant difference between students studying in Private and Government higher secondary with regard to Self Actualization.

Hence the hypothesis – 17 stating that " There is no significant difference between the mean scores of Self Actualization among Higher Secondary Students with regard to " Type of Management" is partially verified.

INFLUENCE OF FAMILY INCOME ON SELF ACTUALIZATION

Hypothesis-18

There is no significant difference in Self Actualization of higher secondary students based on Family Income.

TABLE. 9.18: ANOVA Showing the Significant Difference between the mean Scores of Self Actualization of Higher Secondary Students with Regard to Family Income.

Variable		Sum of Squares	DF	Mean Squares	F Value	L.S
Self Actualization	Between Groups	24.639	2	12.320	0.313	NS
	Within groups	23529.601	597	39.413		
	Total	23554.240	599			

INFERENCE

From the above table, it is clear that the obtained 'F' value (0.313) is lower than the table value (3.01) at 0.05 level. Therefore there is no significant difference between the mean scores of Self Actualization among Higher Secondary Students with regard to Family Income.

Hence the hypothesis – 18 stating that " There is no significant difference between the mean scores of Self Actualization among Higher Secondary Students with regard to Family Income" is accepted.

CORRELATION BETWEEN SOCIAL MATURITY AND EMOTIONAL COMPETENCY

Hypothesis-19

The scores related to correlation between the Social Maturity and Emotional Competency of Higher Secondary Students have been computed and details are furnished in the following table.

TABLE. 9.19: Correlation

Variable	N	'r' Value	L.S
Social Maturity and Emotional Competency	600	0.152	0.01

INFERENCE

From the above table, it is clearly observed that there is significant correlation between Social Maturity and Emotional Competency among higher secondary students at 0.01 level.

Hence the hypothesis 19 stating that "there is no significant correlation between Social Maturity and Emotional Competency among higher secondary students is rejected."

CORRELATION BETWEEN THE SOCIAL MATURITY AND SELF ACTUALIZATION

Hypothesis-20

The scores related to correlation between the Social Maturity and Self Actualization of Higher Secondary Students have been computed and details are furnished in the following table.

TABLE. 9.20: Correlation

Variable	N	'r' Value	L.S
Social Maturity and Self Actualization	600	0.068	NS

INFERENCE

From the above table, it is clearly observed that there is no significant correlation between Social Maturity and Self Actualization among higher secondary students at 0.05 level.

Hence the hypothesis 20 stating that " there is no significant correlation between Social Maturity and Self Actualization among higher secondary school students is accepted."

CORRELATION BETWEEN THE EMOTIONAL COMPETENCY AND SELF ACTUALIZATION

Hypothesis-21

The scores related to correlation between the Emotional Competency and Self Actualization of Higher Secondary Students have been computed and details are furnished in the following table.

TABLE. 9.21: Correlation

Variable	N	'r' Value	L.S
Emotional Competency and Self Actualization	600	0.040	NS

INFERENCE

From the above table, it is clearly observed that there is no significant correlation between Emotional Competency and Self Actualization among higher secondary students even at 0.05 level.

Hence the hypothesis 21 stating that " there is no significant correlation between Emotional Competency and Self Actualization among higher secondary school students is accepted."

CONCLUSION

The analysis and interpretation of the data represent the application of deductive and inductive logic to the research process. The data's are often classified by division into groups and then analyzed and synthesized in such a way that the hypothesis may be accepted or rejected. The final result may be a new principle of generalization. Like interpretation of results, the formulation of conclusion and generalizations also demands keen observations, a wide look and power of logical thinking.

In the succeeding chapter a brief report of the research study together with major findings arrived at along with the educational implication has been presented.

❐

10

Conclusion

"Research is an honest, exhaustive, intelligent searching for facts and their meanings or implications with reference to a given problem. The products of findings of given piece of research should be an authentic, verifiable contribution to knowledge in the field studied". P.M.Cook

This chapter deals with the consolidation of the various findings presented in the previous chapters. Findings are statements of factual information based upon the data analysis. Conclusions are answers to the questions raised or the statements of acceptance or rejection of the hypothesis proposed. In this chapter, the researcher deals with the aspects pertaining to the tools used for investigations objectives and hypotheses of the study, based on analysis the major findings arrived at and finally the educational implications together with suggestions for further study.

STATEMENT OF THE PROBLEM

The present study is entitled as ***"Relationship of Social Maturity and Emotional Competence with reference to Self- Actualization of Higher Secondary students".***

OBJECTIVES OF THE STUDY

1. To find out the level of Social Maturity among higher secondary students.
2. To find out the level of Emotional Competence among higher secondary students.
3. To find out the level of Self Actualization among higher secondary students.
4. To find out the significant difference in Social Maturity among higher secondary students in relation to Gender.
5. To find out the significant difference in Social Maturity among higher secondary students in relation to Number of Siblings.
6. To find out the significant difference in Social Maturity among higher secondary students in relation to Type of Family.
7. To find out the significant difference in Social Maturity among higher secondary students in relation to Type of Management.
8. To find out the significant difference in Social Maturity among higher secondary students in relation to Family Income.
9. To find out the significant difference in Emotional Competency among higher secondary students in relation to Gender.
10. To find out the significant difference in Emotional Competency among higher secondary students in relation to Number of Siblings
11. To find out the significant difference in Emotional Competency among higher secondary students in relation to Type of Family.
12. To find out the significant difference in Emotional Competency among higher secondary students in relation to Type of Management.
13. To find out the significant difference in Emotional Competency among higher secondary students in relation to Family Income.
14. To find out the significant difference in Self Actualization among higher secondary students in relation to Gender
15. To find out the significant difference in Self Actualization among higher secondary students in relation to Number of Siblings.
16. To find out the significant difference in Self Actualization among higher secondary students in relation to Type of Family.
17. To find out the significant difference Self Actualization among higher secondary students in relation to Type of Management.
18. To find out the significant difference in Self Actualization among higher secondary students in relation to Family Income.
19. To find out whether there is significant correlation between Social Maturity and Emotional Competency of higher secondary students.

20. To find out whether there is significant correlation between Social Maturity and Self Actualization of higher secondary students.
21. To find out whether there is significant correlation between Emotional Competency and Self -Actualization of higher secondary students.

HYPOTHESES OF THE STUDY

In the present study, the following hypotheses are formulated based on the objectives of the study.

1. The level of Social Maturity among higher secondary students is moderate in nature.
2. The level of Emotional Competence among higher secondary students is moderate in nature.
3. The level Self Actualization among higher secondary students is moderate in nature.
4. There is no significant difference in Social Maturity among higher secondary students in relation to Gender.
5. There is no significant difference in Social Maturity among higher secondary students in relation to Number of Siblings.
6. There is no significant difference in Social Maturity among higher secondary students in relation to Type of Family.
7. There is no significant difference in Social Maturity among higher secondary students in relation to Type of Management.
8. There is no significant difference in Social Maturity among higher secondary students in relation to Family Income.
9. There is no significant difference in Emotional Competency among higher secondary students in relation to Gender.
10. There is no significant difference in Emotional Competency among higher secondary students in relation to Number of Siblings.
11. There is no significant difference in Emotional Competency among higher secondary students in relation to Type of Family.
12. There is no significant difference in Emotional Competency among higher secondary students in relation to Type of Management.
13. There is no significant difference in Emotional Competency among higher secondary students in relation to family income.
14. There is no significant difference in Self Actualization among higher secondary students in relation to Gender.
15. There is no significant difference in Self Actualization among higher secondary students in relation to Number of Siblings.
16. There is no significant difference in Self Actualization among higher secondary students in relation to Type of Family.

17. There is no significant difference Self Actualization among higher secondary students in relation to Type of Management.
18. There is no significant difference in Self Actualization among higher secondary students in relation to Family Income.
19. There is no significant correlation between Social Maturity and Emotional Competency of higher secondary students
20. There is no significant correlation between Social Maturity and Self Actualization of higher secondary students
21. There is no significant correlation between Emotional Competency and Self Actualization of higher secondary students.

SAMPLE FOR THE STUDY

The present study is mainly concerned with the higher secondary students from different schools in Chennai.

For the present study, a sample of 600 students studying in the higher secondary schools around Chennai during the academic year 2014-2015 were chosen, using stratified random sampling technique.

TOOLS USED IN THE STUDY

The following tools were used for the present study

1. Rao's Social Maturity Scale (1986)
2. Emotional Competence Scale (Latha 2002)
3. John Korte's Self Actualization Scale (2007)

LIMITATIONS OF THE STUDY

The present study had been restricted to the following limitations..

- The study has been restricted only to the Higher secondary students.
- It includes sample size of 600 Higher secondary students.
- The sample has been chosen from Chennai only.

MAJOR FINDINGS OF THE STUDY

The following findings have been arrived through this study.

1. It was found that the level of social maturity among higher secondary students is moderate in nature.
2. It was found that the level of emotional competence among higher secondary students is moderate in nature.
3. It was found that the level self actualization among higher secondary students is moderate in nature.
4. It was found that there is significant difference in social maturity among higher secondary students in relation to Gender.

5. It was found that there is no significant difference in social maturity among higher secondary students in relation to number of sibling.
6. It was found that there is significant difference in social maturity among higher secondary students in relation to type of family.
7. It was found that there is significant difference in social maturity among higher secondary students in relation to Type of management.
8. It was found that there is significant difference in social maturity among higher secondary students in relation to family income.
9. It was found that there is no significant difference in emotional competency among higher secondary students in relation to Gender.
10. It was found that there is no significant difference in emotional competency among higher secondary students in relation to number of sibling.
11. It was found that there is no significant difference in emotional competency among higher secondary students in relation to type of family.
12. It was found that there is significant difference in emotional competency among higher secondary students in relation to Type of management.
13. It was found that there is significant difference in emotional competency among higher secondary students in relation to family income.
14. It was found that there is no significant difference in self actualization among higher secondary students in relation to Gender.
15. It was found that there is no significant difference in self actualization among higher secondary students in relation to number of sibling.
16. It was found that there is no significant difference in self actualization among higher secondary students in relation to type of family.
17. It was found that there is significant difference self actualization in among higher secondary students in relation to Type of management.
18. It was found that there is no significant difference in self actualization among higher secondary students in relation to family income.
19. It was found that there is significant correlation between social maturity and emotional competency of higher secondary students
20. It was found that there is no significant correlation between social maturity and self actualization of higher secondary students
21. It was found that there is no significant correlation between emotional competency and self actualization of higher secondary students.

EDUCATIONAL IMPLICATIONS

Parents and teachers have the most important influence on the children. Sharing with the child his problems, will lead him to develop self-confidence and the bringing about solutions to domestic as well as social and academic problems. Since action speaks louder than words, keeping interest in adolescents' activities will produce a healthy relationship.

Changes in the expression of emotions have been in this phase. Several psychologists have worked out for measuring emotional maturity and expressing it in terms of emotional age.

The higher secondary students with abnormal behaviour are almost always found to have low emotional quotients, coupled with intelligence quotients that are more likely to be low rather than high. The positive values in adolescents can be inculcated with experience of social skills, feeling of loyalty and with getting along with the like-minded people. On the whole, the adolescents are the most valuable unit of society and teachers and parents have to play a definite role in it with proper understanding of adolescents and their concerns.

This effort will be helpful for the higher secondary students in following ways;

1. **Emotional Maturity:** The better understanding will encourage the adolescents to emerge from childish into adult forms of emotional expression. They will learn not to flee from reality. They will aiso substitute rational for emotional reactions at least in situation that recur.
2. **Social Maturity:** The adolescents will get along well with work and with others. They will develop self-reliance in matter of taste and develop tolerance of human differences.
3. **Economic Independence:** Better understanding and helping hands from parents and teachers will help an adolescent to select work for which he is fit and he will learn the proper use of leisure.
4. **Intellectual Adulthood:** The adolescent will begin to develop an attitude towards experience that will give his life a meaning and develop a set of ideals to guide him towards his goals.

The modern adolescents wants to feel secure and to enjoy emotional satisfaction. To overcome their problems, there is a dire need for proper social understanding and good role to follow and training in responsibility, proper moral development and education for character development.

It is the duty of parents, teachers, school administration and the society at large to provide proper atmosphere for the education of emotions and instincts, selection of the vocation and proper use of leisure. Education as per individual differences and attitude will definitely help the higher secondary students to overcome their problems. The Government NGOs and social organization need to give proper attention to the concerns of adolescents, find out the causes and offer solutions.

In the light of the findings of the study the Social Maturity Emotional Competence and Self-Actualization is moderate in nature among Higher Secondary students.

The Higher Secondary students curriculum could have better input and opportunities for developing the Social Maturity, Emotional Competence and Self- Actualization as they play a vital role in moulding the character of the students when they study in school.

The potential and dreams of the Higher secondary school students are to be actualized. It is essential to give them on opportunity to excel and realize those dreams, to live full and healthy lives, enriched with stable and meaningful relationships. Challenges prepare them for an increasing diverse society and build a tradition of tolerance, acceptance and respect for others.

SUGGESTIONS FOR FURTHER STUDY

- Since an attempt has been made to study the Social Maturity Emotional Competence and Self- Actualization towards the Higher secondary students in Chennai. A similar study can be conducted among the college and university students.
- The sample size is restricted to 600 Higher secondary school students only in the present study. Further study can be done by including a large number of Higher secondary students drawn from various parts of Tamilnadu.
- A similar study of the present investigation could be done with other related variables.
- A similar study can be undertaken for the principals and supervisors of selected educational institutions by changing the variables according to the study.
- Other research studies could add a wealth of volume to the educational scenario in the future like Self Esteem, Emotional Intelligence, Self Regulation and Aptitude.

CONCLUSION

The purpose of the present study was to study the Social Maturity, Emotional Competence and Self- Actualization among Higher secondary students. The present study is sure to provide some insight into the field of educational research and the findings of the study can serve as a database for further research.

❐

11

The Problem and its Perspectives

In 21st century learning, students use educational technologies to apply knowledge to new situations, analyze information, collaborate, social problem and make decisions. Utilizing emerging technology to provide expanded learning opportunities is critical to the success of future generations improved options and choice for student will help improve students' completion and achievement.

Education is essential for everyone .It is the level of education that helps people earn respect and recognition. Education is an indispensable part of life both personally and socially. However, the unequal standard of education is still a major problem that needs to be solved.

The importance of education is undeniable for every single person. It goes without saying that education has a positive effect on human life. All people need to study. Only with the advent of education can people gain knowledge and enlarge their view over the world.

THE CONCEPT OF PERSONAL GROWTH

Personal Growth is the only thing which is going to remain with them forever. Therefore, your basic goal in life should be continuously grow physically, mentally and spiritually irrespective of circumstances. Personal growth, in other words, means respecting your own individuality. The more you improve your personal growth in life and you respect yourself so start by recognizing your natural potential for living life to the fullest.

DEFINITIONS OF PERSONAL GROWTH

Personal growth is a lifelong process people are capable of growing, learning and improving throughout their entire lives, and the ability to do so has an impact on many areas, personal growth in necessary both in the work place and in relationships, Doris Ann(2012).

Personal development includes activities that improves awareness and identify, develop talents and potentials builds human capital and facilitates employability, enhances quality of life and contribute to the realizations of dreams and aspirations. Martins Seligman (1998)

Notes that personal growth of all the aspects of psychological well-being is most similar to the pursuits of self-actualization, an aspect often discussed within the realms of personality development. Further, an exploration of the underlying factor structure of well-being, which included component of psychological well-being, life satisfaction, and positive and negative effect, confirmed that personal growth is subsumed under a well-being factor descriptive of meaningful, purposeful striving and engagement. Ryff and singer (2008)

The experiences of personal growth is certainly incorporated into notion of development as well as psychological approaches to well-being (ryff,1989)

Personal growth are reflection of such processes or reflect actual development changes, there is no question that this phenomenological feelings of growth is related to others outcomes of positive functioning, such as and higher well-being (Helgeson, Reynolds and Tomich, 2006).

CHARACTERISTIC OF PERSONAL GROWTH

At the level of the individual, personal development includes the following activities.

1. Improving self –awareness
2. Improving self-knowledge
3. Improving or learning new skills
4. Becoming a self reader
5. Building or renewing identity

6. Developing strength or talents
7. Improving wealth
8. Spiritual development
9. Identifying or improving potential
10. Building employability or human capital
11. Enhancing lifestyle or quality of life
12. Improving health
13. Fulfilling aspiration
14. Initiating a life enterprise or personal autonomy
15. Defining and executing personal development plans
16. Improving social abilities

CONCEPT OF THE COPING BEHAVIOR

In coping with the stress, people tend to use one of the three main coping strategies either appraisal focused, problem focused or emotion focused coping. Appraised focused strategies occur when the person modifies the way they think oneself from the problem.

Virtually all-living beings routinely utilize coping skills in daily life. These are perhaps noticeable in response to physical disabilities an easy examples of the uses of coping skills in the animals kingdom are three legged dogs, which typically learn to overcome the obvious disability to becomes as agile and mobiles as their four-legged counterparts, whether born with the disability or having received it due to an injury.

MEANING OF COPING BEHAVIOR

Coping responses are partly controlled by personality but also partly by the social environment, particularly the nature of the stressful environment. Coping behavior is a trait and frequently default behavior or group of behavior ensued whenever coping with

Coping (psychology) is the process of managing taxing. Circumstances, expending effort minimize, reduce or tolerate stress or conflict, to solve personal and interpersonal problems and seeking to master. A coping skill is a behavioral tool which may be used by individual to offset or overcome or eliminating the underlying condition.

DEFINITION OF COPING BEHAVIOR

Coping refers to the thoughts and actions we used to deal with stress. In large part, feeling stressed or not depends on whether we believe having the coping resources to deal with the challenges facing them.

CHARACTERISTIC OF COPING BEHAVIOR

Caplan identified the seven characteristic of coping behavior as,

1. Active search for information.
2. Free expression of both positive and negative feeling.
3. Asking for help from others people.
4. Breaking problems down into manageable bits and working through them one at a time.
5. Fatigue countered in pacing of one's efforts.
6. Active mastery of feeling where possible but acceptances of lacking control when it occurs.
7. Trust in oneself and optimism about outcome.

COPING MECHANISM

Ones group of coping skills are coping mechanism, defined as the skills used to reduces stress. In psychology terms, these are consciously used skills and defense mechanisms are their unconscious counterpart. Overuse of coping mechanisms and defenses mechanism may exacerbate one's problem rather than remedy it. There are two primary styles of coping with problems such as stress they are Action based coping, Emotion based coping.

Action Based Coping

Action based coping involves actually dealing with the problem that is causing stress. Examples can includes getting a second job in the face of financial difficulties or studying to prepare for exam. Action based coping is generally seen as superior to emotion-based coping, as it can directly reduces a sources of stress. Examples of action-based coping in include planning, suppression of competing activities, confrontation, self control and restraint

Emotional Based Coping

Emotional-based coping skills reduce the symptoms of stress without addressing the sources of the stress. Sleeping or discussing the stress with friends is all emotion-based coping strategies. Others examples includes denial, repression, wishful thinking, distraction, relaxation, reappraisal and humor. There are both positive and negatives coping can be useful to reduces stress to a manageable level, enabling action-based coping, or when the sources of stress cannot be addressed directly.

HARMFUL COPING METHOD

Psychologically, we are equipped to deal with various aspects of a crisis at different times and our reaction can the game at overtime. Some of the appropriate reactions to a crisis are the following:

Acceptances

After time we often become more accepting of what is happening and we are ready to work through the problems and all of their ramification and Impact on our lives.

Shock

At first we are in shock and disbelief that something of crisis nature can be happening to us. This shock can allow us to be in a state of denial for quite sometimes until we are ready to deal with the crisis.

Overwhelming Thoughts or Emotion

As we get over the shock and denial of the situation we are ready to flood our mind with overwhelming thought. We may have day dream, fantasies, depression, shame or anxiety. We often cannot control the representative nature of these thought.

Stress

We all know that there is good stress and bad stress. good stress may come from a challenging project with a tight deadline at work or case of the jitter that may accompany us down the aisle on the wedding day. But stress comes from traumatic events that make us feel unsafe. Bad stress can contribute too many emotional and physical problems. There are some who would say that stress creates all illness as well. Whether we chose to believe that stress is that powerful for those of us who have experienced. It can be very unpleasant.

Fear

It is very common to be afraid when things are happening to us that are completely outside of the normal experiences. They fear safety has been shattered and future is unsecure. This insecurity can rock there foundation and cause fear.

MEANING OF SOCIO-ECONOMIC STATUS

Another aspect of the present investigation deals with the socio-economic status of the society. This is concerned with the socio-economic status of the individual in the society in which he lives. It is the position the individual takes in the socio-economic hierarchy. Different individuals are of different Socio-Economic status in accordance with what they do (which is their vocation), what they are (their educational or professional qualification) and what they have (their income or salary and the sources of wealth).

There are many factors that decide an individual's Socio-Economic status. They are ones vocation, income wealth, Education home and associations and activities, accomplishments (top athlete, musician and movie star). Family background related to the royalty or other distinguished personages) and lastly the kind of marriage a person makes. Among all these the prime factors that are taken into consideration in deciding an individual's Socio-Economic status are vocation, educational qualification and income or salary.

Vocation-an individual's Job-his place in the established hierarchy of vocations is the most important single determiner of his Socio-Economic status. The status a vocation gives is determined by the significance of the work being done, the power and responsibility exercised the capacities, training, skills and experience required the prestige and dignity attached to the vocation and lastly the remuneration or income received. Between the top and bottom of the vocational hierarchy are many other levels, varying in job significance, power capacity and training required prestige and pay, secondary educational qualification is important in itself as the amount of education a person has had is a status factor itself. The higher one climbs the ladder of educational qualification the more he is marked as capable and ambitious. One's association with an institution and its activities has a favorable public standing. The diplomas and degrees are a formal recognition of one's achievement. The third prime determinant of one's Socio-Economic status is the income or salary. Income is closely related to vocation as a status factor. Income tends to group individuals on a solid financial standing and it is a status giving material.

The minor determinants of socio economic status is that one's home and location comprise such an important reflection of the status given by the varying degree of wealth, that it is considered as a discrete status factor. Status is also indicated by the degree and intimacy of a person's association with people of prestige and power-the "people who count". One's personal accomplishments in being a Judge athlete, musician etc. may brighten the family halo family lineage or background and it adds to the socio economic status of an individual. Another factor that is of some importance is the kind of marriage a person makes, marriage is a additionally powerful force in social mobility, whether positive or negative.

Among the prime determinants of socio-economic status, vocation and education are interrelated and independent but there is no perfect relationship between education and income. There are people for example, with high level talents who have not much formal education but who have substantial incomes. Further there are always some people with very creative minds who by-pass the university campus on their fast route to fame. Though education and vocation are inter-related and inter dependent, education and income are not etymologically speaking socio economic status refers to the position a person maintains in his daily business of life both in the family and in the society he interacts with. The determinates of social class are amount of income type and amount of formal education social class position and economic activity Chaplin defines socio-economic status as, the position an individual or family occupies with reference to the prevailing average standards or cultural possessions effective income, material possessions and participation in the group activities of the community.

THE CONCEPT OF SOCIO-ECONOMIC STATUS

Children living in poverty are less likely to complete school Anderson (1988), Lockhead and Verspoor (1990), Rumberger (1987) socio economic status correlated with deep out/push out, is often denoted by parented education, father's occupation, family income, and household items available. Rumberger (1983), in a United States study, found that differences in dropout rates among ethnic groups could be explained mostly by differences in family background. The most uniform predictor among the various ethnic/gender groups was the presence of available reading materials at home.

Surveys of early college dropout underscore the importance of socio economic reasons. According to Veshive and Pita De melo (1988), some families cannot afford to pay for college fees, books and supplies, transportation and uniforms, others cannot afford the opportunity costs, that is the earned income and domestic labor that parents forego when their children are enrolled in school. Still other children report shame at their relative poverty, reflected in their clothes or lack of lunch. In Brazil, where the dropout rate exceeds at the primary level, low income families make up the majority in the public school system Davico (1990) identified a number of schools-related factors that seemed to influence the disengagement process, including inadequately prepared teachers and low expectations for student success.

All are important, though less likely to occur in schools enrolling large numbers of disadvantaged students. If poor children are to have success to the opportunities of mainstream life in the United States, then socialization towards that end must occur both in school and at home.

It is common, particularly under the bureaucratic view, to see home environment as a potential problem that may be "solved" through parent education. In this view, control of education remains with professionals and possible disjunction of home and school values is not addressed directly. This view has been challenged increasingly manifested through efforts towards community control of schools in poor communities. Another option the functional community Coleman and Hoffer (1987) combines the bureaucratic and communitarian perspectives while productive social relations between families and schools are stressed, the school is seen as a limited community focused on educational aims. The professional expertise of college staff retains a special role which is respected by families.

DEFINITION OF SOCIO-ECONOMIC STATUS

Socio-economic status can be defined as the individual's relative position of the community. According to Chaplin J.P there are many factors that decide an individual's socio-economic status. They are one's vocation, income, wealth, education, home and its location, association activities, accomplishment, family backgrounds etc.

DEFINITION OF STRESS

Stress may be defined as a state of psychological in balances resulting from the disparity situational demand and the individual's ability and motivation to meet those demands. Stress can be positive or negative, stress can be positive when the situation offers an opportunity for a person to gain something it acts as a motivator for a peak performance.

Stress can be negative when a person faces social, physical, organization, and emotional problems.

Stress is a term people often use to describe a feeling of pressure, strain, or tension. People often say that they are under stress or feel stressed out when they are dealing with changeling situations or event.

CAUSES OF STRESS ON STUDENTS

Causes of stress on students include both positive and negative stress, but the focus here is on the causes of negative stress on students.

Academic stress

Alphabetically first among the causes of stress on students is academic pressure simply tacking more difficult assignment's can demand stress management techniques.

Dating

Student's life throughout high school and college is filled thinking about dating, trying to date, failing to date, and being "dumped" the mating game is filled with estruses, but it also involves distress, and is among the greatest causes of stress on students.

Environment

The school environment itself can be cause of stress on students. Students moving into secondary education find it changeling to constantly move around to classes. These tertiary education are challenged with leaving home and establishing a new life in a new setting. Both can use cause stress on students.

Extracurricular

Pressure on high school students to engage in extracurricular activities such as choirs, skills, sports band, or volunteer work. The presence of these on a student application can a far toward acceptance. Once in college, extracurricular activities still cause stress on students, since their presence on a job application is also an asset.

Peers

Like dating, peer relationships can provide estruses or stress as peers apply pressure in regard to dress, behavior, choice of friends or music, and many other areas of life, that pressure can become a huge cause of stress on students.

Workload

High school workloads, and later college workloads, are heavy for many students. For secondary students planning on tertiary studies, high school grades are important. So is the number of subjects as a result, students may overload their schedules in college, where financial investment has been, student may overwork to reach their goals and benefit from the money spent workloads at either level are causes of stress on students.

Parental Pressure

Finally, students at either level experiences stress from parental pressures. Parents and their children to succeed in school. They want to see good grades, but they also want to see success in life's other areas in their attempts to guide their children; parents can become one of the major causes of stress on students.

ACADEMIC STRESSORS

Academic stressors among students have long been researched on, and researchers have identified stressor such as too many assignments, competitions with other students (Fair Brother and Warn, 2003)

Academic stressor includes the students' perception of the extensive knowledge base required and the perception of an inadequate time to develop it. (Carveth et al, 1996)

Students report experiencing academic stress at predictable times each semester with the greatest sources of academic stress resulting from taking and studying and for exams, grade competition and the large amount of content to master in a small amount of time (Abouserie,1994).

The academic stress was measured through its four components namely frustration, conflict, pressure and anxiety.

MEANS OF ACADEMIC STRESS

- Increasing amounts of schoolwork
- Assignment deadliness
- Quizzes and Exams
- Class presentation (Public speaking)
- Honors and IB classes
- High stakes tests
- Getting into college
- Selecting a career path
- Balancing school with sports, hobbies and social life
- Expectations of parents and teachers
- competing with siblings
- Fear of failure

Based on the theoretical framework discussed above, an investigation is made by the researcher to find out the effect of personal growth, coping behavior and socio- economic status on academic stress among higher secondary students.

STATEMENT OF THE PROBLEM

The problem is stated as “An Investigation into Personal Growth, Coping Behavior and Socio-Economic Status of Higher Secondary Students in Relation to Their Academic Stress”.

OPERATIONAL DEFINITIONS OF THE KEY TERMS

Personal Growth

Personal growth includes activities that improve awareness and identity, develop talents and potential, build human capital and facilitates employability, enhances quality of life and contributes to realization of dreams and aspiration. In the present investigation, it is assessed by the Personal Growth Initiative scale, prepared by Christine Robitschek (2011)

Coping Behavior

The psychological definition of coping behavior is the process of managing taxing circumstances, expending effort to solve personal and interpersonal problems and seeking to master, reduce or tolerances stress or conflict.

In the present study it is measured by Coping Behavior Inventory, prepared and standardized by Dai Rost and Skermer (1997)

Socio-Economic Status

In determining the socio-economic status of subjects, Kuppuswamy's Socio-economic Status Scale as adapted and modified by Dr.S.Devasahayam Selvakumar has been made use of in the present study.

Higher Secondary Student

Students studying in standard (Grade) XI are considered as Higher Secondary Students.

Academic Stress

Dr. Selye observes that one of the leading authorities on the concept of stress as "the rate of all wear and tear caused life." In the present study, Academic Stress Inventory is prepared and standardized by the Investigator and Dr. S. Devasahayam Selvakumar(2014).

OBJECTIVES OF THE STUDY

The following objectives have been framed in the present study

1. To find out level of personal growth of higher secondary students.
2. To find out level of coping behavior of higher secondary students.
3. To find out level of socio-economic status of higher secondary students.
4. To find out level of academic stress of higher secondary students.
5. To find out whether there is any significant difference between the mean scores of personal growth among higher secondary students in relation to

   Gender : Male/Female
   Type of schools : Boys'/Girls'/Co Education schools
   Type of management of schools : Government/Government Aided/ Self Finance schools
   Medium of instruction : English/ Tamil
   Type of family : Joint/Nuclear
   Locale of residence : Urban/Rural

6. To find out whether there is any significant difference between the mean scores of coping behavior among higher secondary students in relation to

   Gender : Male/Female
   Type of schools : Boys'/Girls'/Co Education schools
   Type of management of schools : Government/Government Aided/

Self Finance schools

Medium of instruction	:	English/ Tamil
Type of family	:	Joint/Nuclear
Locale of residence	:	Urban/Rural

7. To find out whether there is any significant difference between the mean scores of socio-economic status among higher secondary students in relation to

Gender	:	Male/Female
Type of schools	:	Boys'/Girls'/Co Education schools
Type of management of schools	:	Government/Government Aided/ Self Finance schools
Medium of instruction	:	English/ Tamil
Type of family	:	Joint/Nuclear
Locale of residence	:	Urban/Rural

8. To find out whether there is any significant differences between the mean scores of academic stress among higher secondary students in relation to.

Gender	:	Male/Female
Type of schools	:	Boys'/Girls'/Co Education schools
Type of management of schools	:	Government/Government Aided/ Self Finance schools
Medium of instruction	:	English/ Tamil
Type of family	:	Joint/Nuclear
Locale of residence	:	Urban/Rural

9. To find out whether there is any significant correlation between coping behavior and academic stress among higher secondary students.
10. To find out whether there is any significant correlation between socio-economic status and academic stress among higher secondary students.

SIGNIFICANCE OF THE STUDY

It really depends exactly what students mean by personal growth; but it is fair to say this would mean gaining skills that are perhaps outside the basic remit of whatever job that you do and that can be transferred to a different role or enable you to fit into a different environment without too much difficulty. This is important because of several reasons; with computerization and automation, manual labor and repetitive tasks have been made obsolete. The advancement of technology has further made the world a confusing place. The only challenges that remain are with their own ideologies, like politics and religion. The global problem of human relevance is just beginning where our confidence is easily shattered. Problems cannot always be solved in one's own preferred style; however style is not behavior but an influence on it's, so when necessary, everyone is able to tackles their current problems in what is for them a non-preferred way by using coping behavior.

All individuals indulge in coping behavior because of the narrowness of the range of the style within which they at ease, compared with the wide range of style needed to manage the usual array of diverse problems the individual needs to solve. The academic stress can have a negative impact on academic performances and the students' ability to cope up with the school life. It is also one of the factors which affect the mental health, causing depression and anxiety. This may lead to a number of drop outs from the school for the inability to continue the school education and further higher education. Etymologically speaking, socio-economic status refers to the position a person maintains in his daily business of life both in the family and in the society. The determinants of socio-economic class include economic activity amount of income, type and amount of formal education and social class position of one's family.

DELIMITATIONS OF THE STUDY

- The study had the following delimitations
- The sample is limited to 299 students.
- The sample is taken only from Vellore district, Tamil Nadu.
- Higher secondary school students are considered in the present study.

CONCLUSION

The problem of the study has been discussed briefly in this chapter, bringing out the need for the study, objectives of the study, operational definition of the terms used in this study. A review of the related literature available has been scanned to the theoretical perspective in the study to throw light for formulating appropriate hypotheses which cloud be tested. A detailed discussion of the related literature bearing on the problem in hand follow in the next chapter.

❐

12

Review of Literature

"The review of literature promotes a greater understanding of the problem and crucial aspects and ensures avoidances of unnecessary defecation: it is also provides comparative data on the basis of which we evaluate and interpret the significance of one's finding."(George J. Mouly 1970)

The study of the related literature implies locating, reading, and evaluating reports of research as well as reports of casual observation and opinion that are related to the individuals planned research projects. The study of related literature provides helpful orientation for the definition of the problem, background for selection of procedure and comparative data for the interpretation of the result.

STUDIES RELATED TO PERSONAL GROWTH

The essence of personal growth needs for selection or developmental assessment purposes. Further implications for the development of competences within organizations were discussed.

Robitschek, (2003) in his study predicted a positive moderate correlation between PGI and independent self-construal or the focus on the self, as distinct from other people .This hypothesis was based on the assumption that PGI focuses on one's own growth, which may be independent of other's growth. Using a sample of 165 undergraduates of Mexican descent, ROBITSCHEK found a strong relationship between these two variables.

Robitschek (1999) in another study involving 169 undergraduate students, hypothesized that different ways of growing would be differentially correlated with PGI scores. Specifically, participants were asked to report the degree to which they felt they had achieved growth using Ryff's (1989) domains of psychological wellbeing. They were then asked, using a global behavioral self-report measure, to indicate the ways in which they had accomplished this growth. ROBITSCHEK reasoned that in espousing growth as a goal, those high in PGI would be more likely to both recognize growth and report growth as intentional. As hypothesized, findings indicated that participants who had higher PGI scores reported a greater level of growth that demanded both awareness and intentionality. In contrast, these participants reported lower levels of unintentional growth, or growth not based on effort.

In the study of Whittaker and Robitschek (2001), PGI scores were also found to be related to self-reported measures of family functioning. In a co relational study, assessed several family functioning variables in an undergraduate sample of 336 participants. PGI was found to correlate positively with such family variables as problem solving, communication, father differentiation, and mother differentiation.

In the study of Shorey, Little, Snyder, Kluck, &Robitschek, (2007) the sample consisted of 378 undergraduate participants. Researchers used structural equation modeling to determine if hope and AGI are empirically distinct constructs. SHOREY et al. found that a two-factor model (portraying hope and PGI as unique but related constructs) fit the data between than did a one-factor (combined construct) model. The latent variable correlation between PGI and hope was 0.84, indicating that the two constructs are highly related yet somewhat distinct.

T.Dary Erwin, (2010) found that alumni self-ratings of their personal growth were linked to their intellectual development during college four to seven years earlier. Graduates that were satisfied with their personal growth in the arts, creative thinking, making logical inferences, learning independently, exercising initiative, and tolerating other points of view had higher intellectual scores in commitment and empathy as undergraduates years earlier. These findings support a relationship between college student intellectual development and alumni perceptions of their personal growth. The implications of this study support continuing the custom of querying graduates about their earlier education, a practice in wide use already; and add to the validity of the scale of intellectual development as a measure of college impact upon personal dispositions.

According to Robitschek (1998), PGI had also been found to be relatively distinct from social desirability bias, cognitive ability, and age, which helps to establish its discriminate validity, in particular, found that theoretically unrelated constructs such as social desirability, SAT scores, and age showed no significant association with PGI, Although all of the reviewed studies are correlation in nature, they provide initial evidence that supports PGI as a unique construct of potential importance. These studies suggest that PGI scores possess both convergent and discriminate validity.

According to Aaron C. Geise (2008) Personal growth is conceptualized as the phenomenological experience of self-directed growth, which has been found to be related to positive functioning. The question remains, does the phenomenological experience of personal growth also relate to actual personality development? The current research assessed personal growth, well-being (both psychological well-being and subjective well-being), and ego development in two studies. Study 1 assessed a sample of 176 community adults and found that personal growth was related to both ego development and life satisfaction. Study 2 followed a sample of 122 first year college students over the course of a year and a half. Ageing, personal growth was related to both ego development and subjective well-being, concurrently. Further, study 2 also explored the prospective relationships between personal growth, well-being, and ego development. Only subjective well-being at time 1 uniquely predicted personal growth at time 2. Results are discussed in reference to personal growth, personality development, and maturity.

Loevinger, (1996), identified that subjective feeling of personal growth and ego development had been suggested to occur in response to challenging life events, or "pacers". Loevinger described pacers as experiences that challenge an individual to revise their organismic frame. Similarly in adopting PIAGET'S notion of accommodation to personality development.

According to Stremba, Robert (1986), personal growth wilderness outings have been conducted by the counseling center at the University of Puget Sound for the past five years. Using the outdoors as a medium for students to learn about themselves, to communicate and cooperate with one another, and to have fun are purposes consistent with the counseling's center's mission of offering programs for students to achieve success personally, socially, emotionally and academically. The general goals and purposes of the personal growth outings program were described to participants at during meetings.

STUDIES RELATED TO COPING BEHAVIOR

Hammer et al., (1986) conducted a study on, 'coping resources are what propel bring to situations (as opposed to what they do) that enable them to deal with stressors more effectively, allow them to recover faster, or experience fewer or less intense symptoms upon exposure to stressors'. The coping resources inventory (CRI) measures resources in the following domains cognitive, social, emotional, spiritual/philosophical and physical. The CRI was completed by 126 female and 48 college students who also rated their level of stress and physical health. Results included (1) the low stress group students has significantly higher resources than did the high stress group (2)female subjects had significantly higher resource scores on the social, emotional and spiritual scales than did males: (3) counseling center clients had significantly lower cognitive and emotional scale resources than did non-clients (4) eating disorder clients had significantly lower scores than did non-clients on physical and emotional scales. (5) Resident advisors had significantly higher scores on the social and spiritual scales than did other college students. The CRI could be useful in identifying college counseling center students at risk for developing physical or psychological symptoms. Students with high resources could be trained to tutors students low explore in resources. Identifying resources could also be useful in planning prevention activities with groups (ABL).

Robitschek (1999) in another study involving 169 undergraduate students, hypothesized that different ways of growing would be differentially correlated with PGI scores. Specifically, participants were asked to report the degree to which they felt they had achieved growth using Ryff's (1989) domains of psychological wellbeing. They were then asked, using a global behavioral self-report measure, to indicate the ways in which they had accomplished this growth. ROBITSCHEK reasoned that in espousing growth as a goal, those high in PGI would be more likely to both recognize growth and report growth as intentional. As hypothesized, findings indicated that participants who had higher PGI scores reported a greater level of growth that demanded both awareness and intentionality. In contrast, these participants reported lower levels of unintentional growth, or growth not based on effort.

Chapman et al., (2000) conducted an investigation on, 'racial differences in coping strategies and self-esteem'. This study was examined for 361 male and female adolescents in garages. Coping strategies were assessed with the adolescent coping orientation for problem experiences (J.M. Patterson & H.I. MOCUBBIN 1986). Self-esteem was assessed by the coppersmith self-esteem inventory (S. COPPERSMITH, 1987). Multivariate analysis revealed racial difference in adolescent coping strategies of ventilating feelings, seeking diversions, developing self-reliance, avoiding problems, seeking spiritual support, investing in close friends, engaging in demanding activities, solving family problems and relaxing. In particular African American adolescents reported using diversions, self-reliance, spiritual support, close friends, demanding activities, family problems and relaxation more frequently than Caucasian adolescents did. Implications for professionals and recommendations for future research are discussed.

Fickova, (2000) made a study on, 'the prefer once of coping strategies in relation to various categories of hassles and to their total hassles score in adolescents'. Girls with high total score in hassles interfere significantly more often strategies of planning. Religion, focus on the venting of emotions denial behavioural and mental disengagement. Boys with high number of hassles more often prefer emotional social support and drug/alcohol use and also, identically the daily hassles, girls experience significantly more often loneliness and dissatisfaction with oneself need for increased effort and lack of time need for increased effort and lack time.

Grant, K.E., J. H et., (2000) investigated on individual (coping strategies, family (parent/child relationships) and community based (religious involvement) variables'. They were examined as potential factors from 224 low income urban sixth through eighth-grade African American adolescents. Each of those variables was examined as a moderator and analyses were conducted to determine whether the association between stress and psychological symptoms was attenuated for youth endorsing positive coping strategies, strong parent/ child relationships with father figures buffered the effects of stress on externalizing symptoms for boys and for girls. Religious involvement was protective for girls but not for boys. The sole coping strategy to demonstrate a protective effect was avoidant coping, which attenuated the relation between stress and externalizing symptoms for boys. Supplemental analyses focusing on specific subsets of stressful experience indicated that avoidant coping and social support-seeking coping accentuated the relation between daily hassles and internalizing symptoms for girls.

Kristin D. Neff et Al., (2005) examined 'the relationship between self-compassion, academic achievement goals and coping with perceived academic failure among undergraduates'. Self-compassion entails being kind to one self in instances of failure, perceiving one's experiences as part of the larger human experience and holing painful feelings in mindful awareness. Study 1 (N=222) found that self-compassion was positively associated with mastery goals and negatively associated with performance goals, a relationship that was mediated by the lesser fear of failure and greater perceived competence of self-compassionate individuals. Study 2 confirmed these findings among students who perceived their recent midterm grade as also failure (N=110) with results also indicating that self-compassion was positively associated with emotion focused coping strategies and negatively associated with avoidance-oriented strategies.

STUDIES RELATED TO SOCIO-ECONOMIC STATUS

Anita Sharma (2005) studied socio-economic status as determined by the family environment. Whether socio-economic class has bearing on development of family environment in boys and girls. The family environment scale (MOOS &MOOS, 1986) was SPM (Standard Progressive Matrices, RAVEN 1960) was used of measure fluid intelligence. GMAT (General Mental Ability Test) BY JALOTA, 1973 was used to measure the crystallized intelligence achievement oriented and show more crystallization as compared to low socio-economic status families. Girls are more cohesive achievement oriented and high on moral independent. There is a significant interaction effect of socio-economic status and sex on the facto of control of family environment which shows that at the high SES(HSES) level the boys are significantly kept under higher control than girls because they are considered the bread winners.

Madhu Asthana (2004) investigated alienation in relation to gender, socio economic status and streams of study. The concept of alienation rooted deeply in sociological traditions has recently enjoyed a new popularity. The following null hypotheses were framed to be tested. There will be no gender difference and socio-economic status. The study was conducted on a random sample of 400 (200 males and 200 females) undergraduate students of different degree colleges and universities of Varanasi. Following tools were used of collect relevant data in present study students alienation scale developed by Sharma (1988) it consist of 54 items measuring five dimensions socio-economic status scale (urban) developed by Kushreshtha (1987) in Hindi it is a 20 items scale, which consist of sex component variables in order to lower level of measuring lessons indicates that students have sufficient understanding of the events in which they are engaged. The alienation in male students has impacts on SES and course streams are not found significant.

Pakkirisamy M., Elakka Kumar. B (2002) studied various levels of socio-economic status of students and their national integration compares the attitudes of higher secondary students towards national integration. A sample of 981 first year higher secondary students' integration scale and socio-economic scale was developed by the investigator. The number of subjects of very high socio-economic scale was 8 a high SES, average SKS 446, low SES 207, and very low SES 78, the mean score on national integration was maximum for the high SES and minimum for very low SES group. Compression of the group navigated that they significantly differed from each other so far as their attitude towards national integration was concerned. The only exceptions were that the average and very low SES groups as well as the low and very low SES group were comparable with each other.

Mohanasundaram and Kannan (2002) investigated socio economic status and attitude of parents towards women's education. They examined the attitude of 300 parents from rural and urban areas towards women's duration. A scale of attitude of parents towards women's education (constructed by the investigators) and a personal data blank were used. Result indicated that both father and mother had a favorable attitude towards women's education. However urban parents had a significantly more favorable attitude than rural parents, economic and social status did not significantly impact the parents attitude towards women's educations. suggestions to surmount barriers to women's education have been made.

Panjoyar, Rout Muri (2001) studied adjustment as a function of social class and economic status. Assesses the competence of different social class and economic status group in coping with environment dements. The sample comprised 300 respondents.100 from each of the 3 social classes high backward and scheduled. In each class 50 subjects belonged to high middle and low income group. An adaptation of bell adjustment inventory (MOHSIN & HUSSAIN 1970) was used to assess adjustment in home health social and emotional areas. A personal data bank developed by the authors was used for identifications. Status played a significant role in the adjustment of individuals. High class SS were more adjusted then the scheduled class SS white the backward class was the least adjusted compared to the other two groups. The low income groups was found to be best adjusted the high income group was better adjusted than the middle income group.

Sammons, Paneia (1995) did the study on gender, ethnic and socio economic differences in attainment and progress a longitudinal analysis of student achievement over 9 years. Differences in achievement related to gender and socio-economic factors remained consistent and generally increased over time, greater changes was found in patterns of ethnic differences.

Smart, Reginaid (1994) studied neighborhood socio-economic factors in He relation to student drug use and programs. He examined relationships between drug use problems and socio-economic status of neighborhoods where students in grades 11 and 13 reside. He found largest number of alcohol and drug problems in areas with lowest socio- economic characteristic characterized by low-cost substandard housing.

Daly- John (1994) found that eight grater's level of comfort about asking questions in class was positively related to family income, socio-economic status. English language proficiency family intellectual environment, educational aspirations academic performance, self esteem and locus of control and was significantly associated with gender, ethnicity, geographic region, home language background and perceptions of teachers responsiveness to students.

Robinson-Scott (1994) investigated mathematics and science learning milieus in diverse schools in Florida, African American students from small town, low socio-economic backgrounds. This paper presented a description of a northern Florida middle school and of the students enrolled in the school. 92% of whom where African –American. Three quarters of the entire student population was eligible for free or reduced price government assisted lunches. This figure was double the state average. During academic year 1991-1992, expenditure per student enrolled within regular academic programs was 12% below the state average or € 2,920 per student observations of an eight-grade physical science class a sixth-grade mathematics class and an eight-grade social assembly were related. Interviews with the science teacher and mathematics teacher from these classes were given along with a list of needs generated from mathematics and science teachers. Traditional methods of teaching prevailed in these classroom.

Omoniyi, Tope (1993) made an evaluation of policy and conducted a study on the socio-economic and political implications of commercialization of nursery education in Nigeria. The years of nursery educational were crucial in the language development process of the child in Nigeria a nation with over 400 languages, naming a national language for educational and cultural development that foster unity and identity becomes a sensitive issue. It was argued that government encouragement of private efforts in the provision of pre-primary education had led to commercialization and that in this context, language skills that schools supply were in a way product that carries price-tag. As such, government policy was an alternative product and government must change the attitudes of the people in order for its alternative product to be accepted. Eight private nursery schools were consulted for information on clientele, fees payable, quality of staff and language policy. A socio-economic description of nursery schools was offered to government language policy objectives.

Adegoke Alfored, (1992) studied the relationship between parental socio-economic status sex and initial pubertal problems among school going adolescents in Nigeria. He examined relationship between parental socio economic status (SES) sex and initial pubertal problems among Nigerian adolescents (n-700). He found that boys from low SES groups experienced more physical problems than other group's low SES students.

Undheim, Johan Olav, Nordvik, Hilmar (1992) conducted the study on socio-economic factors and sex difference in an egalitarian educational system and academic achievement among 16 year old Norwegian students. Data from 2000 Norwegian 16 year old ninth graders used to study the importance of socio-economic factors and sex differences in an educational system with main streaming no ability grouping, little acceleration and no retention in grade. Analysis illustrates how sex and socio economic differences may be mediated in an egalitarian society.

Omoniyi,Tope (1993) made an evaluation of policy and conducted a study on the socio-economic and political implications of commercialization of nursery education in Nigeria. The years of nursery educational were crucial in the language development process of the child in Nigeria a nation with over 400 languages, naming a national language for educational and cultural development that foster unity and identity becomes a sensitive issue. It was argued that government encouragement of private efforts in the provision of pre-primary education had led to commercialization and that in this context, language skills that schools supply were in a way product that carries price-tag. As such, government policy was an alternative product and government must change the attitudes of the people in order for its alternative product to be accepted. Eight private nursery schools were consulted for information on clientele, fees payable, quality of staff and language policy. A socio-economic description of nursery schools was offered to government language policy objectives.

Adegoke Alfored, (1992) studied the relationship between parental socio-economic status sex and initial pubertal problems among school going adolescents in Nigeria. Examined relationship between parental socio-economic status (SES) sex and initial pubertal problems among Nigerian adolescents (n-700). He found that boys from low SES groups experienced more physical problems than other group's low SES students.

Undheim, Johan Olav, Nordvik, Hilmar (1992) conducted the study on Socio-economic factors and sex difference in an egalitarian educational system and academic achievement among 16 year old Norwegian students. Data from 2000 Norwegian 16 year old ninth graders used to study the importance of socio-economic factors and sex differences in an educational system with main streaming no ability grouping, little acceleration and no retention in grade. Analysis illustrates how sex and socio economic differences may be mediated in an egalitarian society.

Obiakor – Festue. (1992) examined the myth of socio-economic dissonance implications for African American exceptional students. This paper addressed the myth of socio-economic dissonance and its effects on the identification, assessment, Placement and instruction of African-American students with special needs. Socioeconomic status is seen to predetermine the academic success and survival of African –American students. Nontraditional identification, assessment and instructional strategies were recommended. Educators were urged to do-emphasize the family environment and low socioeconomic background of these students and instead provide caring environments.

Soto Lourdee, Diaz (1992) studied Hispanic families as learning environment for young children. The report reviewed research related to the home learning environment and presented a study on the home learning environment of young Hispanic children. Research had progressed from concern with home learning environment variables such as ethnicity, socio-economic variable and demographic characteristics to more relevant issues concerning experiences in the home and their effect on the cognitive and affective performances of children. A study compared the home learning environment of agrarian migrant Puerto Rican families (n -20) and non-migrant puerk) Rican families (n=20) in two Rannsyivania communities. The selected families with one Child between the ages of 5 to 8 participated in a teacher parent education program. Data were collected through community observation and home visits conducted by graduate students using various instruments that measure home environment variable. The study found statistically significant higher mean scores for migrant families on obstacle of parental aspirations for their child, concern for the use of language and parental reinforcement learning theory concerning children's intellectual development, migrant families serve as a critical and facilitative role for newly arriving families in the community developmental differences revealed a more optimistic point of view by parents of younger learners. Implications were discussed for future research, practice and policy in early childhood education of Hispanic children.

Harinesh. S. Kaike (1991) studied on the anxiety among boys in related to their intelligence and socio-economic status. The sample compressed 191 IX class boys selected randomly from five recognized senior secondary schools of Ludhiana city. Tools SRIVASTAVA And TIWARI'S ANXIELY SCALE (1973) and KUPPUSWANY'S SES scale (1981). Students were categorized into three groups on the basis of their socio economic level students in the upper 27% socio-economic level (score 21 and above N-21 and above N-65)j were placed in the high socio-economic group those in the level 27% socio-economic level (scores between (I and 12, N -52) formed the low socio-economic group wherever the removing students (scores between 13 and 20 N=74) were kept in the average socio economic group manor findings. No significant relationship exists between anxiety on one side and intelligence and socio-economic status on the other. There is no significant difference in anxiety among boys belonging to high average and low levels of intelligence as well as socio-economic status.

Bisht. Abhe Rani (1990) viewed the vocational stress in relation to socio –economic status and belongingness to weaker sections of the society and the emerging discontent indifferent sections of society. A total number of 900 students with 480 students each from the non-weaker and the weaker sections comprised the sample of the study. The data were collected through the BISHT battery of stress scale. The socio-economic status scale by UNIGAL and BISHT and the last examination marks. Two-way ANOVA were used to treat the data. vocational stress of students was found to be independent of SES, BWSS (belongingness to weaker section of society) and their interacting influence, respectively as the F-rations were found to be insignificant.

Govwendr Reddy (1989) investigated the impact of socio economic status and parental education on language development. Following the stratified random sampling procedure. A sample of 720 students drawn from 20 schools located in Chithore district in Andhra Pradesh were selected for investigation. Tools family topic father, mother, brother school topic and environmental major findings were SS having high socio economic status families and better language developments as evidence by the large number of sentences written by them compared to the sentences written by them to the subjects (SS) handling from lower socio economic status group who could write a much smaller number of sentences. Children whose parents had high educational background had better language development as evidence by the large number of sentences written by them compared to children whose parents had low educational background.

Malabika Ganguly (1989) conducted a study on socio economic status and scholastic achievement to investigate whether there was any approvable difference in the scholastic achievement of upper, middle and lower socio economic groups of students. For studying the relation of SES to achievement 400 students of class IV of different secondary scattered over both urban, rural areas in the districts of Birbhum, west Bengal were taken. The schools were selected through the stratified random sampling on the basis of their results in Mandhyamik examinations for the three successive years high, average and low bring the three state accepted for the classification of schools. In the identification of urban and rural areas the guidelines of the census report 1971 were followed. Tools used were Socio economic status scale for urban areas and Socio economic status scale for rural areas. The students who belonging to the lower SES group were faced with many adverse circumstances to be academically successful one requires some guidance at home parents should keep an eye at educational status.

Modi B.M (1981) related that the socio economic status was determined by educational qualification monthly income, administrative, authority, residential accommodation, house rent, possession of vehicle, cost of furniture, cost of electrical appliances, and possession of telephone and refrigerator. A sample of 1000 persons supplied the data about the status enjoyed by two real brothers in the family, Caste and locality. The main findings of the study were The status enjoyed by a person depended on his educational level. The study of education and holding had the relation with the socio-economic status of the person.

The influence of education in the case of farmers with education above SSLC not brings about a change in the increase in the rate of their annual income.

Kumar P. (1980) aimed at investigating the socio economic background of high school students in Allahabad city. The relationship and effect of any of these socio economic factors on the demand for higher education and on the educational level sought and the factors other than social and economic which had a bearing on effective educational demand. The sample consisted of 772 students 474 boys and 298 girls from different schools of Allahabad districts. Data were collected through personal meetings with the respondents. The following were some of the findings.

More than 89% students demanded higher education. The proportion of girls demanding higher education was more than that of boys.

The highest dropout rate was in the literary group.

With the increase in their father education, the inclination of girl's income and literately groups towards higher status was increased.

The percentage of high school students who intended to go into professional technical and related occupations was 37.2%

STUDIES ON ACADEMIC STRESS

According to Bartone, Paul.T (2009), academic stress is associated with a variety of negative outcomes such as physical illness and deteriorating mental health. This paper explores the capacity of personality hardiness to buffer the relationship between academic stress and health. Results showed that hardiness was negatively associated with both academic stress and number of health complaints, and showed that hardiness moderated the association between academic stress and health.

Grace,S.M, Daniel.F.K (2010) examined the role of paternal support in the relation between academic stress and the mental health of primary school children in HONGKONG. The participants of this cross-sectional study were 1171 fifth and sixth graders. The results indicated that academic stress was a risk factor that heightened student anxiety levels and that among children. However, paternal informational support delivered to children during times of high academic stress appeared to heighten student anxiety levels.

Lu,Zuhong (2011) examined the longitudinal relationships between adolescents' stress in school and the change rates of their academic achievement. The results indicated that for those academic achievement significantly declined over time, the students 'stress from teacher-student interaction significantly predicted the change rates of their academic achievement. The findings provided support to the notion that stress was a risk factor in students' academic development.

D.Paige, (2009) examined school stress and depression in adolescents with and without learning disabilities. Students from secondary schools in Calgary completed questionnaire on depression in the adolescents with deported significantly higher levels of academic self-concept stress than their non LD peers. However, the groups did not differ significantly on depression or on the other areas of the school related stress. Significant and positive correlation between schools related stress and depression were found, and the stress variables were found to be significant predicators of adolescent depression.

Richard (2012) examined on problem-focused and emotion-focused, academic achievement, life satisfaction, positive feelings towards school and negative feelings towards school. Results demonstrate that coping incrementally predicts all four outcomes above and beyond the effects of the big five personality factors, vocabulary, and demographic variables. Incremental prediction is strongest for school feelings, and 15% of the variance in negative feelings. All three coping styles was important in predicting different outcomes: problem-focused coping predicts grades, life satisfaction, and positive feelings about school; emotion-focused coping predicts negative feelings only; and avoidant-focused coping predicts both positive and negative feelings about school. Results suggest that coping styles was an important variable for school outcomes, and that the effectiveness of different strategies depending on the outcome considered.

Berliner, David.C (2009), in an empirical study, had focused on understanding the academic stress of Chinese international students in the United States. This qualitative inquiry examines the most stressful aspects of their academic lives in the U.S., they characterize their academic stress, and what conditions they believe tend to account for their academic stress findings indicate that academic stress is extremely high for most students in this study. Culture and education disparities between china and America, together with Chinese student's language deficiencies, ineffective interactions with American faculty members, and their high motivations to achieve contribute to their academic stress.

According to Laura.J. (2012), the standard assessment tests (SAT) taken by pupils in their final year of primary schooling in England have been widely criticized for placing children under too pressure and contributing to an increase in test related stress and anxiety. In this exploratory study we set out to explore the experiences of forth coming SATs in a small sample of children using an appraisal model of stress and to reflect on whether these criticisms are justified.

Results from focus groups with pupils and interviews with class and head teachers suggested that there was diversity in pupils experience their tests. The pressure associated with SATs did not necessarily lead to negative outcomes and some children described SATs in more positive ways, as challenging rather than threatening. Self-worth judgments played a central role in individual level appraisal and may also provide a useful link to discourses surrounding the value of academic credentials.

Blazer (2010) expressed that students were under pressure from teachers, parents, and college admissions counselors to maintain high grade point averages, score well on high stakes tests, participate in a variety of extra-curricular activities, and gain admission to top colleges, in fact suggestions for parents and teachers on how they can help gifted kids with stress management.

CONCLUSION

The review of related literature gave the researcher an understanding of the research methodology, which refers to the way the study, is to be conducted. The review of related research work has enabled the investigator to formulate relevant hypotheses for the present study and to know about the tools and instruments, which proved to be useful and promising in the previous studies. Further, based on this review suitable methodology and a well planned strategy for the present investigation could be adopted.

❐

13

Research Design and Methods

Research is the systematic process of collecting and analyzing information to increase our understanding of the phenomenon under study. The main aim of the present study is to investigate the higher secondary students' Attitude towards physics and Achievement in physics.

The present chapter highlights an overall picture of the design of the study in the form of hypotheses to be tested, the research tools used for the data collection, nature and selection of the sample, reliability and validity of the tools a brief description of the procedures adopted for the data collection, scoring and statistical techniques to be employee for the further analysis of the data.

DESIGN OF THE STUDY

Research method is a systematic procedure through which the desired investigation gathers information and draws conclusion on the basis of the collected data. The normative survey method is employed to describe or interpret what exist at present. The survey method gathers data form a relatively large number of cases at a particular time. It is not concerned with the statistics that result when data are abstracted from a number of individual cases.

VARIABLES SELECTED

Major variables under study

The following major variables were selected for the study.

- Personal Growth
- Coping behavior
- Socio economic status
- Academic stress

Personal Variables

- Gender
- Medium of instruction
- Type of family
- Locale of residence

School related variables

- Type of management of schools
- Type of schools

HYPOTHESES OF THE STUDY

The following hypotheses have been framed in the present study:

1. The level of personal growth of higher secondary students is average in nature.
2. The level of coping behavior of higher secondary students is average in nature.
3. The level of socio-economic status of higher secondary students is average in nature.
4. The level of academic stress of higher secondary students is average in nature.
5. There is no significant difference between the mean scores of personal growth among higher secondary students in relation to

Gender	:	Male/Female
Type of schools	:	Boys'/Girls'/Co Education schools
Type of management of schools	:	Government/Government Aided/ Self Finance schools
Medium of instruction	:	English/ Tamil
Type of family	:	Joint/Nuclear
Locale of residence	:	Urban/Rural

6. There is no significant difference between the mean scores of coping behavior among higher secondary students in relation to

   Gender : Male/Female
   Type of schools : Boys'/Girls'/Co Education schools
   Type of management of schools : Government/Government Aided/ Self Finance schools
   Medium of instruction : English/ Tamil
   Type of family : Joint/Nuclear
   Locale of residence : Urban/Rural

7. There is no significant difference between the mean scores of socio-economic status among higher secondary students in relation to

   Gender : Male/Female
   Type of schools : Boys'/Girls'/Co Education schools
   Type of management of schools : Government/GovernmentAided/ Self Finance schools
   Medium of instruction : English/ Tamil
   Type of family : Joint/Nuclear
   Locale of residence : Urban/Rural

8. There is no significant difference between the mean scores of academic stress among higher secondary students in relation to

   Gender : Male/Female
   Type of schools : Boys'/Girls'/Co Education schools
   Type of management of schools : Government/Government Aided/ Self Finance schools
   Medium of instruction : English/ Tamil
   Type of family : Joint/Nuclear
   Locale of residence : Urban/Rural

9. There is no significant correlation between coping behavior and academic stress among higher secondary students.
10. There is no significant correlation between socio-economic status and academic stress among higher secondary students.

METHOD OF THE STUDY

A research design is the arrangement of conditions for collection and analysis of data in a manner that aims to combine relevance to the research purpose with economy in procedure. In fact, the research design is the conceptual structure within which research is conducted. It constitutes the blue print for the collection, measurement and analysis of data.

RESEARCH TOOLS SELECTED FOR PRESENT STUDY

To collect the pertinent data for the present investigation, the following tools have been designed: Personal data sheet consists of details like Gender, Medium of instruction, Type of family, Locale of residence, employed to quantify the variables involved in the study.

1. Personal Growth Initiative Scale by Christine Robitschek (2011)
2. Coping Behavior Inventory prepared and standardized by Dai, Rost and Skermer (1997)
3. Academic Stress Inventory developed and standardized by the Investigator and
4. Dr. S. Devasahayam Selvakumar(2014)
5. Kuppuswamy's Socio-Economic Status Scale as adopted and modified by Dr.S.Devasahayam Selvakumar(2014)

DESCRIPITION AND SCORING PROCEDURE OF THE TOOLS USED IN THE PRESENT STUDY

PERSONAL GROWTH INITIATIVE SCALE

Description

Personal Growth Initiative Scale (Appendix-I) constructed by Christine Robitschek (2011) had been used in order to find the level of personal growth of students. The inventory consists of 9 items. It is measured by a 6 point scale. All items are positive statements.

Administration

Students were asked to sit comfortably and fill personal growth initiative scale given. Even though there was no time limit to finish the questionnaire, students completed the task within 10 minutes. They were also told that their responses would be kept confidential and used strictly on the purpose of research only. The response is to be given on the bracket itself. Against each item of the inventory, alternatives are given in the form of cells indicating the intensity of the four point scale.

Scoring

For each statement, scoring of 6 points for definitely agree, 5 points for mostly agree, 4 points for somewhat agree,3 points for somewhat disagree, 2points for mostly disagree and 1point for definitely disagree were awarded.

COPING BEHAVIOR INVENTORY

Description

The Coping Behavior Inventory (Appendix -II) was mainly adopted from Dai Rost and skermer,1997. There are totally 21 items.

Administration

Students were asked to sit comfortably and fill their tool as the sheet given, Even though there was no time to finish the questionnaire, student completed the task within 20 minutes. They were also told that their responses would be kept confidential and used strictly only for the purpose of research.

Scoring

There are totally 21 items. All the items were scored as almost never (1 mark), rarely (2 marks),often(3 marks), very often(4 marks) and almost always(5 marks). The score ranges from 0 to 105

SOCIO ECONOMIC STATUS SCALE

Description

In determining the socio-economic status of subjects, Kuppuswamy's Socio-Economic Status Scale, as adopted and modified by DrS.Devasahayam Selvakumar (2014) has been made use of the following feature were considered and incorporated in the modified scale (Appendix-III)

1. In giving scores for educational, occupational and economic status for the parents of each student, both father and mother were taken for consideration and scores were assigned separately for each.
2. The distance education programmers have made the access for the graduate and post graduate degrees much easier.
3. The top income range can no longer be taken as Rs.1000/-p.m. since even class IV employees draw more than Rs.3000/-p.m.

Administration

To get the comprehensive socio-economic status score, a copy of the socio-economic status scale was distributed to each student, after explaining the purpose of the scale. Students were encouraged to present a real picture about their socio-economic status. They took 10 minutes to complete the scale.

Scoring

The responses were scored as per the scoring sheet. The maximum possible score are as follows:

Educational status	-	16 points
Occupation	-	20 points
Income status	-	24 points
Total	-	60 points

Based upon the Socio-Economic Status Score, the Students were Classified:

Score range	Socio-economic status level
35-60	High
20-34	Moderate
19 and below	Low

ACADEMIC STRESS INVENTORY

Description

The Academic Stress Inventory ((Appendix-IV) developed and standardized by the Investigator and Dr.S.Devasahayam Selvakumar(2014). The academic stress inventory developed consists of 34 items each one comprising of five alternatives, namely; always, often, frequently, rarely and never. All the 34 items are negative.

Administration

Students were asked to sit comfortably and fill their tool and they took 10 minutes to complete the scale.

Scoring

All the items were scored as follows: 5 marks are allotted to always, 4 marks to often, 3 marks to frequently, 2 marks to rarely and 1 to never. Maximum possible score is 170 and the minimum score is 34. The high score indicates more academic stress and low score indicates low academic stress.

PILOT STUDY

A pilot study was conducted in October, 2014 among fifty XI standard physics students which were not included for the main study, to established the reliability and validity of the different research tools used in this study.

ESTABLISHING RELIABILITY AND VALIDITY OF TOOLS USED

ersonal Growth initiative Scale

Reliability

Reliability of personal growth initiative scale was established using test-re-test method. The reliability was computed and it was found to be (0.83). Hence the tool was highly reliable.

Validity

The index of validity, which is the square root of reliability and it was found to be (0.91). Hence the tool is valid for the present study.

Coping Behavior Inventory

Reliability

The reliability of coping behavior inventory is obtained by test-retest method and it is equal to 0.86, indicating that the tool is highly reliable.

Validity

The index of validity is considered to be the square root of reliability which is equal to 0.93, indicating that coping behavior inventory is highly valid.

Academic Stress Inventory

Reliability

In order to establish the reliability of the academic stress inventory, the odd even method of reliability was used. The reliability of academic stress inventory was found to be 0.72 Hence, academic stress inventory was considered to be reliable and suitable for the present study.

Validity

The index of validity is the square root of reliability. The validity of the academic stress inventory was found to be 0.85 which is more valid suitable for the present study.

SAMPLE

The present study was concerned with higher secondary schools. Hence, the students of standard XI from various government, government aided schools and private schools were taken to constitutes the population for the present study. Stratified random sampling technique was adopted in the present study. The size of the sample was 299.

TABLE. 13.1: Showing the Details of SampleSelected

Types of Management	Sl. No	Name and place of the school	Male	Female
Government school	1	Government boys' higher secondary school, Arakkonam	42	-
Government School	2	Government girls' Higher secondary school, Arakkonam	-	42
Government School	3	Government higher secondary school chitteri,	21	20
Self finance school	4	Vivekanda matric higher secondary school, Arakkonam	25	24
Government aided school	**5**	CSI girls' higher secondary school		42
Government aided school	**6**	St Andrews boys' higher secondary school	42	-
Government aided	7	R.C.M higher secondary school	21	20

MAIN STUDY

The investigator conducted and obtained permission from the principal/ head of the selected schools for data collection in Government schools. The correspondent/secretary of the Government Aided and Self Finance schools were contacted to get permission to collect data from their schools. The willingness and co-operation of the respective class teachers were also sought.

The data were collected personally by the investigator from the selected 299 pupils in the month of November 2014.Proper instruction were given to the pupil before starting to fill the Questionnaires. Each pupil was provided with set of tools containing Personal Data Sheet, a Personal Growth Scale, Coping Behavior Inventory, Socio- economic Status and Academic Stress. Pupil were requested to mark their responses in the space provided in the tools itself. In order to facilitate the clear understanding of the statement in the tools, the investigator read out each statement loudly, using simple terms, wherever necessary.

After having ascertained that the pupils have responded the particular items, the investigator passed on the next. Students were requested not to omit any of the items. Finally the filled in the questionnaire were collected from the students.

STATISTICAL TECHNIQUES USED

i. MEAN

$$\text{Mean } (\bar{X}) = A + \frac{\sum fd}{\sum f} \times i$$

Where,

A = Assumed mean

f = frequency

d = deviation from the assumed mean

i = Class interval

ii. STANDARD DEVIATION

$$\text{Standard Deviation, } SD(\sigma) = \sqrt{\frac{\sum fd^2}{N} - \left[\frac{\sum fd^2}{N}\right]^2} \times i$$

Where,

f = Frequency

d = Deviation from the assumed mean

I = Class interval

N = Total frequency

iii. 't' TEST

To continue the significance of difference between means of various measures test is used: 't' ratio is calculated from the relation.

$$\text{t-ratio} = \frac{M_1 \sim M_2}{\sqrt{\frac{\sigma_1^2}{N_1} + \frac{\sigma_1^2}{N_2}}} = \frac{M_1 \sim M_2}{S \in D}$$

Where,

M_1, M_2 = Means of the groups

SED = Standard Error Deviation

iv. 'F'-TEST

F-ratio = Variance between the group/Variance within the group Correction term 'C'

$$C = \frac{\sum x_1 + \sum x_2 + \sum x_3}{N}$$

$$BSS = \left(\sum x_1\right)^2 / w_1^N + \left(\sum x_2\right)^2 / W_2 + \left(\sum x_3\right)^2 / W_3 - C$$

$$TSS = \sum x_1^2 + \sum x_2^2 + \sum x_3^2 - C$$

WSS = TSS - BSS

Where,

$x_1, x_2, x_3,$ are score in different group

C = correction Term

TSS = Total Sum of Squares

BSS = Between Sum of Squares

WSS= Within Sum of Squares

v. CO-EFFICIENT OF CORRELATION (r)

$$r = \frac{N\sum x \sum y - \sum x \sum y}{\sqrt{\left(N\sum x^2 - \left(\sum x^2\right)\right)\left(N\sum Y^2 - \left(\sum y\right)^2\right.}}$$

x, y – Variables,

N- Total strength.

CONCLUSION

Adopting the methods and the procedures discussed earlier in this chapter tests were administered and marked. This chapter outlined the design of the study, the procedure followed and the nature of the sample. It describes the hypotheses to be tested, selection of tools, and the method of administration and scoring procedures. The obtained data were then analyzed using appropriate statistical techniques. The next chapter presents the analysis and interpretation of the data collected in the light of the hypothesis formulated.

❒

14

Analysis and Interpretation of the Data

Research consists of systematic observation and description of the characteristic of properties for the purpose of discovering relationships starts with the description of the measures of the variables and goes on to the higher levels of statistical analysis. The data collected will be carefully edited, systematically classified and tabulated, scientifically analyzed and interpreted and rationally concluded.

Thus, in the present study the data collected with regard to personal growth, coping behavior, academic stress and socio economic status were analyzed with reference to the objectives and hypotheses of the study. The data have been subjected to the following statistical analysis namely percentile, descriptive, differential and correlation. The results of statistical analysis have been summarized and tabulated.

THE MAJOR CATEGORISATION OF THE SAMPLE BASED ON THE MAJOR VARIABLE OF THE STUDY

Categorisation of the Sample Based on Personal Growth

The scores related to personal growth of higher secondary students have been analysed to find out the level of their personal growth.

TABLE. 14.1: Showing the Level of Personal Growth of Higher Secondary Students.

Variable	No. of Sample	Range	Level	Frequency	Percentage
Personal Growth	299	Below 29	Low	84	28.1
		Between 30 to 39	Moderate	140	46.8
		Above 40	High	75	25.1

INFERENCE

From the table, it is clear that the level of Personal growth of higher secondary students is moderate in nature. Hence, the hypothesis 1 stating that "The level of personal growth of higher secondary students is average in nature" is accepted.

CATEGORISATION OF THE SAMPLE BASED ON COPING BEHAVIOR

The scores related to coping behavior of higher secondary students have been analysed to find out the level of their coping behavior.

TABLE. 14.2: Showing the Level of Coping Behavior of Higher Secondary Students

Variable	No. of Sample	Range	Level	Frequency	Percentage
Coping Behavior	299	Below 69	Low	81	27.1
		Between 70 to 82	Moderate	139	46.5
		Above 83	High	79	26.4

INFERENCE

From the table, it is clear that the level of Coping Behavior of higher secondary students is moderate in nature.

Hence, the hypothesis 2 stating that "The level of coping behavior of higher secondary students is average in nature" is accepted.

CATEGORISATION OF THE SAMPLE BASED ON SOCIO-ECONOMIC STATUS

The scores related to socio-economic status of higher secondary students have been analysed to find out the level of their socio-economic status

TABLE.14.3: Showing the Level of Socio Economic Status of Higher Secondary Students

Variable	No. of Sample	Level	Frequency	Percentage
Socio Economic status	299	Low	141	47.2
		Moderate	142	47.5
		High	16	5.4

INFERENCE

From the table, it is clear that the level of Socio economic status of higher secondary students is moderate in nature.

Hence, the hypothesis 3 stating that "The level of socio-economic status of higher secondary students is average in nature" is accepted.

CATEGORISATION OF THE SAMPLE BASED ON ACADEMIC STRESS

The scores related to academic stress of higher secondary students have been analysed to find out the level of their academic stress.

TABLE.14.4: Showing the Level of Academic Stress of Higher Secondary Students

Variable	No. of Sample	Range	Level	Frequency	Percentage
Academic Stress	299	Below 93	Low	81	27.1
		Between 94 to 129	Moderate	139	46.5
		Above 130	High	79	26.4

INFERENCE

From the table, it is clear that the level of Academic stress of higher secondary students is moderate in nature.

Hence, the hypothesis 4 "The level of academic stress of higher secondary students is average in nature" is accepted.

INFLUENCE OF GENDER ON PERSONAL GROWTH

The scores related to personal growth of male and female higher secondary students have been computed and details are furnished in the following table

TABLE. 14.5: Showing the Significant Difference between the mean Scores of Personal Growth with Respect to Gender.

Variable	Gender	N	Mean	SD	Critical Ratio	L.S
Personal Growth	Boys	151	35.75	7.585	2.931	0.01
	Girls	148	33.13	7.755		

INFERENCE

From the table, it is clear that the obtained C.R value (2.931) is higher than the table value (2.58) at 0.01 level. Therefore there is significant difference between the mean scores of personal growth among higher secondary students with regard to Gender.

It is also noted that male students have significantly higher personal growth than their counterparts.

Hence the hypothesis – 5 (a) stating that "There is no significant difference between the mean scores of Personal growth among higher secondary students based on Gender" is rejected.

INFLUENCE OF TYPE OF SCHOOLS ON PERSONAL GROWTH

The scores related to personal growth of higher secondary students based on type of schools (Boys'/Girls'/co- education schools) have been computed and details are furnished in the following table

TABLE. 14.6: ANOVA Showing the Significant Difference between the mean Scores of Personal Growth with Respect to Type of Schools

Variable		Sum of Squares	df	Mean Squares	F Value	L.S
Personal Growth	Between groups	1069.839	2	534.919	9.366	0.01
	Within groups	16905.887	296	57.114		
	Total	17975.726	298			

INFERENCE

From the table, it is clear that the obtained "F" value (9.366) is higher than the table value (4.68) at 0.01 level. Therefore there is significant difference between the mean scores of personal growth among higher secondary students with regard to Type of schools.

This has been further analysed by comparing the groups among themselves for their personal growth, using 't' test

TABLE. 14.7: Showing the Multiple Comparisons of the Significant Difference between the mean Scores of Personal Growth with Respect to Type of Schools.

Variable	Type of School	N	Mean	S.D	Critical Ratio	L.S
Personal Growth	Boys'	80	37.21	8.039	4.059	0.01
	Girls'	80	32.08	7.971		
	Boys'	80	37.21	8.039	2.892	0.01
	Co-education	139	34.21	7.010		
	Girls'	80	32.08	7.971	2.062	0.05
	Co-education	139	34.21	7.010		

INFERENCE

In the first case, the calculated 't' value (4.059) is greater than the table 't' value (2.58) at 0.01 level, showing that there is significant difference between students studying in Boys' and Girls' higher secondary schools with regard to their Personal growth.

In the second case, the calculated 't' value (2.892) is greater than the table 't' value (2.58) at 0.01 level, showing that there is significant difference between students studying in Boys' and Co-education higher secondary schools with regard to their Personal growth.

In the third case, the calculated 't' value (2.062) is greater than the table 't' value (1.96) at 0.05 level, showing that there is significant difference between students studying in Girls' and Co-education higher secondary school with regard to their Personal growth.

It is also proved that students studying in boys' schools have shown significantly higher personal growth than the students studying in girls' and co education schools.

Hence the hypothesis – 5 (b) stating that "There is no significant difference between the mean scores of Personal growth among higher secondary students based on Type of schools" is rejected.

INFLUENCE OF TYPE OF MANAGEMENT OF SCHOOLS ON PERSONAL GROWTH

The scores related to personal growth type of management higher secondary students based on the type of management of schools(Government,/ government aided/self finances) have been computed and details are furnished in the following table.

TABLE.14.8: ANOVA Showing the Significant Difference between the mean Scores of Personal Growth of Higher Secondary Students based on Type of Management of Schools.

Variable		Sum of Squares	df	Mean Squares	F Value	L.S
Personal Growth	Between groups	913.354	2	456.677	7.922	0.01
	Within groups	17062.372	296	57.643		
	Total	**17975.726**	**298**			

INFERENCE

From the table, it is clear that the obtained "F" value (7.922) is higher than the table value (4.68) at 0.01 level. Therefore there is significant difference between the mean scores of personal growth among higher secondary students with regard to Type of management of schools.

This has been further analysed by comparing the groups among themselves for their personal growth, using ‘t’ test

TABLE. 14.9: Showing the Multiple Comparisons of Significant Difference between the mean Scores of Personal Growth with Respect to Type of Management of Management of Schools.

Types of Management	N	Mean	S.D	CR Value	L.S
Government Vs Government Aided	125 125	35.41 32.48	7.584 7.958	2.978	0.01
Government Aided Vs Self Finance	125 49	32.48 36.98	7.958 6.578	3.513	0.01
Government Vs Self Finance	125 49	35.41 36.98	7.584 6.578	1.274	NS

INFERENCE

In the first case, the calculated ‘t’ value (2.978) is greater than the table ‘t’ value (2.58) at 0.01 level, showing that there is significant difference between students studying in Government and Government-Aided higher secondary schools with regard to their Personal growth.

In the second case, the calculated ‘t’ value (3.513) is greater than the table ‘t’ value (2.58) at 0.01 level, showing that there is significant difference between students studying in Government-Aided and Self-finance higher secondary schools with regard to their Personal growth.

In the third case, the calculated ‘t’ value (1.274) is lesser than the table ‘t’ value (1.96) at 0.05 level, showing that there is no significant difference between students studying in Government and Self-finance higher secondary schools with regard to their Personal growth.

It is also proved that students studying in Government aided schools have shown significantly lesser personal growth than students studying in Government and Self-finance schools.

Hence the hypothesis – 5(c) stating that “There is no significant difference between the mean scores of Personal growth among higher secondary based on Type of management of schools” is partially verified.

INFLUENCE OF MEDIUM OF INSTRUCTION ON PERSONAL GROWTH

The scores related to personal growth of higher secondary students based on medium of instruction (Tamil/English) have been computed and details are furnished in the following table.

TABLE. 14.10: Showing the Significant Difference between the mean Scores of Personal Growth with Respect to Medium of Instruction.

Variable	Medium of Instruction	N	Mean	SD	Critical Ratio	L.S
Personal Growth	Tamil	126	34.67	7.381	0.442	NS
	English	173	34.27	8.053		

INFERENCE

From the table, it is clear that the obtained 't' value (0.442) is less than the table 't' value (1.96) at 0.05 level. Therefore there is no significant difference between the mean scores of personal growth among higher secondary students with regard to medium of instruction.

Hence the hypothesis 5 (d) stating that "There is no significant difference between the mean scores of Personal growth among higher secondary students based on Medium of instruction" is accepted

INFLUENCE OF TYPE OF FAMILY ON PERSONAL GROWTH

The scores related to personal growth of higher secondary students based on type of family(Nuclear/Joint) have been computed and details are furnished in the following table.

TABLE. 14.11: Showing the Significant Difference between the mean Scores of Personal Growth with Respect to Type of Family.

Variable	Type of Family	N	Mean	SD	Critical Ratio	L.S
Personal Growth	Joint	43	34.67	7.612	0.212	NS
	Nuclear	256	34.40	7.806		

INFERENCE

From the table, it is clear that the obtained 't' value (0.212) is lesser than the table 't' value (1.96) at 0.05 level. Therefore there is no significant difference between the mean scores of personal growth among higher secondary students with regard to type of family.

Hence the hypothesis – 5(e) stating that "There is no significant difference between the mean scores of Personal growth among higher secondary students based on Type of family" is accepted.

INFLUENC OF LOCALE OF RESIDENCE ON PERSONAL GROWTH

The scores related to personal growth of higher secondary students based on locale of residence (Rural/Urban) have been computed and details are furnished in the following table.

TABLE. 14.12: Showing the Significant Differences between the mean Scores of Personal Growth with Respect to Locale of Residence.

Variable	Locale of Residence	N	Mean	SD	Critical Ratio	L.S
Personal Growth	Rural	91	35.20	7.556	1.114	NS
	Urban	208	34.11	7.852		

INFERENCE

From the table, it is clear that the obtained 't' value (1.114) is lesser than the table 't' value (1.96) at 0.05 level. Therefore there is no significant difference between the mean scores of personal growth among higher secondary students with regard to Locale of Residence.

Hence the hypothesis – 5 (f) stating that "There is no significant difference between the mean scores of Personal growth among higher secondary based on Locale of Residence" is accepted.

INFLUENCE OF GENDER ON COPING BEHAVIOR

The scores related to coping behavior of higher secondary students have been analysed to find out the level of their coping behavior based on gender

TABLE. 14.13: Showing the Significant Difference between the mean Scores of Coping behavior with Respect to Gender.

Variable	Gender	N	Mean	SD	Critical Ratio	L.S
Coping Behavior	Boys	151	74.87	10.957	1.604	NS
	Girls	148	76.79	9.652		

INFERENCE

From the table, it is clear that the obtained 't' value (1.604) is lesser than the table 't' value (1.96) at 0.05 level. Therefore there is no significant difference between the mean scores of Coping behavior among higher secondary students with regard to Gender.

Hence the hypothesis –6(a) stating that "There is no significant difference between the mean scores of coping behavior among higher secondary students based on Gender" is accepted.

INFLUENCE OF TYPE OF SCHOOLS ON COPING BEHAVIOR

The scores related to coping behavior of higher secondary students based on type of schools (boys'/girls'/co education schools) have been computed and details are furnished in the following table

TABLE. 14.14: ANOVA Showing the Significant Difference between the mean Scores of Coping Behavior with Respect to Type of Schools.

Variable		Sum of Squares	df	Mean Squares	F Value	L.S
Coping Behavior	Between groups	679.188	2	339.594	3.212	0.05
	Within groups	31298.418	296	105.738		
	Total	**31977.605**	**298**			

INFERENCE

From the table, it is clear that the obtained "F" value (3.212) is greater than the table 'f' value (3.03) at 0.05 level. Therefore there is significant difference between the mean scores of Coping behavior among higher secondary students with regard to Type of schools.

This has been further analysed by comparing the groups among themselves for their coping behavior, using 't' test

TABLE. 14.15: Showing the Multiple Comparisons of Significant Differences between the mean Scores of Coping Behavior with Respect to Type of Schools.

Variable	Type of School	N	Mean	S.D	Critical Ratio	L.S
Coping Behavior	Boys'	80	74.49	11.532	0.082	NS
	Girls'	80	74.35	9.459		
	Boys'	80	74.49	11.532	1.990	0.05
	Co-education	139	77.44	9.973		
	Girls'	80	74.35	9.459	2.249	0.05
	Co-education	139	77.44	9.973		

INFERENCES

In the first case, the calculated 't' value (0.082) is lesser than the table 't' value (1.96) at 0.05 level, showing that there is no significant difference between students studying in Boys' and Girls' higher secondary school with regard to their Coping behavior.

In the second case, the calculated 't' value (1.990) is greater than the table 't' value (1.96) at 0.05 level showing that there is significant difference between students studying in Boys' and Co-education higher secondary school with regard to their Coping behavior.

In the third case, the calculated 't' value (2.249) is greater than the table 't' value (1.96) at 0.05 level showing that there is significant difference between students studying in Girls' and Co-education higher secondary school with regard to their Coping behavior.

It is also proved that students studying in coeducation schools have shown significantly higher coping behavior than the students studying in boys' and girls' schools

Hence the hypothesis-6 (b) stating that "There is no significant difference between the mean scores of coping behavior among higher secondary based on Type of schools" is partially verified .

INFLUENCE OF TYPE OF MANAGEMENT OF SCHOOLS ON THE COPING BEHAVIOR

The scores related to coping behavior of higher secondary students based on the type of management of schools have been computed and details are furnished in the following table.

TABLE.14.16: ANOVA Showing the Significant Difference between the Mean Scores of Coping Behavior of Higher Secondary Students based on Type of Management of Schools.

Variable		Sum of Squares	df	Mean Squares	F Value	L.S
Coping behavior	Between groups	1436.620	2	718.310	6.962	0.01
	Within groups	30540.986	296	103.179		
	Total	**31977.605**	**298**			

INFERENCE

From the table, it is clear that the obtained "F" value (6.962) is greater than the table 'F' value (4.68) at 0.01 level. Therefore there is significant difference between the mean scores of Coping behavior among higher secondary students with regard to Type of management of schools.

TABLE.14.17: Showing the Multiple Comparisons of Significant Difference between the mean Scores of Coping Behavior with Respect to Type of Management of Schools.

Types of Management of schools	N	Mean	S.D	CR Value	L.S
Government Vs Government Aided	125	76.98	10.129	2.757	0.01
	125	73.38	10.471		
Government Aided Vs Self Finances	125	73.38	10.471	3.333	0.01
	49	79.10	9.381		
Government Vs Self Finances	125	76.98	10.129	1.271	NS
	49	79.10	9.381		

INFERENCE

In the first case, the calculated 't' value (2.751) is greater than the table 't' value (2.58) at 0.01 level showing that there is significant difference between students studying in Government and Government-Aided higher secondary school with regard to their Coping behavior.

In the second case, the calculated 't' value (3.333) is greater than the table 't' value (2.58) at 0.01 level showing that there is significant difference between students studying in Government-Aided and Self-finance higher secondary school with regard to their Coping behavior.

In the third case, the calculated 't' value (1.271) is lesser than the table 't' value (1.96) at 0.05 level, showing that there is no significant difference between students studying in Government and Self-finance higher secondary schools with regard to their Coping behavior.

It is also proved that students studying in Government aided schools have shown significantly lesser coping behavior than the students studying in Government and Self-finance schools.

Hence the hypothesis – 6 (c) stating that "There is no significant difference between the mean scores of coping behavior among higher secondary based on Type of management of schools" is partially verified.

INFLUENCE OF MEDIUM OF INSTRUCTION ON THE COPING BEHAVIOR

The scores related to coping behavior of higher secondary students based on the medium of instruction have been computed and details are furnished in the following table

TABLE.14.18: Showing the Significant Difference between the mean Scores of Coping Behavior with Respect to Medium of Instruction.

Variable	Medium of Instruction	N	Mean	SD	Critical Ratio	L.S
Coping Behavior	Tamil	126	75.78	10.366	0.064	NS
	English	173	75.86	10.384		

INFERENCE

From the table, it is clear that the obtained "t" value (0.064) is lesser than the table value (1.96) at 0.05 level. Therefore there is no significant difference between the mean scores of Coping behavior among higher secondary students with regard to medium of instruction.

Hence the hypothesis –6(d) stating that "There is no significant difference between the mean scores of Coping behavior among higher secondary students based on Medium of instruction" is accepted.

INFLUENCE OF TYPE OF FAMILY ON THE COPING BEHAVIOR

The scores related to coping behavior of higher secondary school students based on type of family(Nuclear/Joint) have been computed and details are furnished in the following table

TABLE. 14.19: ANOVA Showing the Significant Difference between the Mean Scores of Coping Behavior with Respect to Type of Family.

Variable	Type of Family	N	Mean	SD	Critical Ratio	L.S
Coping Behavior	Joint	43	77.07	9.202	0.853	NS
	Nuclear	256	75.61	10.543		

INFERENCE

From the table, it is clear that the obtained "t" value (0.853) is lesser than the table 't' value (3.03) at 0.05 level. Therefore there is no significant difference between the mean scores of Coping behavior among higher secondary students with regard to Type of family.

Hence the hypothesis –6 (e) stating that "There is no significant difference between the mean scores of Coping behavior among higher secondary students based on type of family" is accepted.

INFLUENCE OF LOCALE OF RESIDENCE ON THE COPING BEHAVIOR

The scores related to coping behavior of locale of residences higher secondary students based on locale of residence (Rural/Urban) have been computed and details are furnished in the following table

TABLE. 14.20: Showing the Significant Difference between the mean Scores of Coping Behavior with Respect to Locale of Residence.

Variable	Locale of Residence	N	Mean	SD	Critical Ratio	L.S
Coping Behavior	Rural	91	77.38	10.428	1.730	NS
	Urban	208	75.14	10.279		

INFERENCE

From the table, it is clear that the obtained "t" value (1.730) is lesser than the table 't' value (1.96) at 0.05 level. Therefore there is no significant difference between the mean scores of Coping Behavior among higher secondary students with regard to locale of residence.

Hence the hypothesis-6(f) stating that "There is no significant difference between the mean scores of Coping Behavior among higher secondary based on Locale of Residence" is accepted.

INFLUENCE OF GENDER ON SOCIO-ECONOMIC STATUS

The scores related to socio-economic status of male and female higher secondary students have been computed and details are furnished in the following table

TABLE. 14.21: Showing the Significant Difference between the mean Scores of Socio Economic Status with Respect to Gender.

Variable	Gender	N	Mean	SD	Critical Ratio	L.S
Socio Economic Status	Boys	151	15.96	6.214	0.570	NS
	Girls	148	16.36	6.067		

INFERENCE

From the table, it is clear that the obtained C.R value (0.570) is lesser than the table value (1.96) at 0.5 level. Therefore there is no significant difference between the mean scores of socio – economic status among higher secondary students with regard to Gender.

Hence the hypothesis – 7 (a) stating that "There is no significant difference between the mean scores of Socio- Economic Status among higher secondary students based on Gender" is accepted.

INFLUENCE OF TYPE OF SCHOOLS ON SOCIO- ECONOMIC STATUS

The scores related to socio- economic status of higher secondary students based on type of schools (Boys'/Girls'/co- education schools) have been computed and details are furnished in the following table

TABLE. 14.22: ANOVA Showing the Significant Difference between the mean Scores of Socio-Economic Status with Respect to Type of Schools.

Variable		Sum of Squares	df	Mean Squares	F Value	L.S
Socio Economic Status	Between groups	819.540	2	409.770	11.669	0.01
	Within groups	10394.755	296	35114		
	Total	**11214.294**	**298**			

INFERENCE

From the table, it is clear that the obtained "F" value (11.669) is higher than the table value (4.68) at 0.01 level. Therefore there is significant difference between the mean scores of socio- economic status among higher secondary students with regard to Type of schools.

This has been further analysed by comparing the groups among themselves for their socio- economic status, using 't' test

TABLE. 14.23: Showing the Multiple Comparisons of the Significant Difference between the mean Scores of Socio- Economic Status with Respect to Type of Schools.

Variable	Type of School	N	Mean	S.D	Critical Ratio	L.S
Socio Economic Status	Boys'	80	14.71	3.064	0.364	NS
	Girls'	80	14.53	3.460		
	Boys'	80	14.71	3.045	3.480	0.01
	Co-education	139	17.94	7.947		
	Girls'	80	14.53	3.460	3.642	0.01
	Co-education	139	17.94	7.947		

INFERENCE

In the first case, the calculated 't' value (0.364) is lesser than the table 't' value (1.96) at 0.05 level, showing that there is no significant difference between students studying in Boys' and Girls' higher secondary schools with regard to their socio- economic status.

In the second case, the calculated 't' value (3.480) is greater than the table 't' value (2.58) at 0.01 level, showing that there is significant difference between students studying in Boys' and Co-education higher secondary schools with regard to their socio- economic status.

In the third case, the calculated 't' value (3.642) is greater than the table 't' value (2.58) at 0.01 level, showing that there is significant difference between students studying in Girls' and Co-education higher secondary school with regard to their socio- economic status.

It is also proved that students studying in co education schools have shown significantly higher socio- economic status than the students studying in boys' and girls' schools.

Hence the hypothesis – 7(b) stating that "There is no significant difference between the mean scores of socio- economic status among higher secondary students based on Type of schools" is partially verified.

INFLUENCE OF TYPE OF MANAGEMENT OF SCHOOLS ON SOCIO-ECONOMIC STATUS

The scores related to socio-economic status of higher secondary students based on the type of management of schools (Government,/government aided/ self finance)have been computed and details are furnished in the following table.

TABLE. 14.24: ANOVA Showing the Significant Difference between the mean Scores of Eocio-Economic Status of Higher Secondary Students based on Type of Management of Schools.

Variable		Sum of Squares	df	Mean Squares	F Value	L.S
Socio Economic status	Between groups	7820.350	2	3910.175	341.023	0.01
	Within groups	3393.944	296	11.466		
	Total	**11214.294**	**298**			

INFERENCE

From the above table, it is clear that the obtained "F" value (341.023) is greater than the table 'F' value (4.68) at 0.01 level. Therefore there is significant difference between the mean scores of Socio-economic status among higher secondary students with regard to Type of management of schools.

This has been further analysed by comparing the groups among themselves for their socio-economic status, using 't' test.

TABLE.14.25: Showing the Multiple Comparisons of the Significant Difference between the mean Scores of Socio- Economic Status with Respect to Type of Management of Schools.

Types of Management	N	Mean	S.D	CR - Value	L.S
Government Vs Government Aided	125	13.58	2.982	1.568	0.01
	125	14.22	3.378		
Government. Aided Vs Self Finance	125	14.22	3.378	21.908	0.01
	49	27.67	4.273		
Government Vs Self Finance	125	13.58	2.982	24.681	0.01
	49	27.69	4.273		

INFERENCE

In the first case, the calculated 't' value (1.5681) is lesser than the table 't' value (1.96) at 0.05 level, showing that there is no significant difference between students studying in Government and Government-Aided schools with regard to their socio- economic status.

In the second case, the calculated 't' value (21.908) is greater than the table 't' value (2.58) at 0.01 level, showing that there is significant difference between students studying in Government-Aided and Self-finance higher schools with regard to their socio- economic status.

In the third case, the calculated 't' value (24.681) is greater than the table 't' value (2.58) at 0.01 level, showing that there is significant difference between students studying in Government and Self-finance higher secondary schools with regard to their socio- economic status.

It is also proved that students studying in Self finance schools have shown significantly higher socio- economic status than students studying in Government and Government-Aided schools.

Hence the hypothesis – 7 (c) stating that "There is no significant difference between the mean scores of socio- economic status among higher secondary based on Type of management of schools" is partially verified.

INFLUENCE OF MEDIUM OF INSTRUCTION ON SOCIO-ECONOMIC STATUS

The scores related to socio- economic status of higher secondary students based on medium of instruction (Tamil/English) have been computed and details are furnished in the following table.

TABLE. 14.26: Showing the Significant Difference between the mean Scores of Socio-Economic Status with Respect to Medium of Instruction.

Variable	Medium of Instruction	N	Mean	SD	Critical Ratio	L.S
Socio Economic status	Tamil	126	14.80	3.255	3.324	0.01
	English	173	17.15	7.427		

INFERENCE

From the table, it is clear that the obtained 't' value (3.324) is greater than the table 't' value (2.58) at 0.01 level. Therefore there is significant difference between the mean scores of socio- economic status among higher secondary students with regard to medium of instruction.

Hence the hypothesis 7(d) stating that "There is no significant difference between the mean scores of socio- economic status among higher secondary students based on Medium of instruction" is rejected.

INFLUENCE OF TYPE OF FAMILY ON SOCIO- ECONOMIC STATUS

The scores related to socio- economic status of higher secondary students based on type of family (Nuclear/Joint) have been computed and details are furnished in the following table.

TABLE. 14.27: Showing the Significant Difference between the mean Scores of Socio- Economic Status with Respect to Type of Family.

Variable	Type of Family	N	Mean	SD	Critical Ratio	L.S
Socio Economic status	Joint	43	15.56	5.552	0.695	NS
	Nuclear	256	16.26	6.231		

INFERENCE

From the table, it is clear that the obtained 't' value (0.695) is lesser than the table 't' value (1.96) at 0.05 level. Therefore there is no significant difference between the mean scores of socio- economic status among higher secondary students with regard to type of family.

Hence the hypothesis – 7 (e) stating that "There is no significant difference between the mean scores of socio- economic status among higher secondary students based on Type of family" is accepted.

INFLUENC OF LOCALE OF RESIDENCE ON SOCIO- ECONOMIC STATUS

The scores related to socio- economic status of higher secondary students based on locale of residences(Rural/Urban) have been computed and details are furnished in the following table.

TABLE. 14.28: Showing the Significant Difference between the mean Scores of Socio-Economic Status with Respect to Locale of Residence.

Variable	Locale of Residence	N	Mean	SD	Critical Ratio	L.S
Socio Econom-ic status	Rural	91	15.98	5.937	0.340	NS
	Urban	208	16.24	6.231		

INFERENCE

From the table, it is clear that the obtained't' value (0.340) is lesser than the table 't' value (1.96) at 0.05 level. Therefore there is no significant difference between the mean scores of socio- economic status among higher secondary students with regard to Locale of Residence.

Hence the hypothesis – 7(f) stating that "There is no significant difference between the mean scores of socio- economic status among higher secondary based on Locale of Residence" is accepted.

INFLUENCES OF GENDER ON THE ACADEMIC STRESS

The scores related to academic stress of male and female higher secondary students have been computed and details are furnished in the following table.

TABLE. 14.29: Showing the Significant Difference between the mean Scores of Academic Stress with Respect to Gender

Variable	Gender	N	Mean	SD	Critical Ratio	L.S
Academic Stress	Boys	151	109.50	24.829	1.398	NS
	Girls	148	113.67	26.688		

INFERENCE

From the table, it is clear that the obtained "t" value (1.398) is lesser than the table 't' value (1.96) at 0.05 level. Therefore there is no significant difference between the mean scores of Academic stress among higher secondary students with regard to Gender.

Hence the hypothesis – 8 (a) stating that "There is no significant difference between the mean scores of Academic stress among higher secondary students based on Gender" is accepted.

INFLUENCE OF TYPE OF SCHOOLS ON ACADAMIC STRESS

The scores related to academic stress of higher secondary students based on type of schools(Boys'/Girls'/Co education) have been computed and details are furnished in the following table.

TABLE. 14.30: ANOVA Showing the Significant Difference between the Mean Scores of Academic Stress of Higher Secondary Students based on Type of Schools.

Variable		Sum of Squares	df	Mean Squares	F Value	L.S
Academic Stress	Between groups	1491.951	2	745.976	1.121	N.S
	Within groups	196975.53	296	665.458		
	Total	**198467.48**	**298**			

INFERENCE

From the table, it is clear that the obtained "F" value (1.121) is lesser than the table 'F' value (3.03) at 0.05 level. Therefore there is no significant difference between the mean scores of Academic stress among higher secondary students with regard to type of schools.

Hence the hypothesis –8 (b) stating that "There is significant difference between the mean scores of Academic stress among higher secondary students based on Type of schools" is accepted.

INFLUENCE OF TYPE OF MANAGEMENT OF SCHOOLS ON ACADAMIC STRESS

The scores related to academic stress of higher secondary students based on type of managements of schools (government/government aided/self finances) have been computed and details are furnished in the following table.

TABLE. 14.31: ANOVA Showing the Significant Difference between the mean Scores of Academic Stress of Higher Secondary Students based on Type of Management of Schools.

Variable		Sum of Squares	df	Mean Squares	F Value	L.S
Academic Stress	Between groups	20071.544	2	10035.772	16.652	0.01
	Within groups	178395.93	296	602.689		
	Total	198467.48	298			

INFERENCE

From the table, it is clear that the obtained "F" value (16.652) is greater than the table 't' value (4.68) at 0.01 level. Therefore there is significant difference between the mean scores of Academic stress of higher secondary students with regard to Type of management of schools.

This has been further analysed by comparing the group among themselves for their academic stress, using 't' tests.

TABLE. 14.32: Showing the Multiple Comparisons of Significant Difference between the mean Scores of Academic Stress with Respect to Type of Management of Schools.

Types of Management	N	Mean	S.D	CR - Value	L.S
Government Vs Government Aided	125	111.22	22.498	2.015	0.05
	125	105.10	25.425		
Government Aid Vs Self Finances	125	105.10	25.425	5.460	0.01
	49	128.96	27.187		
Government Vs Self Finances	125	111.22	22.498	4.405	0.01
	49	128.96	27.187		

INFERENCE

In the first case, the calculated 't' value (2.015) is greater than the table 't' value (1.96) at 0.05 level showing that there is significant difference between students studying in Government and Government-Aided higher secondary students with regard to their Academic stress.

In the second case, the calculated 't' value (5.460) is greater than the table 't' value (2.58) at 0.01 level showing that there is significant difference between students studying in Government-Aided and Self-finance higher secondary students with regard to their Academic stress.

In the third case, the calculated 't' value (4.405) is greater than the table 't' value (2.58) at 0.01 level showing that there is significant difference between students studying in Government and Self-finance higher secondary students with regard to their Academic stress.

It is also proved that the students studying in self finance schools have shown significantly higher academic stress than the government and government aided schools students.

Hence the hypothesis –8(c) stating that "There is no significant difference between the mean scores of Academic stress among higher secondary based on Type of management of schools" is rejected.

INFLUENCE OF MEDIUM OF INSTRUCTION ON ACADAMIC STRESS

The scores related to academic stress of higher secondary students based on medium of instruction have been computed and details are furnished in the following table.

TABLE. 14.33: Showing the Significant Difference between the mean Scores of Academic Stress with Respect to Medium of Instruction.

Variable	Medium of Instruction	N	Mean	SD	Critical Ratio	L.S
Academic Stress	Tamil	126	110.79	22.358	0.441	NS
	English	173	112.13	28.104		

INFERENCE

From the table, it is clear that the obtained "t" value (0.441) is lesser than the table 't' Value (1.96) at 0.05 level. Therefore there is no significant difference between the mean scores of Academic stress among higher secondary students with regard to medium of instruction.

Hence the hypothesis – 8 (d) stating that "There is no significant difference between the mean scores of Academic stress among higher secondary students based on Medium of instruction" is accepted.

INFLUENCE OF TYPE OF FAMILY ON THE ACADAMIC STRESS

The scores related to academic stress of higher secondary students based on type of family have been computed and details are furnished in the following table.

TABLE. 14. 34: Showing the significant difference between the mean scores of Academic stress with respect to type of family.

Variable	Type of Family	N	Mean	SD	Critical Ratio	L.S
Academic Stress	Joint	43	114.37	29.232	0.770	NS
	Nuclear	256	111.09	25.219		

INFERENCE

From the table, it is clear that the obtained "t" value (0.770) is lesser than the table value (1.96) at 0.05 level. Therefore there is no significant difference between the mean scores of Academic stress among higher secondary students with regard to Type of family.

Hence the hypothesis – 8 (e) stating that "There is no significant difference between the mean scores of Academic stress among higher secondary students based on Type of family" is accepted.

INFLUENCES OF LOCALE OF RESIDENCE ON THE ACADAMIC STRESS

The scores related to academic stress of higher secondary students based on locale of residence have been computed and details are furnished in the following table.

TABLE. 14.35: Showing the Significant Difference between the mean Scores of Academic Stress with Respect to Locale of Residence.

Variable	Locale of Residence	N	Mean	SD	Critical Ratio	L.S
Academ-ic stress	Rural	91	114.03	25.084	1.094	NS
	Urban	208	110.49	26.103		

INFERENCE

From the table, it is clear that the obtained "t" value (1.094) is lesser than the table 't' value (1.96) at 0.05 level. Therefore there is no significant difference between the mean scores of Academic stress among higher secondary students with regard to locale of residence.

Hence the hypothesis – 8 (f) stating that "There is no significant difference between the mean scores of Academic stress among higher secondary students based on Locale of Residence" is accepted.

CORRELATON BETWEEN COPING BEHAVIOR AND ACADEMIC STRESS

The correlation between coping behavior and academic stress of higher secondary students has been computed the details of which are presented in the following table.

TABLE. 14.36: Showing the Correlation between the Coping Behavior and Academic Stress of Higher Secondary School Students.

Variables	N	r value	L.S
Coping Behavior Vs Academic Stress	299	0.190	0.01

INFERENCE

From the above table, It is clear that there is significant and Positive correlation between the Coping behavior and academic stress among higher secondary students.

Hence the hypothesis –09 stating that "There is no significant correlation between coping behavior and academic stress of higher secondary students" is rejected.

CORRELATON BETWEEN SOCIO-ECONOMIC STATUS AND ACADEMIC STRESS

There is no significant correlation between Socio-economic Status in relation to their Academic Stress of higher secondary students.

TABLE.14.37: Showing the Correlation between the Socio-Economic Status and Academic Stress of Higher Secondary School Students.

Variables	N	r value	L.S
Socio-Economic Status Vs Academic Stress	299	0.173	0.01

INFERENCE

From the above table, it is clear that there is significant and positive correlation between the Socio-economic Status and Academic Stress among higher secondary students.

Hence the hypothesis – 10 stating that "There is no significant correlation between Socio-economic Status and Academic Stress of higher secondary students" is rejected.

CONCLUSION

This chapter explains the analysis of data, testing of hypotheses and interpretation of the data. A brief report of the research study together with the major findings, educational implications and the suggestion for further research has been presented in succeeding chapter.

❐

15

Findings and Summary

This chapter will discuss a detailed account of the research experiences from selection and definition of the problems, formulation of hypothesis, tools used, major findings, implications of the study and so on.

This chapter provides a brief summary of the entire study giving interpretation of results obtained from the statistical analysis of the data presented in the previous chapter; also highlights the main findings of the study, points of the implication and recommendations for future study.

STATEMENT OF THE PROBLEM

The problem is stated as "An Ivestigation into Personal Growth, Coping Behavior and Socio-Economic Status of Higher Secondary Students in Relation to Their Academic Stress"

OBJECTIVES OF THE STUDY

The following objectives have been framed in the present study

1. To find out level of personal growth of higher secondary students.
2. To find out level of coping behavior of higher secondary students.
3. To find out level of Socio-economic status of higher secondary students.
4. To find out level of academic stress of higher secondary students.

5. To find out whether there is any significant difference between the mean scores of personal growth among higher secondary students in relation to

Gender	:	Male/Female
Type of schools	:	Boys'/Girls'/Co Education schools
Type of management of schools	:	Government/Government Aided/ Self Finance schools
Medium of instruction	:	English/ Tamil
Type of family	:	Joint/Nuclear
Locale of residence	:	Urban/Rural

6. To find out whether there is any significant difference between the mean scores of coping behavior among higher secondary students in relation to

Gender	:	Male/Female
Type of schools	:	Boys'/Girls'/Co Education schools
Type of management of schools	:	Government/Government Aided/ Self Finance schools
Medium of instruction	:	English/ Tamil
Type of family	:	Joint/Nuclear
Locale of residence	:	Urban/Rural

7. To find out whether there is any significant difference between the mean scores of Socio-economic status among higher secondary students in relation to

Gender	:	Male/Female
Type of schools	:	Boys'/Girls'/Co Education schools
Type of management of schools	:	Government/Government Aided/ Self Finance schools
Medium of instruction	:	English/ Tamil
Type of family	:	Joint/Nuclear
Locale of residence	:	Urban/Rural

8. To find out whether there is any significant differences between the mean scores of academic stress among higher secondary students in relation to.

Gender	:	Male/Female
Type of schools	:	Boys'/Girls'/Co Education schools

Type of management of schools	:	Government/Government Aided/ Self Finance schools
Medium of instruction	:	English/ Tamil
Type of family	:	Joint/Nuclear
Locale of residence	:	Urban/Rural

9. To find out whether there is any significant correlation between coping behavior and academic stress among higher secondary students.
10. To find out whether there is any significant correlation between Socio-economic status and academic stress among higher secondary students.

HYPOTHESES OF THE STUDY

The following hypotheses have been framed in the present study

1. The level of personal growth of higher secondary students is average in nature.
2. The level of coping behavior of higher secondary students is average in nature.
3. The level of Socio-economic status of higher secondary students is average in nature.
4. The level of academic stress of higher secondary students is average in nature.
5. There is no significant difference between the mean scores of personal growth among higher secondary students in relation to

Gender	:	Male/Female
Type of schools	:	Boys'/Girls'/Co Education schools
Type of management of schools	:	Government/Government Aided/ Self Finance schools
Medium of instruction	:	English/ Tamil
Type of family	:	Joint/Nuclear
Locale of residence	:	Urban/Rural

6. There is no significant difference between the mean scores of coping behavior among higher secondary students in relation to

Gender	:	Male/Female
Type of schools	:	Boys'/Girls'/Co Education schools
Type of management of schools	:	Government/Government Aided/ Self Finance schools
Medium of instruction	:	English/ Tamil

Type of family	:	Joint/Nuclear
Locale of residence	:	Urban/Rural

7. There is no significant difference between the mean scores of Socio-economic status among higher secondary students in relation to

Gender	:	Male/Female
Type of schools	:	Boys'/Girls'/Co Education schools
Type of management of schools	:	Government/Government Aided/
Self Finance schools		
Medium of instruction	:	English/ Tamil
Type of family	:	Joint/Nuclear
Locale of residence	:	Urban/Rural

8. There is no significant difference between the mean scores of academic stress among higher secondary students in relation to

Gender	:	Male/Female
Type of schools	:	Boys'/Girls'/Co Education schools
Type of management of schools	:	Government/Government Aided/
Self Finance schools		
Medium of instruction	:	English/ Tamil
Type of family	:	Joint/Nuclear
Locale of residence	:	Urban/Rural

9. There is no significant correlation between coping behavior and academic stress among higher secondary students.
10. There is no significant correlation between Socio-economic status and academic stress among higher secondary students.

RESEARCH TOOLS SELECTED FOR PRESENT STUDY

To collect the pertinent data for the present investigation, the following tools have been designed. Personal data sheet consists of details like Gender, Medium of instruction, Type of family, Locale of residence, employed to quantify the variables involved in the study.

1. Personal Growth Initiative scale by Christine Robitschek (2011)
2. Coping Behavior Inventory prepared and standardized by Dai, Rost and Skermer(1997)
3. Academic stress inventory developed and standardized by the Investigator and
4. Dr. S. Devasahayam Selvakumar(2014)

5. Kuppuswamy's socio-economic status scale as adopted and modified by Dr.S.Devasahayam Selvakumar(2014)

MAJOR FINDINGS OF THE STUDY

The following are the findings of the present investigation

1. The level of Personal growth of higher secondary students is average in nature.
2. The level of Coping behavior of higher secondary students is average in nature.
3. The level of Socio-economic status among higher secondary students is average in nature.
4. The level of Academic stress among higher secondary students is average in nature.
5. There is significant difference between the mean scores of Personal growth among higher secondary students based on Gender and the male students have significantly higher Personal growth than their counter parts.
6. There is significant difference between the mean scores of Personal growth among higher secondary students based on Type of schools and the students studying in boy's schools have shown significantly higher Personal growth than the students studying in girls' and co education school.
7. There is significant difference between the mean scores of Personal growth among higher secondary students based on Type of management of schools and the students studying in Government aided schools have shown significantly lesser Personal growth than students studying in Government and Self finance schools.
8. There is no significant difference between the mean scores of Personal growth among higher secondary students based on Medium of instruction.
9. There is no significant difference between the mean scores of Personal growth among higher secondary students based on Type of family.
10. There is no significant difference between the mean scores of Personal growth among higher secondary students based on Locale of residence.
11. There is no significant difference between the mean scores of Coping behavior among higher secondary students based on Gender.
12. There is significant difference between the mean scores of Coping behavior among higher secondary students based on Type of schools and the students studying in co education schools have shown significantly higher coping behavior than the students studying in boy's and girls' schools.

13. There is significant difference between the mean scores of coping behavior among higher secondary students based on Type of management of schools and the students studying in Government aided schools have shown significantly lesser Coping behavior than the students studying in Government and Self finance schools.
14. There is no significant difference between the mean scores of Coping behavior among higher secondary students based on Medium of instruction.
15. There is no significant difference between the mean scores of Coping behavior among higher secondary students based on Type of family.
16. There is no significant difference between the mean scores of Coping behavior among higher secondary students based on Locale of residence.
17. There is no significant difference between the mean scores of Socio-economic Status among higher secondary students based on Gender.
18. There is significant difference between the mean scores of Socio-economic status among higher secondary students based on Type of schools and the students studying in co education schools have shown significantly higher Socio-economic status than the students studying in boy' and girls' schools.
19. There is significant difference between the mean scores of Socio-economic status among higher secondary students based on Type of management of schools and the students studying in Self finance schools have shown significantly higher Socio- economic status than students studying in Government and Government-Aided schools
20. There is significant difference between the mean scores of Socio-economic status among higher secondary students based on Medium of instruction and the English medium students have significantly higher Socio- economic status than Tamil medium students. .
21. There is no significant difference between the mean scores of Socio-economic status among higher secondary students based on Type of family.
22. There is no significant difference between the mean scores of Socio-economic status among higher secondary students based on Locale of Residence.
23. There is no significant difference between the mean scores of Academic stress among higher secondary students based on Gender.
24. There is no significant difference between the mean scores of Academic stress among higher secondary students based on Type of schools.

25. There is significant difference between the mean scores of Academic stress among higher secondary students based on Type of management of schools and the students studying in self finance schools have shown significantly higher Academic stress than the students studying in Government and Government aided schools.
26. There is no significant difference between the mean scores of Academic stress among higher secondary students based on Medium of instruction.
27. There is no significant difference between the mean scores of Academic stress among higher secondary students based on Type of family.
28. There is no significant difference between the mean scores of Academic stress among higher secondary students based on Locale of residence.
29. There is significant correlation between Coping behavior and Academic stress of higher secondary students.
30. There is significant correlation between Socio-economic Status and Academic stress of higher secondary students.

EDUCATIONAL IMPLICATIONS

Boys have higher personal growth than the girls. It shows that boys have more exposure than girls. They learn a lot through their peer group. They are well versed in using internet so that they can get more information and grow in all the aspects of personal growth. Girls should be given training to boost up their personal growth on par with that of boys. When compared to the girls' schools and co education schools, boys' schools have higher rate of personal growth, because boys are very strong, they can handle any type of situations.

The following may be undertaken in order to develop coping behavior among students:

- Proper guidance should given to the students
- Teacher teach moral values to the students
- Teacher should give counseling to the students to behave emotionally natured persons

The Socio-economic status is higher for the students in co educational schools, when compared to boys' and girls' because the parents of the students are educated and they find co education schools are the best place for their children to have a healthy relationship among themselves. As they are well educated and settled, their economic status high.

The students in Self financed schools have higher Socio-economic status than the students studying in Government and Government aided schools. The people who are higher in their economic status choose self financed schools because of the facilities available and good environment.

The Socio-economic status of the students in English medium is high, because the economically strong people admit their children in English medium schools to provide quality education to their children.

The teacher can train the students with various coping strategies which can help the students overcome from their academic stress. Academic stress among the students may also be attributed to over work load on the students. Sometimes the incapability to cope up with such pressure may also cause for the lowering confidences among them. The students can be given physical activities like performing physical exercise, involving them in few games etc, which can serve as stress busters.

The Academic stress is high for the students in self financed schools because such schools are result oriented. These schools have to strive for moulding the overall personality of the children rather than producing cent percent pass rate in academics.

DELIMITATIONS OF THE STUDY

The study had the following delimitations:

- The sample is limited to 299 students.
- The sample is taken only from Vellore district, Tamil Nadu.
- Higher secondary students are considered in the present study.

SUGGESTIONS FOR THE FURTHER STUDY

A number of problems were raised in the course of discussion of the finding in the present study. Following are some of the suggestions given by the investigator for the undertaking further research.

1. A similar study may be conducted in other districts in the state of Tamil Nadu
2. This study may add some more variables too
3. This study can be undertaken to college level students too

CONCLUSION

This chapter gives overall picture of the thesis work, which consists of the major findings, summary, suggestions for the further research and educational implications of the study, which is the goal to be reached. The present study is sure to provide some insight into the field of educational research and the findings of the study can serve a database for further.

❐

16

Introduction

Literally and from the social, economic and political perspectives the statement is valid even today. "My idea of Village Swaraj is that it is a complete republic, independent of its neighbours for its own wants and yet interdependent for many others in which dependence is necessary.....It should have a reserve for its cattle, recreation and playground for adults and children....The village will maintain a village theatre, school and public hall. It will have its own waterworks ensuring clean water supply. This can be done through controlled wells or tanks"

—**Mahatma Gandhi.**

Around 65% of the State's population is living in rural areas. People in rural areas should have the same quality of life as is enjoyed by people living in sub urban and urban areas. Further there are cascading effects of poverty, unemployment, poor and inadequate infrastructure in rural areas on urban centers causing slums and consequential social and economic tensions manifesting in economic deprivation and urban poverty.

Hence Rural Development which is concerned with economic growth and social justice, improvement in the living standard of the rural people by providing adequate and quality social services and minimum basic needs becomes essential. The present strategy of rural development mainly focuses on poverty alleviation, better livelihood opportunities, provision of basic amenities and infrastructure facilities through innovative programmes of wage and self-employment.

The above goals will be achieved by various programme support being implemented creating partnership with communities, non-governmental organizations, community based organizations, institutions, PRIs and industrial establishments, while the Department of Rural Development will provide logistic support both on technical and administrative side for programme implementation. Other aspects that will ultimately lead to transformation of rural life are also being emphasized simultaneously.

The prosperity of Tamil Nadu, like that of India, depends on the development of rural areas. As per the 2001 Census, Tamil Nadu's rural population was 3.62 crores, amounting to 58% of the total population. Ariyalur (88.6%), Villupuram (85.5%), Dharmapuri (84.9%), Pudukottai (84.6%), Krishnagiri (84.3%), Perambalur (83.9%), Tiruvannamalai (82.1%), Tiruvarur (79.8%) and Nagapattinam (77.8%) districts are predominantly rural in character. At the same time, Kanniyakumari (34.6%), Coimbatore (38.3%), the Nilgiris (41.8%), Theni (45.9%) and Madurai (48.3%) districts are relatively urban in character with less than 50 % of their population living in rural areas.

Firmly committed to reducing rural poverty in the semi-arid region of India, the Aga Khan Development Network (AKDN) and its partners are working to improve rural livelihoods in select and environmentally degraded areas in the states of Andhra Pradesh, Gujarat, Madhya Pradesh and Rajasthan. These are states characterised by erratic rainfall, depleting or contaminated groundwater, poor soil conditions and prone to natural calamities, primarily affecting agricultural incomes, still the mainstay of India's predominantly rural economy.

The profile of livelihoods in India, especially in these states shows that agriculture and animal husbandry still remain the main sources of livelihood for rural communities, though there is a significant shift to non-farm sectors such as mining and quarrying, construction and manufacturing during periods of drought.

The ultimate goal is for communities to have the confidence to make informed choices from a range of appropriate options that leads to sustainable and equitable development. AKDN's rural development programmes in India include community federations that have been promoted by the Aga Khan Rural Support Programme (India). Increasingly, these federations are taking over the roles and responsibilities of AKRSP (I) in promoting and strengthening community institutions at the village level. Support for watershed development activities by rural beneficiaries has given rise to savings amongst beneficiaries of 28.2 million rupees (US$ 622,222), increased amounts of water for drinking and irrigation, higher agricultural productivity, greater capability to cope with drought and lower payments to moneylenders. Community-based irrigation management, efficient water resource management and joint forest management approaches have been successfully piloted. A 1995-2000 impact study undertaken in certain areas showed beneficiaries' incomes increased between 40 and 80 percent, while expenditure on food increased by 85 percent. Female literacy levels rose by 10 percent while distress migration declined from 80 percent to 35 percent and distress migration declined from 150 to 90 days per year.

Socio-Economic Factors Affecting Rural Livelihoods

The poor have meager holdings or access to land, little or no capital and off-farm employment is seasonal. It is almost impossible for farmers to secure credit and loans needed to purchase agricultural inputs except at prohibitive rates from private moneylenders leading to risk-prone farming. Markets are under-developed or difficult to access. Extension services are few and far between, and development initiatives aimed specifically at their needs is sparse.

Few employment opportunities and low levels of education and skill result in low cash incomes. This in turn affects the ability to purchase basic needs (such as medicines, education for children, etc). Women and children in particular are the hardest hit especially when access to safe and adequate sources of water are low, resulting in high vulnerability in terms of health. Women are also more affected by underemployment.

The relevance of this is all too clear when one realizes that 29 percent of India's population still lives below the poverty line, earning less than US$ 1 per day. A comparison with other countries in South Asia reveals that 33 percent of Pakistan's population is below the poverty line while it 34 percent for Bangladesh, 42 percent for Nepal and 25 percent for Sri Lanka.

Major components of AKDN's rural development programme include: institution building, social organisation, natural resource management (especially in the area of water management and water-use efficiency including in coastal areas), productive infrastructure development and human resource development (especially of women), enterprise promotion, increased agricultural productivity and credit and savings services.

Promoting Self-Reliance

A central strategy of the rural livelihoods approach is to put people at the centre of development, thereby increasing the effectiveness of development assistance and therefore improving performance in poverty reduction. Involving the poor results in local empowerment, which in turn leads to opportunities for local leadership, including that of women, to emerge.

These leaders play a critical role in bringing about and sustaining development and consequent social change such as pluralism, public participation and democratic principles. Village institutions form the basis of community organisation and function through 'Village Development Committees,' comprising of representatives of all communities in the village (including at least 30 percent women's representation). These Committees develop village development plans and work closely with the Panchayat (the lowest unit of the government that functions at the village level).

Other community organisations such as farmers' federations and women's self-help groups also facilitate the process of community driven development. These institutions work best if they have some independent means of sustaining themselves which is usually enabled by introducing them to micro-credit schemes.

For example, a women's federation in Bharuch district in Gujarat state recently accessed a loan-based scheme for animal husbandry. Likewise, federations of farmers groups have considerably reduced agriculture input costs (seeds, fertilizers and pesticides) through bulk purchases based on demand from member institutions, simultaneously ensuring the quality of inputs supplied.

These organisations have also contributed to improved cropping techniques, rational use of fertilizers and the adoption of appropriate low-cost technologies. Communities eventually go on to form "apex institutions" (federations of various community institutions) at the block (a unit of a district) and "taluka" (a unit of a block) level. These institutions also act as forums where regional issues are discussed and solutions formulated. These institutions also dialogue with the government and other agencies (including banks) to get access to and benefit from various schemes.

The federations also serve as agriculture extension agents, and transfer information from agriculture institutes related to cropping practices, thereby ensuring that information reaches farmers in remote areas. Collective marketing of agricultural produce and enabling member institutions to sell their produce at the best price possible is another important activity.

Farmers' federations and the women's federations have also led social campaigns in the regions such as reducing unnecessary expenditure on social customs, promoting the education of girls, anti-liquor campaigns, and the promotion of organic farming. Mass awareness campaigns by women's groups in Surendranagar in Gujarat for example, have led to a reduction in wasteful and extravagant expenditure on weddings and on social customs such as 'funeral feasts.'

Skills Development

In addition to institution building, programme activities also include human resource development including skills development to build up the skills base of villagers, especially women. For example, in the Netrang programme area of Bharuch district, women have been trained to repair and maintain hand-pumps. In another area women have been trained as masons.

Communities receive organisation and financial management training to support the effectiveness and sustainability of village-level institutions, and key resource people are provided with technical skills to plan, implement and maintain the development activities. The ultimate goal is for people in the participating communities to have the access, confidence and competence to make informed choices from a range of appropriate development options.

In 2001 alone, over 300 training programmes benefited almost 6000 villagers, 64 % of which were women. These were essentially to increase awareness about savings and credit programmes, provide exposure to 'model' villages and orient rural communities to the principles of natural resources management. In addition, over 50 NGOs and 400 government staff have also been trained in various participatory processes.

Creating Rural Assets

Institutional structures are created at the village level through which the rural poor can priorities their needs and decide how best to manage common resources.

Communities build personal and community capital through efficient management of their natural resource base such as water storage and enhanced water use efficiency, irrigation systems, soil conservation or forestry. These efforts include the construction of small scale infrastructure, such as check-dams, irrigation canals and water harvesting structures or agricultural storage facilities.

Over 400 structures have been created for harvesting and storage of rainwater that is directly lifted for irrigation, or recharging the groundwater aquifers for more rational extraction through wells. These have led to an additional 4000 hectares of irrigated croplands in the programme areas, which is being further expanded through the adoption of water saving devices such as drip irrigation and sprinklers.

Income growth is promoted by increasing agricultural productivity through improved farming methods such as using drip-irrigation, provision of better seeds, creation and improvement of markets, land development, micro-credit, increasing off-farm incomes and supporting enterprise development. Local capital is mobilised by promoting savings and developing financial services to enable broad access to credit. Programmes are designed to have a combined effect so as to create a critical mass of economic activities that raise living standards.

In Surendranagar area in Gujarat for example, it was found that a severely degraded natural environment would not allow rural communities to rear cattle and therefore the only viable option was to rear goats.

The rural development programme stepped in to help create a viable market for goat milk in the area and helped the community to get the government to set up a cheese making plant. In another water scare area, a women's federation lobbied with the government to buy them a water tanker which they now use to sell safe drinking water to local communities practically at their doorsteps and at fixed and mutually agree to prices. This has considerably reduced water scarcity in the area by providing households assured water supply and also saves women the time they earlier spent on collecting water.

Benefits and Impact on Quality of Life

Assets thus created often result in more than just increased income generation. AKDN's rural development programmes have benefited over 300,000 households in over 1,000 villages in western and central India since 1983. Development activities have ensured more water for drinking and irrigation, higher agricultural productivity and rural incomes (including household savings), greater resilience to droughts and the ability to manage the natural resource base better.

With over 10,000 households now accessing assured sources of safe drinking water, women have benefited significantly. Since they no longer have to walk long distances to collect water, the time saved can now be spent with family or education of their children. Alternatively they have more time for income generation activities.

Health improvements due to improved diets and access to safe drinking water also lead to a reduction in the costs of medicines and trips to the doctor. Similarly, the number of days of illness has been reduced by 50 percent (down to 15 days per year, as compared to about 30 days per year earlier).

Simultaneously, literacy levels have risen by 10 percent (8 percent in the case of women). Growing gender sensitivity and changing gender equations is also evident from a phenomenal 350 percent increase in the expenditure incurred on medicines for women. School attendance levels show an improvement, especially in the case of girls who now no longer have to accompany their mothers at dawn to collect water.

Impact studies conducted in some areas reveal an average increase of beneficiary incomes by about 60 percent, going up to 80 percent in some cases. More savings and increased access to credit reduces the dependence of the poor on local moneylenders. Even the landless benefit from increased demand for farm labour when improved agricultural practices results in two or three crops instead of just one every year, leading to, among other things, a reduction in migration. In 147 villages in four states, savings amongst beneficiaries was estimated to be approximately US$ 0.6 million (28 million rupees approximately).

As rural employment has improved, stress-migration levels have shown a marked reduction (down to 35 percent from 80 percent earlier). Even the duration of migration has reduced to 90 days per year (down from 150 days a year earlier).

Women's empowerment has also led to them participating in the local political process. In recent local village level elections in a programme area, 52 elected members (including 15 women) out of a total of 179 (approximately 30 percent) who were elected belonged to village institutions established by AKDN's rural development programmes.

Sustainability and Partnerships

Long-term commitment is the key to creating sustainable impact. Consequently rural development programmes in India have now run 20 years and helped create replicable models that can be quickly adapted to a variety of contexts; as well as long-term relationships with donor agencies and peer organisations for the mobilisation of funds, human resources and expertise.

In terms of organisational elements, programmes are usually area-based programmes that serve a defined population, are implemented over a long time frame and at a significant scale and are characterized by comparatively thorough coverage of all of the population within their target area.

Ensuring sustainable impact requires consistent efforts over considerable time periods. In the case of rural development programmes, this has meant at least ten years of concerted efforts at the grassroots level before results and subsequent impact on the quality of life of the poor is visible for all to see.

Step taken by Government for Rural Development

The Government's policy and programmes have laid emphasis on poverty alleviation, generation of employment and income opportunities and provision of infrastructure and basic facilities to meet the needs of rural poor. For realising these objectives, self-employment and wage employment programmes continued to pervade in one form or other.

As a measure to strengthen the grass root level democracy, the Government is constantly endeavouring to empower Panchayat Raj Institutions in terms of functions, powers and finance. Grama sabha, NGOs, Self-Help Groups and PRIs have been accorded adequate role to make participatory democracy meaningful and effective.

Aga Khan Rural Support Programme (India)

The Aga Khan Rural Support Programme (India), the rural development partner of the Aga Khan Foundation (AKF), is an internationally recognized, community-based, non-denominational, non-government development organisation, based in Gujarat. Since the early 1980s, it has focused on enhancing rural livelihoods through sustainable management and use of natural resources in degraded and resource poor regions of western and central India, often characterized by limited economic opportunities as well.

AKRSP (I) goes beyond merely addressing problems of food self-sufficiency and looks at the wider issue of poverty alleviation and improvements in the quality of life. Its programmes aim for broader, long-term economic and social development. The underlying philosophy is that rural economic development is best catalyzed and sustained through village-level institutions that are autonomous and transparent, contributing to democratic norms of behaviour and to the growth of civil society.

The "rural support programme" works in close partnership with local communities and the government to implement strategies that lead to

1. Income growth - by increasing agricultural productivity through improved farming methods, input supply, marketing, land development and management or by increasing on-farm and off-farm incomes and supporting micro-enterprise development;
2. Asset building - through community management of natural resources; water storage, irrigation infrastructure, soil conservation and forestry;
3. Mobilising local capital - by promoting savings and developing financial services to enable access to credit on a sustainable basis;
4. Technical innovations - that on one hand help halt environmental degradation and on the other, help reduce the drudgery of poor people, particularly women, who can then utilize time saved more productively.
5. Human skills development - through training programmes that support the effectiveness and sustainability of village-level and community-led institutions by providing the management and technical skills needed to plan, implement and maintain local development activities;
6. Social Development - especially women's empowerment, equity and social justice and pluralism.
7. The ultimate goal is for communities to have the confidence and competence to make informed choices from a range of appropriate options for sustainable and equitable development. Particular success

has been achieved in improving the management of micro watersheds and creating a variety of water harvesting structures in different agro-climatic regions.

Goals, Objectives and Strategy for Rural development

The prime goal of rural development is to improve the quality of life of the rural people by alleviating poverty through the instrument of self-employment and wage employment programmes, by providing community infrastructure facilities such as drinking water, electricity, road connectivity, health facilities, rural housing and education and promoting decentralization of powers to strengthen the Panchayat raj institutions. The Chief Minister's 15 Point Programme is a visionary programme which seeks to make Tamil Nadu the best State in the country by way of creating growth opportunities in rural areas and eradicating rural poverty. To achieve the above objectives.

The following priorities and thrust areas have been identified during the Tenth Five Year Plan period.

1. The goal is reduction of poverty from 21.12% in 1999- 2000 to 10% by 2006-07 and near elimination by 2012. Poverty reduction will be attempted
   a. By organizing the rural masses into self-help groups and the establishment of micro-enterprises, training, credit linkages, market support, etc.
   b. By substantial flow of investment in physical infrastructure like roads, water supply and social infrastructure like health, education and nutrition.
2. Special efforts for generation of adequate employment and creation of durable community assets to improve the rural people especially the small farmers, marginal farmers, rural artisans etc., through programmes like Sampoorna Grameen Rozgar Yojana (SGRY).
3. Decentralization of the process of planning by entrusting major role to the Panchayat raj bodies in the preparation of local level planning.
4. Improving the efficiency and capacity of the officials and elected local body representatives.
5. Providing all weather roads to all rural habitations having a population above 500 by 2004.
6. Strengthening of Grama Sabha the governing body of village assembly as an agency of social audit and to review the implementation of programmes.
7. Special efforts will be made to converge various schemes and programmes for accelerating the development process through special schemes like Village Self-sufficiency scheme etc.

8. Emphasis will be given for the maintenance of the assets created under various schemes.

Centrally Sponsored Schemes

1. Poverty Alleviation programmes Swarnajayanthi Gram Swarozgar Yojana (SGSY).

The magnitude of poverty and disparities that existed between the various social groups necessitated planned state intervention to provide succor and relief particularly to the disadvantaged and marginalized groups such as SC/ST, women etc. Keeping this in view and having regard to the positive aspects as well as deficiencies, the earlier self employment programmes like TRYSEM, SITRA, GKY, DWCRA, IRDP and MWS were merged and a new self employment programme viz., SGSY was launched w.e.f.1-4-1999.

SGSY Methodology:

- Group Approach
- Organisation of rural masses into Self-help groups
- Establishment of Micro enterprises
- Training for improvement of skill & capacity building
- Credit linkages
- Market support
- Provision of infrastructure facility

2. Sampoorna Grameen Rozgar Yojana (SGRY)

Creation of sustained employment opportunities for securing a minimum level of employment and income for the rural poor necessitated continuous need for special employment programmes. Keeping the above aim and to strengthen the need based infrastructure at the village level to boost the rural economy the erstwhile wage employment programmes JGSY and EAS were merged and a new scheme namely SGRY was launched from 15th August 2001.

3. Rural Housing

The aim of the State Government is to provide a dwelling for each family giving special emphasis to rural poor and deprived. The ongoing rural housing programmes will be given a new thrust.

3.1. Indira Awaas Yojana

With a view to meeting the housing needs of the rural poor, Indira Awaas Yojana (IAY) was launched in May 1985 as a subscheme of Jawahar Rozgar Yojana. It is being implemented as an independent scheme since 1 January 1996.

3.2. Credit cum Subsidy Scheme

The Credit-cum-Subsidy Scheme has been conceived for rural households having an annual income upto Rs. 32,000/-. Subsidy upto Rs. 10,000/- and loan up to Rs. 40,000/- from commercial or co-op. banks is provided to eligible households for construction of houses. Out of the total outlay of Rs. 9.15 crores, 25% share of the State Government will be Rs. 2.29 crores. The physical target under the scheme will be 914.

3.3. Innovative Stream for Rural House and Habitat Development Scheme

This scheme intends to popularize low cost technology and usage of locally available materials in construction of buildings in rural areas.

3.4. Pradhan Mantri Gramodaya Yojana (PMGY) (Rural Shelter Component)

This scheme has been introduced by the Government of India under additional Central assistance for providing shelter in the rural areas to supplement the efforts in the sphere of rural housing considering the magnitude of the task.

4. Pradhan Manthri Gram Sadak Yojana (PMGSY)

The Pradhan Mantri Gram Sadak Yojana (PMGSY) is a Government of India Scheme introduced in the year 2000-2001 with the objective of providing road connectivity through good all weather roads to all unconnected rural habitations having population above 1000 by 2003 and all unconnected habitations having population of 500 and above by end of Tenth Plan period (2007).

Under this programme the approved works are grouped into packages costing more than Rs. 1 crore but less than Rs.5 crores and executed through tender system. The guidelines stipulate that district master plans would be prepared.

A District Rural Road Plan is prepared for each district indicating the habitations in each block with the existing status of road connectivity. The scheme will be fully funded by the Government of India and an allocation of Rs.750 crores has been proposed for the Tenth Plan, which will be shown under the chapter Rural Roads.

5. National Project on Biogas Development

Biogas Development programme aims to promote an eco-friendly Non conventional Energy Source with multiple benefits. The role of biogas as a major source of renewable energy has been recognized by the Government of India by including this scheme as an item in the 20 Point Programme. Prevention of deforestation, production of enriched manure and to improve sanitation and hygiene by linking sanitary toilets with biogas plants are the objectives of this rural energy programme.

This is a centrally sponsored programme with a subsidy component of Rs.1800/- for general category and Rs. 2300/-for scheduled category and Rs. 3500/- for hilly areas. An amount of Rs. 500/-is provided in addition for installation and maintenance of the plant to the Turnkey agent. 10,000 bio-gas plants will be constructed during the Tenth Plan. The scheme is fully funded by the Government of India and Rs. 8.05 crores is provided for the Tenth Plan which will be directly released to the District Collectors.

6. Eleventh Finance Commission Grant

This grant is provided to Village Panchayats and Panchayat Unions for maintenance of civic services. Under Eleventh Finance Commission grant, a sum of Rs 186.45 crores for 2000-01 and 2001-02 was allocated. Out of this, Rs. 171.92 crores is provided to Village Panchayats and Panchayat Unions for maintenance of civic services and Rs. 14.53 crores for maintenance of accounts and audit and for development of database. An outlay of Rs. 659.47 crores has been proposed during the Tenth Plan period under this scheme.

7. Rashtriya Sam Vikas Yojana (RSVY)

During Tenth Plan a new scheme viz, Rashtriya Sam Vikas Yojana (RSVY)-Development and Reform Facility will be launched by Government of India. The prime objective of RSVY is to address the problems of pockets of high poverty, low growth, low agricultural productivity, unemployment and poor governance by putting in place programmes and policies, which would remove barriers to growth and accelerate the development process. An 98' 3. Rural Development amount of Rs. 15 crores per year will be provided for implementation of various developmental programmes such as drought proofing (soil conservation, afforesation, social forestry, wasteland development and minor irrigation), agriculture, horticulture etc. infrastructure (road and power), social sector (health and education) and livelihood support (income generating activities such as handloom, information technology, agricultural processing etc.). Under the scheme 15% of the funds will be earmarked for maintenance of assets in health, education and veterinary sectors.

The main focus and strategy of the scheme will be on infrastructure development and income generation for under-privileged. The scheme will be implemented through people's participation, involvement of PRIs, NGOs and Self Help Groups at every stage including plan formulation, implementation and monitoring. Tiruvannamalai district has been selected on pilot basis for implementation of RSVY scheme. During Tenth Plan period the total amount of Rs.225 crores is proposed under the scheme.

Various Rural Development Schemes Implemented by Central & State Government before Nregs:

I. State Government Sponsored Schemes:

- Anaithu Grama Anna Marumalarchi Thittam.
- Member of Legislative Assembly Constituency Development Scheme (MLACDS).
- Panchayat Union School Renovation Programme .
- Namakku Naame Thittam.
- Periyar Ninaivu Samathuvapuram .
- Rural Roads under NABARD - Rural Infrastructure Developement Fund (RIDF).
- Twelfth Finance Commission Road works.
- Programme for Comprehensive Development of Dharmapuri and Krishnagiri districts.
- Rural Infrastructure Scheme.
- Mahalir Thittam by the Tamil Nadu Corporation for development of women Ltd. (TNCDW).
    1. Mahalir Thittam
    2. Credit rating and Linkage
    3. Revolving Fund to Urban SHGs
    4. Panchayat Level Federation (PLF)
    5. Skill Training for Youth
    6. Manimegalai Awards
    7. Cultural Competitions
    8. ID Cards to SHGs

II. Central Government Sponsored Schemes

1. Indira Awaas Yojana (IAY)
    - New houses
    - Upgradation of kutcha houses
2. Sampoorna Grameen Rozgar Yojana (SGRY)_
3. National Rural Employment Guarantee Scheme – Tamil Nadu
    - Objectives of the Scheme
    - Funding pattern
    - Priority of works
    - Special steps taken to ensure successful implementation of NREGS
4. Swarnjayanthi Gram Swarozgar Yojana (SGSY)
5. Total Sanitation Campaign (TSC)
    - Nirmal Gram Puraskar

6. Member of Parliament Local Area Development Scheme (MPLADS)
7. Pradhan Mantri Gram Sadak Yojana (PMGSY)
8. National Project on Bio-gas Development
9. Rajiv Gandhi Rehabilitation Package (RGRP) funded by Government of India
    - Schemes which are implemented
    - Provision of basic amenities in NGOs built sites
    - Construction of houses and provision of basic amenities in NGOs backed out sites
    - Reconstruction of vulnerable houses

A History of Programmes under Nrega

India has three decades of experience in implementing employment generation programmes. The concept of creating employment in public works is not new: the Maharashtra model of rural employment has existed since the 1970s. The most critical difference now is that people's entitlement, by law, to employment, is mandated through NREGA for the entire country. Not much has changed in the form and substance of the public work programmes in the past 30-odd years, however. In many ways the NREGA is a replication of earlier schemes in letter and spirit, of course, with a legal guarantee. So past failures do haunt the NREGA.

The first set of programmes, the National Rural Employment Programme and the Rural Landless Employment Programme, began in the 1970s as clones of the Maharashtra EGS. In 1989, the Rajiv Gandhi government integrated the two schemes into one, revamped the schemes and decided delivery would occur through the panchayati raj institutions (village-level elected institutions).

Thus born the Jawahar Rozgar Yojana (JRY); but it was radically different. The bureaucratic machinery was bypassed; funds would be deposited in the accounts of each village institution responsible for planning development activities used to create employment creation, and overseeing implementation. The scheme began but it was never given a chance to succeed. In retrospect, JRY was perhaps an idea before its time (See Box: Rural wage employment programmes in India).

In 1990, when prime minister V P Singh ambushed the Rajiv Gandhi government over the Bofors gun scandal, the election call was a promise to 'guarantee' Maharashtra-type employment for all. Instead the subsequent, Narasimha Rao-led, government diluted what existed. By 1993, JRY received little political leadership or attention. It was agreed (from largely anecdotal and some official reports) that the scheme, controlled by people's representatives, was leading to increased corruption and even greater inefficiency in delivery. Therefore, it needed to be re-vamped.

In 1993, the Employment Assurance Scheme (EAS) was launched. Now, half the allocated funds for rural employment would be channelised through the bureaucracy, not the panchayati raj institutions. The big brother was back in business, to the tune of roughly Rs 2,000 crore each year.

In April 2002 another re-naming took place. These times the two schemes - JRY and EAS-were merged to create the Sampoorna Grameen Rozgar Yogana (SGRY). Its spending, too, was divided between the panchayati raj institutions and the administration. Incidentally, in the National Democratic Alliance period the name of JRY had been changed into the Jawahar Gram Samridhi Yogana (JGSY). A component of SGRY provided foodgrain to calamity-stricken states for relief work. Now the cost increased to about Rs 4,000 crore per year.

Then came the semi-final reincarnation. In late 2004, the National Food for Work Programme (NFWP) WAS launched, targeting 150 backward districts. These districts were identified through a task force set up by the ministry of rural development, which used three variables to compute 'backwardness' - agricultural productivity per worker, agricultural wage rate and the scheduled caste and schedule tribe population in the district. This programme was to be implemented through the district administration and a menu of "labourintensive projects" would be prepared, to be undertaken over a five-year period. In the 2005-06 budget, the allocation was enhanced. NFWP got Rs 6,000 crore in addition to the SGRY's Rs 4,000 crore. The NFWP remains the programme design for the NREGA.

The final change came in December 2004, when the National Rural Employment Guarantee Bill was tabled in Parliament. The bill provided a guarantee of 100 days of unskilled manual work in a financial year to every poor household, in rural areas, whose adult members volunteered for work.

The first phase would cover 200 districts. But many believed the bill 'diluted' what the common minimum programme of the government had promised. The bill was referred to a parliamentary standing committee, which gave its report after two and a half sessions, called the legislation as "path-breaking" but observed that organisations and individuals who deposed before it were "almost unanimous" in objecting to several provisions.

National Rural Employment Guarantee Act (Nrega)

The Parliament enacted an Act No. 42 of 2005 called the National Rural Employment Guarantee Act. The Act provides a guarantee for rural employment to households whose adult members volunteer to do un-skilled manual work not less than 100 days of such work in a financial year in accordance with the scheme made under the Act.

The scheme

Has been launched on February 2nd 2006 in 200 districts of the Country. In J&K State it has been introduced in the Districts of Kupwara, Poonch and Doda in the first instance. Is being extended to all other districts within 5 years in a phased manner. Is expected to enhance people's livelihood on sustained basis by developing economic and social infrastructure in rural areas. Is a direct attack on the causes of chronic poverty such as drought, deforestation and soil erosion?

The scheme is different from the earlier wage employment programmes in different ways

It provides legal guarantee of 100 days work to every rural house hold whose adult member volunteer to do un-skilled manual work. If an applicant is not provided employment within 15 days he/she shall be entitled to unemployment allowance. Rural Employment Guarantee Scheme is demand -driven instead of being supply-driven.

The focus of the scheme shall be on

1. Water conservation and water harvesting.
2. Drought proofing including afforest ration and tree plantation.
3. Irrigation canals including micro and minor irrigation works,
4. Provision of irrigation facilities to land owned by households belonging to SC/ST or to land of beneficiaries of land reforms or that of the beneficiaries under IAY.

Conditions for Guaranteed Rural Employment under the scheme

1. Registration to be made at the level of Gram Panchayat for issuance of job cards.
2. Duty of the Gram Panchayat to issue the job card after making such an enquiry as it may deem fit.
3. The registration for not less than 5 years and to be renewed from time to time.
4. Every job card holder entitled to apply for unskilled manual work under the scheme.
5. All registered persons belonging to a house hold entitled to employment in accordance with the scheme for as many days as each applicant may request, subject to a maximum of 100 days per house hold in a given financial year.
6. Such job to be provided within a period of 15 days of the receipt of an application or from the date he/she seeks work in case of advance application whichever is later.

Main features of Rural Employment Guarantee Scheme

1. The focus of the scheme shall be on the following works in their order of priority:
   - Water conservation and water harvesting.
   - Drought proofing (including afforestration and tree plantation.
   - Irrigation canals including micro and minor irrigation works.
   - Provision of irrigation facility to land owned by households belonging to the scheduled Castes/Schedule Tribes or to land of beneficiaries of land reforms or that of the beneficiaries under the IAH of Govt.l India.
   - Renovation of traditional water bodies including desilting of tanks.
   - Land Development.
   - Flood control and protection works including drainage in water logged areas.
   - Rural connectivity to provide all weather access and
   - Any other work which may be notified by the Central Government in consultation with the State government.
2. Creation of durable assets and strengthening the livelihood resource base of the rural poor shall be an important object of the scheme.
3. The works taken up under the scheme shall be in rural areas.
4. The state council shall prepare a list of preferred works for different areas based on their ability to create durable assets.
5. The scheme shall be subject to appropriate arrangements as may be laid down by the State Government under the rules issued by it for proper maintenance of the public assets created under the scheme.
6. Under no circumstances shall the labourers be paid less than the wage rate, notified by the State Government.
7. When wages are directly linked with the quantity of work, the wages shall be paid according to the scheme of rates fixed by the state government for different types of work in every year, in consultation with the state council.
8. The schedule of rates of wages for unskilled labourers shall be so fixed that a person working for 7 hours would normally earn a wage equal to the wage rate.
9. The cost of material component of projects including the wages of the skilled and semi skilled workers taken up under the scheme shall not exceed 40% of the total project costs.

10. It shall be open to the programme officer and Gram Panchayat to direct any person who applied for employment under the scheme to do work of any type permissible under it.
11. The scheme shall not permit engaging any contractor for implementation of the projects under it.
12. As far as practicable, a task funded under the scheme shall be performed by using manual labourers and not machines.
13. Every scheme shall contain adequate provisions for ensuring transparency and accountability at all levels of implementation.
14. Provisions for regular inspection and supervision of works taken up under the scheme shall be made to ensure proper quality of work as well as to ensure that the total wages paid for the completion of the work is commensurate with the quality and quantity of work done.
15. The District Programme Coordinator, The Programme Officer and the Gram Panchayat implementing the scheme shall prepare annually a report containing the facts and figures and achievements relating to the implementation of the scheme within his or its jurisdiction and a copy of the same shall be made available to the public on demand and on payment of such free as may be specified in the scheme.
16. All accounts and records relating to the scheme shall be made available for public scrutiny and any person desirous of obtaining copy or relevant extracts there from may be provided such copies of extracts on demand and after paying such fee as may be specified in the scheme.
17. A copy of the muster rolls of each scheme or project under a scheme shall be made available in the office of the Gram Panchayat and Programme Officer for inspection by any person interested after paying such fee as may be specified in the scheme.

Conditions for Guaranteed Rural Employment under a Scheme and Minimum Entitlements of labourers

1. The adult members of every household who-
    - Reside in any rural areas; and
    - Are willing to do unskilled manual work, may submit their names, age and the address of the household to the Gram Panchayat at the village level (hereafter in this Schedule referred to as the Gram Panchayat) in the jurisdiction of which they reside for registration of their household for issuance of a job card.
2. It shall be the duty of the Gram Panchayat to register the household, after making such enquiry as it deems fit and issue a job card containing such details of adult members' of the household affixing their photographs, as may be specified by the State Government in the Scheme.

3. The registration made under paragraph 2 shall be for such period as may be lapidate Scheme, but in any case not less than five years, and may be renewed from time to time.
4. Every adult member of a registered household whose name appears in the job card shall is entitled to apply for unskilled manual work under the Scheme.
5. All registered persons belonging to a household shall be entitled to employment in accordance with the Scheme made under the provisions of this Act, for ash any days as each applicant may request, subject to a maximum of one hundred days per household in a given financial year.
6. The Programme Officer shall ensure that every applicant referred to in paragraph 5 shall be provided unskilled manual work in accordance with the provisions of the Scheme within fifteen days of receipt of an application or from the date he seeks work in case of advance application, whichever is later: Provided that priority shall be given to women in such a way that at least one-third of the beneficiaries shall be women who have registered and requested for work under this Act.
7. Applications for work must be for at least fourteen days of continuous work.
8. There shall be no limit on the number of days of employment for which a person may apply, or on the number of days of employment actually provided to him subject to the aggregate entitlement of the household.
9. Applications for work may be submitted in writing either to the Gram Panchayat or to the Programme Officer, as may be specified in the Scheme.
10. The Gram Panchayat and Programme Officer, as the case may be, shall be bound to accept valid applications and to issue a dated receipt to. The applicant. Group applications may also be submitted.
11. Applicants who are provided with work shall be so intimated in writing, by means of a letter sent to him at the address given in the job card and by a public notice displayed at the office of the Panchayats at the district, intermediate or village level.
12. As far as possible, employment shall be provided within a radius of five kilometers of the village where the applicant resides at the time of applying.
13. A new work under the Scheme shall be commenced only if-
    - At least fifty labourers become available for such work; and
    - The labourers cannot be absorbed in the ongoing works: Provided that this condition shall not be applicable for new works, as determined by the State Government, in hilly areas and in respect of afforest ration.

14. In cases the employment is provided outside such radius, it must be provided within the Block, and the labourers shall be paid ten per cent. Of the wage rate as extra wages to meet additional transportation and living expenses.
15. A period of employment shall ordinarily be at least fourteen days continuously with not more than six days in a week.
16. In all cases where unemployment allowance is paid, or due to be paid, the Programme officer shall inform the District Programme Coordinator in writing the reasons why it was not possible for him to provide employment or cause to provide employment to the applicants.
17. The District Programme Coordinator shall, in his Annual Report to the State Council, explain as to why employment could not be provided in cases where payment of unemployment allowance is involved.
18. Provision shall be made in the Scheme for advance applications, that is, an application which may be submitted in advance of the date from which employment is sought.
19. Provision shall be made in the Scheme for submission of multiple applications by the same person provided that the corresponding periods for which employment is sought do not overlap.
20. The Gram Panchayat shall prepare and maintain or cause to be prepared and maintained such registers, vouchers and other documents in such form and in such manner as may be specified in the Scheme containing particulars of job cards and passbooks issued, name, age and address of the head of the household and the adult members of the household registered with the Gram Panchayat.
21. The Gram Panchayat shall send such list or lists of the names and addresses of households and their adult members registered with it and supply such other information to the concerned Programme Officer at such periods and in such form as may be specified in the Scheme.
22. A list of persons who are provided with the work shall be displayed on the notice board of the Gram Panchayat and at the office of the Programme Officer and at such other places as the Programme Officer may deem necessary and the list shall be open for inspection by the State Government and any person interested.
23. If the Gram Panchayat is satisfied at any time that a person has registered with it by furnishing false information, it may direct the Programme Officer to direct his name to be struck off from the register and direct the applicant to return the job card: Provided that no such action under this paragraph shall be directed unless the applicant has been given an opportunity of being heard in the presence of two independent persons.

24. If any personal injury is caused to any person employed under the Scheme by accident arising out of and in the course of his employment, he shall be entitled to, free of charge, such medical treatment as is admissible under the Scheme.
25. Where hospitalization of the injured worker is necessary, the State Government shall arrange for such hospitalization including accommodation, treatment, medicines and payment of daily allowance not less than half of the wage rate required to be paid had the injured been engaged in the work.
26. If a person employed under a Scheme dies or becomes permanently disabled by accident arising out of and in the course of employment, he shall be paid by the implementing agency an ex gratia payment at the rate of twenty- five thousand rupees or such amount as may be notified by the Central Government, and the amount shall be paid to the legal he irs of the deceased or the disabled, as the case may be.
27. The facilities of safe drinking water, shade for children and periods of rest, first-aid box with adequate material for emergency treatment for minor injuries and other health hazards connected with the work being performed shall be provided at the work site.
28. In case the numbers of children below the age of six years accompanying the women working at any site are five or more, provisions shall be made to depute one of such women worker to look after such children.
29. The person deputed under paragraph 28 shall be paid wage rate.
30. In case the payment of wages is not made within the period specified under the Scheme, the labourers shall be entitled to receive payment of compensation as per the provisions of the Payment of Wages Act, 1936 (4 of 1936).
31. The wages under a Scheme may be paid either wholly in cash or in cash and kind provided that at least one- fourth of the wages shall be paid in cash only.
32. The State Government may prescribe that a portion of the wages in cash may be paid to the labourers on a daily basis during the period of employment.
33. If any personal injury is caused by accident to a child accompanying any person who is employed under a Scheme, such person shall be entitled to, free of charge, such medical treatment for the child as may be specified in the Scheme and in case of death or disablement, through an excreta payment as may be determined by the State Government.
34. In case of every employment under the Scheme, there shall be no discrimination solely on the ground of gender and the provisions of the Equal Remuneration Act, 1976 (25 of 1976), shall be complied with.

The National Rural Employment Guarantee Scheme (Nregs)

The National Rural Employment Guarantee Scheme has been launched in ,more than150 most backward districts of the country, identified by the Planning Commission in consultation with the Ministry of Rural Development and the State Governments. This Programme was formely known as National Food for Work Programmme.

Need

The existing resources in the SGRY were not sufficient to meet the requirement of additional wage employment in most backward districts. Moreover, it was felt that the additional resources should be channelised into some focus areas like water conservation and drought proofing which is the principal problem in some States and a major cause of backwardness of certain regions. Some areas are flood-prone and measures for flood control require special attention in these areas in a planned manner.

The States were finding difficult to provide State share of funds and therefore, a 100% Centrally Sponsored Scheme was proposed so that the investment in backward areas does not suffer because of lack of resources available with the States.

A need for the preparation of Perspective Plan under the NREGS was felt, to assess the work force/wage seekers available in the villages and to identify need based optimum infrastructure at the Panchayat Level for creation of a sound base, for self sustaining economy to remove poverty and bring this district at least on par with other developed areas of the state and country. The Perspective Plan aims at creation of need based optimum infrastructure at the Panchayat Level

During the preparation of Perspective Plan, National Rural Employment Guarntee Act 2006, came in to force. This plan has been transformed under the light of the said act, an act to provide, enhancement of livelihood security of the households in rural areas of the district by providing at least one hundred days of guaranteed wage employment in every financial year to every household whose adult members volunteer to do unskilled manual work.

Nregs In Ariyalur District

National Rural Employment Guarantee Scheme - Tamil Nadu

The National Rural Employment Guarantee Scheme was initially implemented in six notified (Phase I) districts viz. Cuddalore, Villupuram, Tiruvannamalai, Nagapattinam, Dindigul and Sivagangai districts from 2.2.06. In the second phase, it was extended to Thanjavur, Tiruvarur, Karur and Tirunelveli districts with effect from01.04.2007. From 01.04.2008 onwards, the Scheme has been extended to all the remaining 20 districts (Phase III) of Tamilnadu viz. 1. Ariyalur, 2. Dharmapuri, 3. Perambalur, 4. Pudukottai, 5. Ramanathapuram, 6. Namakkal, 7. Vellore, 8. Thoothu kudi, 9. Virudhunar 10. Salem, 11. Erode, 12. Tiruchirapalli, 13. Kancheepuram 14. Theni, 15. Tiruvallur, 16. Madurai, 17. Nilgiris, 18. Kanniyakumari, 19. Coimbatore and 20. Krishnagiri.

Objectives of the Scheme

The National Rural Employment Guarantee Act, 2005 (NREGA) guarantees 100 days of employment in a financial year to any rural household whose adult members are willing to do unskilled manual work. This Act is an important step towards the realization of the right to work. It is also expected to enhance people's livelihoods on a sustained basis, by developing the economic and social infrastructure in rural areas.

The Village Panchayat will issue job cards to every registered individual. Payment of the statutory minimum wage and equal wages for men and women are the notable features of the scheme.

Funding PatternThe cost of the scheme is shared between the Centre and the State in the ratio of 90:10. The Central Government will bear the following costs:

1. The entire cost of wages for unskilled manual workers.
2. 75 percent of the cost of material and wages for skilled and semi-skilled workers.
3. Administrative expenses, which will include, inter alia, the salary and allowances of Programme Officers and their support staff and work site facilities.
4. Administrative expenses of the Central Employment Guarantee Council.

The State Government will bear the following costs

1. 25 percent of the cost of material and wages for skilled and semi-skilled workers.
2. Unemployment allowance payable in case the State Government cannot provide wage employment within 15 days of application.
3. Administrative expenses of the State Employment Guarantee Council.

Priority of works

Taking into account the field conditions in Tamil Nadu, the works are being taken up in Tamil Nadu in the following priority:

1. Formation of new ponds.

2. Renovation of existing Ponds, Kuttais, Kulams, Ooranies, and Temple tanks etc.
3. Desilting of channels.
4. Desilting and strengthening of bunds of irrigation tanks.
5. Formation of new roads.
6. Other water conservation/soil conservation measures/flood protection measures.

Special steps taken to Ensure Successful Implementation of NREGS

On assumption of office in the month of May 2006, this Government noticed that the scheme had not taken off properly. This was evident from the fact that the expenditure made was only Rs. 3 crores and that works had been taken up only in 924 Village Panchayats out of a total of 3,830 Village Panchayats in the six districts.

This Government was quick to identify the issues and bottlenecks that were responsible for the poor progress in the implementation of the programme and came out with a series of initiatives to address those issues and to remove the implementation bottlenecks.

The following special steps were initiated to streamline and expedite the implementation of the scheme

1. A separate Rural Schedule of Rates was approved exclusively for this scheme in the G.O.Ms. No. 77, RD & PR (CGS-1) Department dated 14.07.2006, thereby removing a major hurdle in getting the statutory minimum wage of Rs.80 per day for seven hours of prescribed work. Rates for working on laterite rock, which is common in Sivaganga district, were added to the Schedule vide G.O M.S No 35 RD & PR Department dated 12.3.2007. The Rural Schedule of Rates under National Rural Employment Guarantee Scheme for the year 2007-08 was ordered in G.O.No.101 RD & PR (CGS-I) Department dated 13.06.2007.
2. A minimum of 30% registrations has been insisted upon in each Village Panchayat. The average percentage of registration in the Phase-I districts is over 65%. In the Phase-II districts, the average registration has crossed 50%, which indicates that there is widespread awareness about the scheme.
3. The existing formats of Job Cards and Nominal Muster Rolls have been revised to make these documents more transparent informative and difficult to manipulate in the process of scheme implementation.
4. Since the scheme requires intensive touring, the Government has sanctioned additional fuel of 50 litres per month for each of the vehicles

in the Panchayat Unions. The Government have also sanctioned additional fuel of 75 litres for the vehicles of the Assistant Executive Engineers (RD) vide G.O.Ms.No.27 RD&PR (CGS-I) Department dated 20.02.2008.

5. Makkal Nala Paniyalars (MNPs) have also been made responsible for the implementation of the scheme at the field level.
6. Additional ministerial, technical and computer staff has been sanctioned at District, Division, Block and Village levels in order to ensure proper implementation and close supervision of the scheme.
7. Only 100% labour intensive works have been taken up in order to prevent the entry of contractors who are strictly banned as per the NREG Act.
8. Only bigger works not less than Rs. 3 lakhs in value have been taken up in order to ensure that i) adequate numbers of workers get sustained employment at a work site for at least 30 days, ii) the assets created are visible, durable and genuinely beneficial to the community, iii) resources are not wasted by being spread too thinly, iv) the works are monitored closely and leakages are minimised.
9. In order to ensure greater transparency and fair play, it has been ordered to disburse the wages to the workers in the presence of at least four members of the following committee:
    - President of the Village Panchayat.
    - Vice–President of the Village Panchayat
    - Ward Member of the area where the work is executed
    - An SC/ST Ward Member, if none of the persons in Sl.Nos. 1, 2 and 3 belongs to SC/ST Community.
    - Two animators of graded Self Help Groups.
    - A representative of the Panchayat Level federation.
10. A 25-member Tamil Nadu State Employment Guarantee council has been constituted vide the G.O Ms No. 117, RD & PR (CGS-I) Department, dated 14.09.2006 to monitor and review the implementation of the scheme. The first, second and third meetings of this council were held on 25.11.2006, 11.06.2007 and 03.03.2008 respectively.
11. In order to ensure efficient monitoring of the scheme through Management Information System (MIS), three computers and a printer have been sanctioned to each of the 141 block offices of Phase-I and II NREGS districts. In 2008-09, computers, printers and computer room facilities will also be provided for the block offices of Phase-III NREGS districts.

12. In order to ensure a total transparency in the implementation of the Scheme, the Government ordered for the conduct of Social Audit of the Scheme in all Village Panchayats of NREGS districts along with the conduct of Grama Sabha meeting on 15th August, 2nd October and 26th January in 2007-08. Likewise, the conduct of Social Audit of the scheme will be conducted along with Grama Sabha meetings in the year 2008-09 also. As a result of the concerted efforts taken by this Government, a sum of Rs.619 crores has been utilized and over 800 lakh mandays of employment have been generated up to 31.03.2008. About 82% of the work force comprises women and 56% are Scheduled Castes. A notable feature of the scheme is that it has had a buoyant effect on rural wages.

National Rural Employment Guarantee Scheme (NREGS)

I. Central Government

- Rural development ministry nodal ministry
- Ensure fund flow
- Set up employment guarantee council for advisory
- Independent monitoring and evaluation

II. State Government

- Evolve regulations
- Set up Employment Guarantee Council
- Facilitating resource flow

III. District Panchayat

- Prepare district annual plan
- Prepare five-year perspective plan based on village plans
- Implement works (not mandatory)
- District level coordination of activities

IV. Block Panchayat

- Coordinate block level plans
- Identify possible works based on village plan
- Design and implement works (not mandatory)
- Monitoring

V. Village Panchayat

- Prepare village plan
- Identify, design and implement 50% works
- Set up local institutions to facilitate implementation
- Evaluate and monitor implementation

❐

17

Review of Literature

Review of literature is an important part of the research process. Studies related to the research problem have been reviewed and documented in this chapter. The present study focuses on the implementation of NREGS, Awareness on the programme and various other topic related to the scheme. The researcher could get only studies that were related in some ways or other with the key variables and such studies have been reviewed and classified under different related areas as follows.

1. Implementation of NREGS
2. Significance of NREGS
3. Awareness on NREGS.
4. Impact of NREGS.
5. Women and Child Care.
6. Social Audit.

Implementation of NREGS

Sharma and Bajpai (2006), Studied the implementation of NREGS in selected Districts of U.P. The government identified 22 districts as backward. For the implementation of NREGS but has increased 17 more districts later on. However the author has taken four districts namely Barabanki, Raebareli, Sitapur and Unnao for the Study. The objectives of the Study were as follows.

1. There is general awareness about the scheme among the villages.
2. The scheme is providing jobs to the application without hassles.
3. The beneficiaries and the village people appreciate the implementation of the scheme.
4. The project has potential to create job opportunities in the area and
5. To make suggestion for effective implementation of NREGS to benefit the poor people living in the rural areas.

The survey exercise was conducted by administering a structured questionnaire schedule on the beneficiaries of the scheme at the worksite in the 16 villages spread over four select districts on the basis of convenient sampling. He has selected two blocks from each district and two villages from each block on random basis. The sample at each village's worksite was 25. Thus 100 beneficiaries were interviewed making the total sample size of 400 beneficiaries.

The study of four districts identified most backward districts of Uttar Pradesh underscores the important role of panchayat Raj Institutions. It revealed the ground realities of the implementation of the scheme. The scheme has provided relief and seccurence to poor village people. It was also found that the people were happy about getting the job opportunities in their own villages. However they want increase in wage and worksite facilities. But the participation of women has not been found encouraging. The author concludes that efforts to create quality awareness on massive scale can provide fillip to efficient and effective implementation of the NREGS.

Rao (2008), presents a overall view on the implementation of the NREGS scheme. In his report published in kurukshetra, June 2008. The author states that according to the latest figures employment provided to 3.08 households as against the demand by 3.10 households. A total of 121.64 crore person days have been created. This includes 32.89 crore person days of scheduled castes and 36.50 crore persondays of Schedule Tribes. Women constituted 51.24 crore persons days.

The author further states that the NREGS programme has strengthened the bargaining capacity of the workers in fixing the minimum wages. It also gave a big boost to the water conservation. It's implementation in some of the nexal-affected areas was very effective. It has helped in reducing the distress of migration of labourers from rural areas to the urban locations.

Pattanaik (2009), studied on the implementation of NREGS in Hoshiarpur district. The primary data was collected from 10 village panchayats of the two blocks i.e. Mahilpur and Dasus of Hashiarpur during the financial year 2007-2008.

The researcher states that initial findings of the study shows that the scheme has been successful in achieving the equity, while its efficiency is still a question to be efficiently dealt by the implementers of the programme the better nexus and coordination between the government and the panchayats would enable efficient implementation of the scheme at the village level.

Significance of the NREGS

Singh (2008), states that with the experience and learning of the past two years, NREGA will be more effectively implemented. The act covered 200 districts in its first phase and was extended to 330 additional districts in 2007-2008. The author lists out the significance of NREGA thus. It creates a social safety for the vulnerable. It adds a dimension of equity to the process of growth. It creates right-based frame work for wage employment and the right to demand employment in a time bound manner.

The author has presented the salient features of the act as follows. The scheme has a right based frame work and it has time bound guarantee which provides employment within 15 Days. It provides opportunity for women empowerment. The scheme has got worksite facilities such as crèche, drinking water and shade. Social audits have been done by Gram Sabha. All accounts and records relating to the scheme are to be made available to any person on demand. There is a list of permissible work and has a definite funding procedure.

The author has also stated that the scheme has reached out to the rural poor, 117.54% of BPL rural households have benefited from the scheme. There is increased women workforce participation ratio. SC/ST households 62% have employment under this scheme. All the above features and significance are presented by the author as the design of the scheme by the government.

Awareness on the Scheme

Singh (2008), conducted a study. It was published in YOJANA. The author took up Sonbhadra which is the most backward district in Uttar Pradesh. The author concludes after the study as follows" In view of the cited Scenario and problems, we can unhesitatingly say that there is a huge need for spreading awareness in this area. Only awareness can save them from the unscrupulous village and district officials.

Rao (2008), conducted a study on the NREGA. The study was carried out in Raichur district of Karnataka and Anantpur district of Andhra Pradesh in May-September 2007 to access the process of awareness of NREGA in the sample districts. The role of the civil society was aptly acknowledged in creating awareness. Further the author suggests the following for creating better awareness. Community radio concepts can effectively be used to give information to the target population. Local associations and teachers can be roped support the awareness.

Impact of NREGS

Mamidipatty Rajanna and Gundeti Ramesh (2009), studied the impact of NREGS in 22 districts in Andra Pradesh by selecting 500 beneficiaries. Out of the beneficiaries 68.6% of them were women and the rest were men. The objective of the study was to know the impact of NREGP in the area. At the end of the study the following finding were arrived. NREGP increased the economic conditions by reducing the income imbalance in rural area, reduction of wage differences by creating equal wages to male and female workers reduced the migration level and helped to reduce seasonal unemployment. The study reveals that the beneficiaries expressed the following changes in the programme in order to be more comprehensive. Effective social audit is necessary to eliminate bogus beneficiaries. At the field level the qualified persons require to maintain the accurate records of the beneficiaries and nature of the worker should be amicable to all the beneficiaries who are willing to participate in this programme.

Women and Childcare

Sudha Narayan (2008), carried out a survey on women and childcare in the NREGA works in viluppuram district. The study was conducted in 11 villages and covered about 104 workers. The objective of the study was to find the changes in the lives of women involved in the NREGA works. The author states that NREGA holds a powerful prospect of bringing major changes in the lives of women. This is especially true in a state like Tamil Nadu. Where women constitute an over whelming proportion more than 80 per cent of NREGA workers. At the same time, however, some significant challenges frustrate this transformative promise of NREGA. One of them is the issues of childcare. The findings indicate that childcare is a significant problem for many of the young mothers with children below the age of three years. However the scheme plays a positive role in the lives of women. The researcher concludes that provision of effective childcare facilities like the crèches at NREGA worksites is an important action to be taken.

Tamilnadu – A report (2008), published in YOJANA August states. Employment has been generated on a massive scale. While the programme was at a virtual standstill last year (in 2006-08) employment generation has surged during the last few months. The average job card holders in villupuram have already been employed for nearly 25 days since 1 April 2007. Nearly 70 per cent of all rural households in the district have a job card. More than 80 percent of NREGA workers in villupuram are women. In most villages, workers know very little about their entitlements under NREGA. Very few worksites had child care facilities of any sort, even when children were presented at the site.

Social Audit

Siwach and Sunil (2009), selected two districts in Haryana under NREGA for the study. Out of the 7 blocks, the researcher took Sirsa block consisting of 54 villages for the analysis of the impact of Social Audit. The basic aim of the study was to investigate the impact of Social Audit in the selected villages.

The author concludes that the NREGS, by and large, has the potential not only to strengthen social security in India, but also strengthens community's mobilization to ensure better responsiveness of local government to communities needs and priorities.

❐

18

Research Methodology

India is the second most populated country in the world. It is highly impossible to give employment to all the people in the country. However the government has to catter to the needs of the people. A scheme one such as the NREGS is the most wanted of all to the rural people as it provides employment and wages. The researcher has taken this scheme for his study.

This chapter deals with the methodology adopted for the study by the researcher. It includes the significance and scope of the study its aim and objectives, research assumptions, conceptual and operational definitions, the researcher design, description of the respondents of the study selected by the researcher, variables, tools of data collection, pilot study, pre testing, limitations of the study and the outline of the presentation of the various chapters of the researcher report.

Statement of the Problem

India is the largest democratic country with rich and varied culture and life styles. There are industrious cities and fertile villages. The villagers depend on agriculture for their living. More than 80% of the Indians live in villages. When agriculture fails them, they hurl in poverty. They central and state governments have implemented various schemes to eradicate the poverty of the rural people. National Rural Employment Guarantee Scheme (NREGS) is one such a scheme which has gained popularity in recent times. It is one of the schemes that has reached the people directly and is popularly known as 100 days employment scheme.

The scheme has gained popularity among the poor and has many salient features. Has this scheme reached the people? This is a key point to be researched upon. More over the study on this scheme becomes essential as it has affected the rural people and agricultural works both directly and indirectly and in a positive and negative way. These should be studied closely to identify the negative aspects and the central reason behind them. So that they can be rectified in order to make the scheme more successful.

The implementation of the scheme nationwide has many practical difficulties. Only a direct research with those who help in implementing the scheme and the beneficiaries will help to remove these difficulties.

Significance of the Study

This research becomes significant since it studies the effects of the NREGS on the individual, society and economic status of the rural people, both directly and indirectly. The study also helps in identifying the defects of the scheme and suggests ways to rectify them. Hence this research becomes important. This research also reflects the social status of the people, effects of the scheme on agriculture and the present situation of the rural people therefore it can be called as the mirror of the society.

Scope of the Study

The research tries to analyse the effects of the NREGS in the 20 panchayats that comes under the Thirumanur Union of the Ariyalur District. It presents a vivid picture with the statistical data collected from the target area.

The target area has agricultural land of both wet and dry nature. All communities (SC, BC, MBC) of people live in this area. They are dependent on agriculture for their living.

The researcher has taken the beneficiaries (Workers), Farmers and those who implement the Scheme (Village Presidents and MNP) as the respondents and subjects of the study.

A careful effort has been taken to prepare a questionnaire that covers the economic and social status of the people, education and condition of the family. The research also studies the salient features of the scheme, it's implementation, works and wages, measurements and social audits. The study involves direct interview method with detailed questionnaire that studies the scheme from different dimensions.

The researcher presents suggestions to make the scheme more effective. Since this study suggests ways to implement the scheme without affecting the agriculture, which is the lifeline of the Indian economy. It stands as the tool for the government to develop this scheme as well as many more such Schemes without affecting any of the standards in the society in the near future.

AREA PROFILE ARIYALUR DISTRICT

District Profile

Ariyalur district came into existence by bifurcating Perambalur as per G.O.Ms.No.683 Revenue RA1(1) Department dated 19.11.07. It is bounded on the North by Cuddalore, South by Thanjavur, East by Cuddalore and Thanjavur and West by Perambalur and Tiruchirapalli districts. The new Ariyalur district is functioning from 23.11.2007Ariyalur district consists of 2 divisions viz., Ariyalur and Udayarpalayam, three Taluks viz., Ariyalur, Udayarpalayam and Sendurai and six blocks.

Brief History of the District

In 1741 the Marathas invaded Tiruchirappalli and took Chanda Saheb as captive. Chanda Saheb succeeded in securing freedom in 1748 and soon got involved in famous war for the Nawabs place in the Carnatic against Anwardeen, the Nawab of Arcot and his son Mohammed Ali.

Mohammed Ali annexed the two palayams of Ariyalur and Udayarpalayam located with troops were in the Ariyalur district on the grounds of default in payment of Tributes and failure to assist him in quelling the rebellion of Yusuf Khan. In November 1764, Mohammed Ali represented the issue to Madras Council and obtained military assistance on 3rd January 1765. The forces led by Umdat-Ul-Umara and Donald Campbell entered Ariyalur and captured it. The young Poligar together with his followers there upon fled to Udayarpalayam. On the 19th January the army marched upon Udayarpalayam. The Poligar's troops were defeated and the playams were occupied. The two poligars fled their town and took refuge in Tharangampadi, then a Danish Settlement. The annexation of the palayam gave the Navab un-interrupted possession of all his territories extending Arcot to Tiruchirapalli.

The history followed was a power struggle between Hyder Ali and later Thippu Sultan with the British. After the death of Thippu Sultan the English took the civil and military Administration of the Carnatic in 1801. Thus Tiruchirappalli came in to the hands of the English and the District was formed in 1801. In 1995 Tiruchirappalli was trifurcated and the Perambalur and Karur districts were formed. Perambalur district was divided into Perambalur and Ariyalur district in the year 2001 and merged with Perambalur in the year 2002. Then now the district is bifurcated from Perambalur and .now functioning from 23.11.2007.

Physical Features

As per 2001 census, the population of Ariyalur is 695524, with male 346763 and female 348761. Ariyalur District is centrally located in Tamil Nadu and is 265 K.M. away in southern direction from Chennai. The District has an area of 1949 Sq.Km.

It is an inland district without coastal line. The District has Vellar River in the North and Kollidam River in the South and it has no well marked natural divisions.

Industry

Five major Cement factories in the district reveal the abundant deposit of limestone. The availability of Lignite at Jayankondam and nearby places is a gift by Mother Nature. The Fossil is said to have been a national asset according to Geologists.

Agriculture

Sugar cane is grown as a major commercial crop. One private sugar factory near keelapalur is functioning in the district with a capacity of crushing 3000 Tonnes per day. One of the main crop in Ariyalur district is cashew. The pre-dominate soil in the district is red sanding with scattered packers of black soil. The soil in the district is best suited for raising dry crops. The district has a high means of temperature and low degree of humidity.

Aim of the Study

The aim of the research is to study the impact of NREGS on the social and economic conditions of the rural people.

Specific Objectives of the Study

1. To study the socio-economic background of the beneficiaries under the National Rural Employment Guarantee Scheme (NREGS) in Ariyalur District.
2. To study the awareness regarding the NREGS among the respondents.
3. To evaluate the usefulness of NREGS in study area.
4. To study the effect of NREGS on agriculture in the study area.
5. To evaluate if the objectives of the NREGS are achieved.
6. To find out whether NREGS helps to promote the infrastructure of the villages.
7. To find out the difference in the standard of living of the village people before and after implementation of NREGS.
8. To suggest ways and means to improve NREGS.

Background Variables

1. Gender
2. Age
3. Marital Status
4. Educational qualification
5. Religion
6. Community
7. Family type

Key Variables

1. Salient features of the Programme
2. Annual Income of the Individual
3. Employment opportunities
4. Type of Farmers
5. Awareness on the Scheme
6. Worker scarcity for agricultural work.
7. Implementation of the Scheme.

Assumptions

1. People under the NREGS scheme have higher wages than the people involved in the agricultural work.
2. The Agricultural works had more labourers before the implementation of NREGS than after the implementation of the scheme.
3. The involvement of women labourers in agricultural works has reduced after the implementation of NREGS than before.
4. People with higher level of education are likely to have a higher level of awareness on the scheme when compared to people with lower level of education.
5. People with higher age have less involvement in the scheme than the people with lower age who have more involvement.
6. People of the rural area get higher employment opportunity through NREGS than before its implementation.
7. People with higher tendencies to migrate in search of work fail to register in the NREGS than the people with lesser tendencies to migrate.
8. The scheme has reduced poverty among the people when compared to agricultural work.

CONCEPTUAL DEFINITIONS

Village

"Village" means a village specified by the Governor by public notification to be a village for the purposes of this part and includes a group of villages so specified.

Panchayat

"Panchayat" means in institution (by whatever name called) of Self-government constituted under article 243B, for the rural areas;

Gram Sabha

"Gram Sabha" means a body consisting of persons registered in the electoral rolls relating to a village comprised within the area of panchayat at the village level;

NREGS

NREGS is a historic employment scheme in India for providing 100 days guaranteed wage employment for all employment seekers above 18 years of age and willing to do work and convert rates on unskilled manual work. The scheme came into force on 5th September 2005 in 200 districts in India and extended to another 130 districts later.

Beneficiary

A beneficiary is one who is benefited by something. In the study it refers to a person who gets 100 days of employment from the NREGS and wages due to him through the scheme.

Employment Opportunity

Employment opportunity in the study refers to the opportunities in various field of work such as agriculture, NREGS and other works. It also refers to opportunities for all communities of people living in the target area.

Wage

Wage can be defined as the money paid to a worker on daily basis depending on the amount of work put in by the individual.

Farmer

A person who operates a farm. A farmer is a person who raises living organisms for food or raw materials. A person who works the land or who keeps livestock, especially on a farm.

OPERATIONAL DEFINITIONS

Socio-economic Condition

Socio-economic condition of the people is a key point to be noted in the study. The condition of the people in the society and in economic standards before and after the implementation of the scheme is being rested through different questions asked to the respondents.

Awareness about the Programme

The Success of any programme lies in the awareness of the people about it. Awareness in the study considers the various methods adopted to create awareness and the reach of the methods to create awareness and the reach of the methods to the last member of the society.

Involvement of People

The study takes into consideration the involvement of the people. By this term the researcher means the measures carry out to find if the people do really like the scheme and are benefited by it.

Scarcity of Agricultural Labourer

Scarcity of agricultural labourer means the demand for people for agricultural work, which causes agriculture to suffer. It does not mean the lack of labourers because there are enough labourers but their involvement in agricultural work has become less due to lower wages.

Pilot Study

The researcher had a deep longing to make a study on one such a popular scheme implemented by the government. The researcher made a visit to the District Collector's office at Ariyalur to gather initial statistical information and necessary permissions to carry out the study. Then he made a visit to the Thirumanur Union Office for getting details regarding the panchayats where the scheme is being implemented and discussed with the officials regarding the feasibility, purpose, aim and objectives of the present study. The researcher made visits to different panchayats and gathered useful ideas which helped in the designing of the interview schedule. The researcher also met quiet a number of people informally and had discussions with them regarding the awareness on the scheme, salient features of the scheme and so on. These discussions gave a lot of insights to the researcher which helped in going about with the study.

Research Design

Descriptive research study is concerned with describing the characteristics of the particular individual. Descriptive Research Design has been used for the present study.

An attempt has been made, initially, to describe the background socio-demographic characteristics of the respondents, and then the key variables namely awareness of the people on the scheme, salient feature of the programme, employment opportunity, and then finally to study the association between variables such as employment opportunity, annual income of the individual and worker scarcity for agricultural works.

Universe and Sampling

The universe of the present study includes all the people living within 6 blocks that falls under Ariyalur district. From the total number of 6 blocks, one block was selected by lottery method. Thirumanur block, which was selected, has 36 panchayats. Among them only those panchayats with families that completed the full 100 days under the NREGS were selected by the researcher for the study. There were 20 such panchayats that came under the study. This had 107 families that completed 100 days of employment.

Census method was used to select the panchayat presidents and beneficiaries (107 families) as respondents and purposive sampling method was used to select the farmers as respondents. In all the 20 panchayats one small farmer, one marginal farmer and one large farmer was taken for the study. (Total number of 60 farmers: 20 small farmers, 20 marginal farmers and 20 large farmers based on official criteria of land holding).

Observational Design

The main source of data for the present study was primary in the sense that the researcher collected first hand information directly from the respondents using the structured interview schedule. However, the researcher used secondary sources of data such as published official reports and other documents, for getting the statistical information about the people registered for the NREGS, funds allotted for each panchayat and the list of works selected for the NREGS. And also the census reports for getting data related to households and population of the area.

Tools of Data Collection

The researcher used a self-prepared structured Interview-Schedule which included the respondent's personal details such as age, gender, education, occupation, income etc, and awareness of the people on regarding NREGS the scheme, registering for the scheme, getting employment and wage and socio-economic conditions of the respondents were included in the schedule. The schedule also includes questions on the salient features of the scheme and questions to know the effects of the NREGS on agriculture. The panchayat presidents as respondents had questions on administration and social audit.

Pre-Testing

The pre-testing experience would always extend effective support to the researcher to have clarity in understanding various aspects pertained to the research topic.

The researcher went to 6 panchyats in Thirumanur block in order to find out the feasibility of applying the interview schedules for the beneficiaries, farmers and panchayat presidents. The researcher had interacted with all the respondents and was able to add more questions and deleted certain questions. The researcher was able to reframe certain questions after conducting pretest with few beneficiaries, farmers and panchyat presidents.

Data Collection

The researcher went to the Union office at Thirumanur and with their guidance and support met the 20 panchayat presidents. The panchayat president offered to help the researcher in all possible ways. They gave the list of families that completed 100 days of work. The panchayat presidents also introduced the researcher to the beneficiaries at the worksite. The researcher developed a cordial relationship with the beneficiaries and estimated a good rapport with them before the collection of data. The panchayat presidents and beneficiaries gave all the information needed by the researcher. Then he also met the farmers in their fields and houses who also helped open heartedly in the collection of data. The observation in the worksite and lands of the farmers added reliability to the data collected.

The structured interview schedule was prepared in Tamil so that it could be understood by the respondents. The collection of data was done from 19th June to 31st August, 2009.

Analysis of the Data

The data collected were carefully analysed and processed. All the questions in the structural interview schedule were given due importance and were processed into a simple table with the different variables.

Problems encountered by the Researcher

The researcher found it very difficult to travel to various villages in the Thirumanur block. The researcher himself went to 20 panchayats to collect data. It was time consuming to finish the process of data collection. The researcher had to go to their worksites, farms and houses to collect data from the respondents. The three types of respondents such as the presidents, farmers and beneficiaries also made data collection a time consuming process.

Limitations of the Study

The researcher took only those who completed 100 days of work as the respondents. The reasons for the non-completions of 100 days could be analysed only when the other beneficiaries were also met and their awareness of the scheme could not be analysed.

The study could not consider the effects of NREGS on other works. It takes into consideration the effects on agriculture only, as the target area is agriculture dependent and has negligible percentage of other works.

The researcher has limited his analysis of the data to the simple table and has not done any tests.

❐

19

Statistical Analysis and Findings

Research consists of systematic observation and description of the characteristic of properties for the purpose of discovering relationships, starts with the description of the measures of the variables and goes on to the higher levels of statistical analysis. The data collected will be carefully edited, systematically classified and tabulated, scientifically analyzed and interpreted and rationally concluded.

Thus, in the present study, the data were collected with regard to Mental Imagery and Academic Stress. The data have been subjected tothe following statistical analysis, namely percentile, descriptive, differential, correlation and association. The results of the statistical analysis have been summarized and tabulated.

For the investigator, analysis of collected data turns out to be a very important task. The information collected through the tools have been quantified as detailed in the following tables. For deciding the Academic Stress of the higher secondary school students with respect to Mental Imagery, the following tables were prepared.

Panchayat Presidents

TABLE. 19.1: Distribution of Respondents by their Age

S. No.	Age	No. of Respondents	Percentage
1.	20 – 30 years	01	5.0 %
2.	31 – 40 years	04	20.0 %
3.	41 – 50 years	10	50.0 %
4.	51 – 60 years	02	10.0 %
5.	61 – 70 years	03	15.0 %
	Total	**20**	**100.0 %**

The table above shows the age of respondents. The maximum of 50 per cent respondents belong to the age group between 41 to 50.

TABLE. 19.2: Distribution of Respondents by their Gender

S. No.	Gender	No. of Respondents	Percentage
1.	Male	13	65.0 %
2.	Female	07	35.0 %
	Total	**20**	**100.0 %**

The gender wise distribution table shows that 65 per cent of the respondents are male and 35 per cent of them are female respondents.

TABLE. 19.3: Distribution of Respondents by their Community

S. No.	Community	No. of Respondents	Percentage
1.	SC	03	15.0 %
2.	BC	12	60.0 %
3.	MBC	05	25.0 %
	Total	**20**	**100.0 %**

The distribution of panchayat presidents according to caste shows that 60 per cent of them belong to Backward Community. 25 per cent belong to Most Backward Community and 15 per cent belong to the Schedule Community.

TABLE. 19.4: Distribution of Respondents by their Educational Qualification

S. No.	Educational Qualification	No. of Respondents	Percentage
1.	Primary	05	25.0 %
2.	Secondary	08	40.0 %
3.	Higher secondary	01	05.0 %
4.	College	06	30.0 %
	Total	**20**	**100.0 %**

The education level of the panchayat presidents are shown in this table 40 per cent of them have completed secondary education and it is very important to note that 30 per cent of the village presidents have completed college studies.

TABLE. 19.5: Distribution of Respondents by their Family Type

S. No.	Type of Family	No. of Respondents	Percentage
1.	Joint	12	60.0 %
2.	Nuclear	08	40.0 %
	Total	**20**	**100.0 %**

The above table shows that 60 per cent of the respondents live in joint families and 40 per cent live in single families.

TABLE. 19.6: Methods of Creating Awareness

S. No.	Methods of Creating Awareness	No. of Respondents	Percentage
1.	Announcement	05	25.0 %
2.	Announcement and Bit Notices	09	45.0 %
3.	Announcement, Bit Notices and Banner	01	05.0 %
4.	Announcement, Bit Notice and Advertisement Board	05	25.0 %
	Total	**20**	**100.0 %**

The above table lists the methods of awareness carried out in different panchayats. Among the respondents 45 per cent of them stated that announcements and bit notices were used to create awareness about the NREGS scheme 25 per cent of the presidents said that only announcement were used and the same percentage of them agreed that announcement, bit notices and advertisement boards were also used for creating awareness among the public.

TABLE. 19.7: Verifying the Application

S. No.	Method of Verification	No. of Respondents	Percentage
1.	Ration Card	12	60.0 %
2.	Electoral Roll	01	5.0 %
3.	BPL Census	01	5.0 %
4.	Ration card and Electoral Roll	06	30.0 %
	Total	**20**	**100.0 %**

This table studies the percentage of responses on the methods of verification used to check the applicants. 60 per cent of the beneficiaries produced ration cards and 30 per cent were verified with both ration cards and electoral roll.

TABLE. 19.8: Number of Gram Sabha Convened to Finalize the List

S. No.	Number of Gram Sabha	No. of Respondents	Percentage
1.	One	12	60.0 %
2.	Two	08	40.0 %
	Total	**20**	**100.0 %**

From the above table we come to know that 60 per cent of the respondents have agreed that only on gramsabha meeting was held to finalize the list of works while 40 per cent of them said that two meetings were held.

TABLE. 19.9: List of Work done under NREGS - 2008 - 2009

S. No.	Name of the Panchayat	Type of work			Total
		Water conservation	Renovation	Rural Roads	
1	Alagayamanavalam	1	-	1	2
2	Chinnputtakadu	-	2	1	3
3	Kamarasvalli	1	1	1	3
4	Kandiratheertham	1	2	-	3
5	Keelakolathur	-	2	1	3
6	Malathankulam	-	1	2	3
7	Kovilesanai	2	-	1	3
8	Kovilur	-	1	1	2
9	Koman	1	2	1	4
10	Kuruvadi	-	1	1	2
11	Manjamedu	1	1	1	3
12	Melapulur	1	1	1	3
13	Parpanacheri	-	-	2	2
14	Poondi	-	1	2	3
15	Sullangudi	-	2	1	3
16.	Thirumalaipadi	1	1	1	3
17.	Varanavasi	1	1	1	3
18.	Villupankurichi	1	1	-	2
19.	Venganoor	1	1	1	3
20.	Vettriyur	-	2	1	3
	Total	**12**	**23**	**21**	**56**

Source : from District Collector Officer, Ariyalur

The table above shows that among the 20 panchayats, 23 works were renovation of ponds and lakes. There were 21 works on rural roads and 12 water conservation works were carried out.

TABLE. 19.10: Average Proportion of SC / ST working under NREGS

S. No.	Percentage of SC / ST Beneficiaries	No. of Respondents	Percentage
1.	Below 25%	01	5.0 %
2.	25% - 50%	09	45.0 %
3.	50% - 75%	10	50.0 %
4.	Above – 75%	-	-
	Total	**20**	**100.0 %**

The above table shows the percentage of SC / ST beneficiaries working under this scheme. Among the 20 panchayat taken for the study, 10 panchayats have 50-75 per cent of SC / ST workers 9 panchayats have 25-50 per cent of them.

TABLE. 19.11: Social Audit at Panchayat Level

S. No.	Interval of Social Audit	No. of Respondents	Percentage
1.	Yearly	-	-
2.	Half yearly	11	55.0 %
3.	Quarterly	09	45.0 %
4.	Monthly	-	-
	Total	**20**	**100.0 %**

This table studies the regularity of the social audits. 55 per cent of the panchayats have half yearly audit and 45 per cent of the panchayats have Quarterly audit.

This shows that the scheme is being regularly monitored and the funds are utilized properly.

TABLE. 19.12: Allocation of fund at Panchayat Level Under NREGS – 2008 - 2009

S. No.	Name of the Panchayat	Provident Funds 2008 – 2009	Expenditure Funds 2008 – 2009	Balance Fund 2008-2009
1	Alagayamanavalam	686000	495784	190216
2	Chinnputtakadu	1192000	767453	424547
3	Kamarasvalli	931000	693898	237102
4	Kandiratheertham	908000	346507	561493
5	Keelakolathur	1103000	613419	489581
6	Malathankulam	1050000	905446	144554
7	Kovilesanai	964000	596527	367473
8	Kovilur	680000	393908	286092
9	Koman	1303000	720997	582003

10	Kuruvadi	921000	498006	422994
11	Manjamedu	962000	500599	461401
12	Melapulur	1185000	893171	291829
13	Parpanacheri	625500	409654	215846
14	Poondi	1074000	1065610	8390
15	Sullangudi	1042000	308272	733728
16.	Thirumalaipadi	900000	512010	387990
17.	Varanavasi	630000	557303	72697
18.	Villupankurichi	626000	324801	301199
19.	Venganoor	118000	390467	789533
20.	Vettriyur	1061000	487820	573180

Source : from District Collector Officer, Ariyalur

Awareness on the NREGS

The survey on awareness about the NREGS list out various questions and the responses by the panchayat presidents. The presidents have given 100 per cent responses to all the questions. They all agree that they know about the scheme and have attended special training on it. They also affirm that the ward members and MNP and others co-operate with them. The presidents have registered people for NREGS in their villages.

The villagers apply both orally and in written. All the applications are processed in 15 days by the president himself. All the presidents agree that no applications were refused and Gram Sabha meetings were convened to recommend the list of works. All the presidents disagreed only on one point that is a separate meeting was not convened on the scheme and receipts for the applications received were not issued to the applicants.

Issue of Job card and Approved list of works

The survey also lists the topics on which there were 100 per cent responses from the presidents. The presidents agree that job cards were issued to all, free of cost, with their photographs, in 15 days from the date of registration. There was a meeting convened in the Gram Panchayat to finalize the list of approved works and the finalized list was put on display for the public to see and all the works were selected from the permissible list of works under NREGS.

Execution of Works

The survey on progress of work brings out the responses by the presidents. There are 100 per cent responses all the responses were positive.

Payment of Wage

The topic lists eight questions on the wages provided to the beneficiaries. All the answers by the panchayat presidents were positive and they agreed that the wages were issued to the beneficiaries as per procedure.

Monitoring and Evaluation

The responses by the presidents on the registers and audit were all positive and the register was maintained as per the procedure laid down by the NREGS scheme and audits were done regularly.

Grievance Redressal

From the survey we come to know that complaint registers are maintained in all the panchayats. All the presidents agree that the complaints are disposed within time limits. The presidents also agreed that no help lines were setup for redressing grievances. The president's 100 per cent are of the opinion that the scheme should be implemented during times of less agricultural works. They also agreed that the scheme reduced migration and provided employment opportunity to all the people.

Beneficiaries

TABLE. 19.13: Distribution of Respondents by Age

S. No.	Age	No. of Respondents	Percentage
1.	20 – 30 years	12	11.2 %
2.	31 – 40 years	25	23.4 %
3.	41 – 50 years	36	33.6 %
4.	51 – 60 years	26	24.3 %
5.	61 – 70 years	7	6.5 %
6.	Above 70 years	1	1.0 %
	Total	**107**	**100.0 %**

TABLE. 19.14: Distribution of Respondents by Gender

S. No.	Gender	No. of Respondents	Percentage
1.	Male	52	48.5 %
2.	Female	55	51.5 %
	Total	**107**	**100.0 %**

TABLE. 19.15: Distribution of Respondents by Age Vs Gender

S. No.	Age	Male	Female	No. of Respondents	Percentage
1.	20 – 30 years	3	9	12	11.2 %
2.	31 – 40 years	8	17	25	23.4 %
3.	41 – 50 years	19	17	36	33.6 %
4.	51 – 60 years	15	11	26	24.3 %
5.	61 – 70 years	6	1	7	6.5 %
6.	Above 70 years	1	-	1	1.0 %
	Total	**52**	**55**	**107**	**100.0 %**

The tables above show the age and gender of the respondents. It is clear from the table that the maximum number of respondents i.e. 33.6 per cent of them belong to the age group of 41-50 years and the male and female beneficiaries in the age group are comparatively equal.

About 92.5 per cent of the respondents belong to the working age group between 20-60 years. It shows that NREGS has been successful in employing the right age group for the works and Table No.2 shows that it is equally beneficial to the male as well as the female.

TABLE. 19.16: Distribution of Respondents by their Religion

S. No.	Religion	No. of Respondents	Percentage
1.	Hindu	97	90.6 %
2.	Christian	10	9.4 %
	Total	**107**	**100.0 %**

The above table shows that the majority of the beneficiaries 90.6 per cent belong to the Hindu religion. It also shows that even the people from the minority community benefit from the scheme.

TABLE. 19.17: Distribution of Respondents by their Community

S. No.	Community	No. of Respondents	Percentage
1.	SC	27	25.2 %
2.	BC	72	67.3 %
3.	MBC	8	7.5 %
	Total	**107**	**100.0 %**

Distribution table above shows the community wise difference among the respondents. Among the respondents 67.3 per cent of them belong to the Backward Community. The Scheduled Community 25.2 per cent and the Most Backward Community 7.5 per cent have also benefited from the scheme. Though there is a vast difference between each community, still when compared with the population in the target area, the scheme has provided equal opportunity to every community.

TABLE. 19.18: Distribution of Respondents by their Educational Qualification

S. No.	Educational Qualification	No. of Respondents	Percentage
1.	Primary	30	28.0 %
2.	Secondary	38	35.5 %
3.	Higher Secondary	2	2.0 %
4.	Technical	1	1.0 %
5.	Illiterate	36	33.5 %
	Total	**107**	**100.0 %**

The table above states that 28 per cent of the beneficiaries have only completed primary education and 35.5 per cent have done secondary education while 33.5 per cent of them are illiterate.

TABLE. 19.19: Distribution of Respondents by their Marital Status

S. No.	Marital Status	No. of Respondents	Percentage
1.	Married	100	93.5 %
2.	Unmarried	7	6.5 %
	Total	**107**	**100.0 %**

The above distribution table shows explicitly that 93.5 per cent of the beneficiaries are married and the scheme helps them in the daily expenses of the family.

TABLE. 19.20: Distribution of Respondents by their Type of Family

S. No.	Type of Family	No. of Respondents	Percentage
1.	Nuclear	88	82.2 %
2.	Joint	19	17.8 %
	Total	**107**	**100.0 %**

TABLE. 19.21: Distribution of Respondents by their Family Size

S. No.	Family Size	No. of Respondents	Percentage
1.	1 – 4 Members	90	84.1 %
2.	5 – 8 Members	13	12.2 %
3.	More than 8 member	4	3.7 %
	Total	**107**	**100.0 %**

The above table distribution of respondents by the type of family shows that 82.2 per cent of the respondents live in nuclear family. While only 17.8 per cent of them live in joint family. It is clear that people from the nuclear families make good use of the scheme and the next table also shows that most of the beneficiaries 84.1 per cent are from smaller families, with only 1-4 members in the family.

TABLE. 19.22: Distribution of Respondents by their Occupation

S. No.	Type of Occupation	Before NREGS	Percentage	After NREGS	Percentage
1.	Agricultural Labourers	70	65.4 %	25	23.4 %
2.	Own agricultural	20	18.7 %	8	7.5 %
3.	Others works	17	15.9 %	-	-
4.	NREGS works	-	-	74	69.1 %
	Total	**107**	**100.0 %**	**107**	**100.0 %**

Occupation wise distribution table shows a very salient point about the scheme. The table clearly shows that people who were agricultural labourers (70) and even those who had their own agricultural land (20) have opted to work under the scheme. About (74) of the respondents have left agricultural work and have joined the NREGS scheme. This study shows that agricultural labour has been affected by the scheme. Even the (17) who have done others works before the scheme have left them and joined the scheme after its implementation.

TABLE. 19.23: Employment Opportunity of the Respondents

S. No.	Employment Opportunity per month (In Days)	Before NREGS	Percentage	After NREGS	Percentage
1.	5 – 10	5	4.7 %	-	-
2.	10 – 15	89	83.2 %	10	9.3 %
3.	15 – 20	13	12.1 %	80	74.8 %
4.	20 – 25	-	-	17	15.9 %
	Total	**107**	**100.0 %**	**107**	**100.0 %**

The above table studies the employment opportunity of the respondents before and after the implementation of the scheme. Maximum number of respondents have expressed that NREGS has given them more number of days of employment per month. (89) of them have said that they had 10-15 days of employment per month before the scheme and (80) of them have agreed that the days of employment has increased to 15-20 days per month after the implementation of the scheme.

TABLE. 19.24: Income Variation Before and After NREGS

S. No.	Annual Income of the Individual	Before NREGS	Percentage	After NREGS	Percentage
1.	10,000 – 12,000	7	6.6 %	-	-
2.	12,000 – 14,000	78	72.9 %	13	12.2 %
3.	14,000 – 16,000	18	16.8 %	71	66.4 %
4.	16,000 – 18,000	4	3.7 %	14	13.0 %
5.	Above – 18,000	-	-	9	8.4 %
	Total	**107**	**100.0 %**	**107**	**100.0 %**

The above table shows clearly that the annual income of the beneficiaries has increased after the implementation of the scheme. The maximum number of respondents (78) have stated that their annual income was 12,000 – 14,000 before the scheme and (71) among (107) accepted that their annual income has increased to 14,000-16,000 after the implementation of the scheme.

TABLE. 19.25: Family Expenditure Per Year

S. No.	Spending Per Year	No. of Respondents	Percentage
1.	**Food**		
	Below – 5,000	21	19.6 %
	5,000 – 7,500	82	76.6 %
	7,500 – 10,000	04	3.8 %
	Above – 10,000	-	-
2.	**Clothes**		
	Below – 1,000	20	18.6 %
	1,000 – 2,000	62	58.0 %
	2,000 – 3,000	25	23.4 %
	3,000 – 4,000	-	-
3.	**Education**		
	Below – 1,000	40	37.4 %
	1,000 – 2,000	52	48.6 %
	Above – 2,000	15	14.8 %
4.	**Medicine**		
	Below – 1,000	48	44.8 %
	1,000 – 2,000	54	50.5 %
	2,000 – 3,000	05	4.7 %
	Above – 3,000	-	-
	Total	**107**	**107 %**

The above table studies the expenditure pattern of the respondents. The respondents 76.6 per cent spend at an average 500 – 7500 rupees per year on food. Their spending on clothes ranges from 1000 to 2000 rupees per year. The maximum number of respondents 86 per cent spend below 2000 rupees on education and 95.3 per cent spend the same amount on medicine. The above facts show clearly that their spending on basic needs are very meager.

TABLE. 19.26: Wage and Working Hours

S. No.	Type of Work	Working Hours		Wage	
		Male	Female	Male	Female
1.	Agricultural Works	5 Hours	5 Hours	100	50
2.	NREGS works	7 Hours	7 Hours	80	80

The above table explains the working hours and wage of the respondents in agricultural works and in NREGS works. The working hours have increased from 5 to 7 hours in the NREGS works. The wages for the men have reduced by 20 rupees whereas for the women it has increased by 30 rupees. There is equal wage for men and women in the NREGS works. The differences in the wages and working hours have not affected the involvement of people in NREGS works as they have regular work.

From the above table we also come to the conclusion that the male workers get less wages in the NREGS works comparing to agricultural works.

Whereas the female workers get more wages through NREGS comparing to agricultural works. The female workers benefit more from this scheme.

TABLE. 19.27: Saving and Debts

S. No.	Particulars	No. of Respondents	Percentage
1.	Saving Habit		
	Saving	80	74.8 %
	Not Saving	27	25.2 %
2.	Saving Money Through		
	Post Office	17	15.9 %
	Self Help Group (SHG)	33	30.9 %
	Others	30	28.0 %
3.	Details of Debt		
	Debt	73	68.2 %
	No Debt	34	31.8 %
	Total	**107**	**100 %**

The savings and Debts table shows that about 74.8 per cent of the respondents have the habit of saving and 58.9 per cent of the respondents prefer saving through, Self help groups and other methods rather than postal saving schemes. More than half 68.2 percent of the respondents also agree that they also have small debts. It is clear from table No. 13 and 15 that the scheme helps them to meet their daily expenses.

TABLE. 19.28: Respondents Having Movable Assets

S. No.	Particulars	No. of Respondents	Percentage
1.	Fan	91	85.0 %
2.	Grinder	51	47.6 %
3.	Mixe	27	25.2 %
4.	Television	81	75.7 %
5.	Radio	36	33.6 %
6.	Bicycle	101	94.3 %
7.	Motor cycle	10	9.3 %
8.	Bullock cart	2	1.8 %
9.	Cattle's	68	63.5 %

The above table shows the movable assets owned by the respondents. The maximum number of respondents has only essential assets like fan, TV, bicycle and Cattle's. Very few of them own comforts like motor cycle and mixe.

TABLE. 19.29: Respondents Having Immovable Property

S. No.	Particulars	No. of Respondents	Percentage
1.	**Land**		
	Own Land	24	22.4 %
	Land less	83	77.6 %
2.	**Type of House**		
	Thatched	47	43.9 %
	Tiled	36	33.7 %
	Concrete	24	22.4 %
3.	**Electrification**		
	Electrified	101	94.4 %
	Non – Electrified	6	5.6 %
4.	**Drinking Water**		
	Hand Pumb	17	15.9 %
	Street Tap	90	84.1 %
5.	**Toilet**		
	Own House Toilet	32	30.0 %
	Open Toilet	75	70.0 %

The studies about the immovable property reveal the following facts. The maximum numbers of beneficiaries 77.6 per cent are landless. The same percentages of them live in thatched 43.9 per cent and tiled 33.7 per cent houses. They have the free electrification done by the government and many of them use open toilets and street taps for drinking water.

TABLE. 19.30: Participation of Physically Challenged

S. No.	Type of People	No. of Respondents	Percentage
1.	Physically challenged	2	1.8 %
2.	Normal	105	98.2 %
	Total	**107**	**100 %**

The above table shows that the physically challenged people are also benefited by the NREGS scheme.

TABLE. 19.31: Gram Sabha Meeting

S. No.	Particulars	No. of Respondents	Percentage
1.	Participants	38	35.5 %
2.	Non-Participants	69	64.5 %
	Total	**107**	**100 %**

TABLE. 19.32: Method of Registration

S. No.	Particulars	No. of Respondents	Percentage
1.	Written	71	66.4 %
2.	Oral	36	33.6 %
	Total	**107**	**100 %**

The above tables bring out the fact that only 35.5 per cent of the beneficiaries attend the Gram Sabha meeting while 64.5 per cent do not participate in the meetings The table also shows that 66.4 per cent of the beneficiaries register for the work in writing. The scheme is flexible in accepting even the oral registration.

TABLE. 19.33: Awareness on Salient Features of the Scheme

S. No.	Salient Features of the Scheme	Know	Percentage
1.	Free medical Treatment for those injured during the work	105	98.1 %
2.	50 per cent of the wage will to be given during the period of treatment	105	98.1 %
3.	There should be an open administration	100	93.4 %
4.	In case of any accident or death during work 25,000/- to be given as compensation	104	97.1 %
5.	The work should be in accordance with Right Information Act.	75	70.0 %
6.	Aged people and Physically Challenged to be allotted suitable work.	100	93.4 %
7.	Social audit reports to be displayed for the public to see	60	56.0 %

The salient features table shows that the people are aware of the benefits of the scheme. We can come to the conclusion that most of the beneficiaries are aware about the salient features of the programme.

Their awareness about openness of administration right to information act, work to be allotted for physically challenged and aged people and audit reports are very little since it does not personally concern them.

TABLE. 19.34: Facilities at Worksite

S. No.	Facilities at worksite	Yes	No	Total
1.	Drinking water	107	-	107
2.	Creche	107	-	107
3.	First Aid	101	6	107
4.	Shade	107	-	107

From the table above we come to a conclusion that facilities like drinking water, crèche and shades are given to all the beneficiaries in the target area. A few respondents (6) have said that first aid was not given properly. Whereas majority of them (101) have accepted that all the facilities were provided.

TABLE. 19.35: Fulfillment of 100 days of Employment

S. No.	No of Person in a family Jointly Fulfilled the 100 Days	No. of the Family	Percentage
1.	Single person	20	18.7 %
2.	Two person	61	57.0 %
3.	Three person	21	19.6 %
4.	Four person	5	4.7 %
	Total	**107**	**100.0 %**

The table above shows that the scheme provides an opportunity for the beneficiaries to arrange a substitute from their family when they are unable to attend the work. The family members can compensate and complete the 100 days work. The real beneficiary in the scheme is the family. From the table we come to know that (61) respondents have expressed that two persons of the same family completed the 100 days. This provides opportunity for substituting during times of sickness and other personal reasons. So that the family gets 100 full days of work and wages to manage the family expenses.

Awareness, Registration, Job Card, Employment and wages (100 per cent responses from the beneficiaries)

The respondents agree that they all know well about the scheme and its implementation in their village. They all accept that there were awareness programmes held by the panchayat to introduce the scheme to them. The Gram Sabha meetings are held in their villages. They all know how to apply and register their names for NREGS scheme. They accept that they had no difficulty in applying for the scheme. They were also give employment within 15 days from the date of registration. All the respondents have ID cards with photograph and it was given to them free of cost. The respondents agreed that ID card was compulsory in the worksite and it is being verified in the worksite. All respondents said that the wages were given in cash once a week and as per the procedure.

Awareness on Salient Features of the Scheme (100 per cent Responses from the beneficiaries)

1. The beneficiaries are aware that they must be given 100 days employment per family and they accept that their families were given 100 days of work.
2. The beneficiaries are aware that the male and female workers have equal wages.
3. They accept the fact that the works are not given in contract basis.
4. They also expressed their awareness that machineries should not be used and it was done so.
5. Beneficiaries are aware that women also have equal rights to participate in the NREGS work in the ratio of 1:3.
6. The respondents agree that drinking water, first aid, child care and resting place are provided for the NREGS workers at the worksite.
7. The beneficiaries also know that construction works should not be given under the NREGS scheme and they agree that no such works were given to them.
8. The workers are aware that the worksite should be within 5 kilometer radius from the place of registration and they agree that it was arranged likewise.
9. They agree that when the worksite could not be found within 5 kilometers 10 per cent of the daily wage is given in addition as travel expenses.

Evaluation of the Scheme
(100 per cent Responses from the beneficiaries)

1. All the respondents agree that NREGS is very much useful to them
2. They agree that it removes poverty in their family.
3. They are able to meet out their daily expenses and they get employment in their own villages. It also helps them to spend on education, medicine and clothes.
4. The beneficiaries also agree that the NREGS works should be given during days of less agricultural works.
5. The beneficiaries agree that works are given on piece and time basis and for 7 hours only.
6. The beneficiaries agree that the wage details are read out aloud while making payment and it is done at a designated place and time.

Opinion of the Beneficiaries Under NREGS
(100 per cent Responses from the beneficiaries)

Positive

1. Beneficiaries get work in their own village.
2. Both men and women get work under this scheme and they also get equal wage. Women do not get so much wage in other works. Even the aged people get work under this scheme.
3. Women beneficiaries say that they could be self dependent with the help of the wages.
4. The scheme helps in managing the daily family expenses.
5. Both men and women welcome the scheme, the scheme is useful more to the women in villages
6. The scheme provides opportunity for compensating the worker with any other family member.
7. The beneficiaries are of the opinion that the scheme is very much beneficial to them as there are no middle men as in contract works. The funds allotted by the government reaches the public directly.

Negative

1. Wages for the men is less and insufficient
2. The piece basis work should be allotted for individual workers so that all the workers give equal share of work.
3. The scheme should be implemented during times of less agricultural works so that there is work throughout the year.
4. Machineries can be used for the most difficult work at the beginning. So that the work is completed quickly and without any danger to life.

Farmers

TABLE. 19.35: Distribution of Respondents by Age

S. No.	Age	No. of Respondents	Percentage
1.	25 – 35 years	13	21.7 %
2.	36 – 45 years	17	28.3 %
3.	46 – 55 years	15	25.0 %
4.	56 – 65 years	14	23.3 %
5.	66 – 75 years	01	1.7 %
	Total	**60**	**100.0 %**

The above table we come to know that the farmers of the target area belong to the age group between 25 - 75

TABLE. 19.36: Distribution of Respondents by their Gender

S. No.	Gender	No. of Respondents	Percentage
1.	Male	60	100.00 %
	Total	**60**	**100.00 %**

The above table states clearly that the agricultural work is done only by male farmers.

TABLE. 19.37: Distribution of Respondents by their Religion

S. No.	Religion	No. of Respondents	Percentage
1.	Hindu	57	95.00 %
2.	Christian	03	5.00 %
	Total	**60**	**100.0 %**

The distribution of respondents table above shows that the targets area consists mostly 95 per cent of Hindu farmers

TABLE. 19.38: Distribution of Respondents by their Community

S. No.	Community	No. of Respondents	Percentage
1.	SC	06	10.0 %
2.	BC	40	66.7 %
3.	MBC	14	23.3 %
	Total	60	100.0 %

The above table states that among the respondents 66.7 per cent of them belong to the backward class. It is thus clear that most of the farmers in the target area belong to the backward community.

TABLE. 19.39: Distribution of Respondents by their Educational Qualification

S. No.	Educational Qualification	No. of Respondents	Percentage
1.	Primary	09	15.0 %
2.	Secondary	34	56.7 %
3.	Higher Secondary	05	8.3 %
4.	College	07	11.7 %
5.	Illiterate	05	8.3 %
	Total	60	100.0 %

The above table shows that the respondents are not illiterate about 91.7 per cent of them have completed their secondary education.

TABLE. 19.40: Distribution of Respondents by their Marital Status

S. No.	Marital Status	No. of Respondents	Percentage
1.	Married	59	98.3 %
2.	Unmarried	01	1.7 %
	Total	**60**	**100.0 %**

Regarding the marital status majority 98.3 per cent of the respondents are married and only 3.7 per cent of them are unmarried

TABLE. 19.41: Distribution of Respondents by their Family Type

S. No.	Type of Family	No. of Respondents	Percentage
1.	Joint	20	33.3 %
2.	Nuclear	40	66.7 %
	Total	**60**	**100.0 %**

Regarding the type of family the table above shows that 66.7 per cent of the farmer's family are nuclear in type and 33.3 per cent of them are joint families.

TABLE. 19.42: Economic Characteristics of the Respondents

S. No.	Particulars	No. of Respondents	Percentage
1.	**Type of Farmer**		
	Marginal Farmer	20	33.3 %
	Small Farmer	20	33.3 %
	Large Farmer	20	33.3 %
2.	**Type of Land they Own**		
	Wet land	24	40.0 %
	Dry land	13	21.7 %
	Wet and Dry land (both)	23	38.3 %

3.	**Power Motor of their** own Have Do not have	28 32	46.7 % 53.3 %
4.	**Cattle** Have Do not have	24 36	40.0 % 60.0 %
5.	**Own Farming Tools** and Machinery Have Do not Have	06 54	10.0 % 90.0 %

The above table studies the economic status of the respondents. The target area had 33.3 per cent marginal farmers and the same percentage of small farmers and large farmers. Among the 60 farmers 40 per cent of them have wet lands and 38.3 per cent of them have both wet and dry lands. And 53.3 per cent of them have power motors of their own while others do not have. The maximum numbers of farmers 60 per cent of them have cattle. Among the farmers taken for study 90 per cent of them do not own farming tools and machinery.

TABLE. 19.43: Distribution of Respondents by Type of Irrigation

S. No.	Type of irrigation	No. of Respondents	Percentage
1.	Canal	26	43.3 %
2.	Well	10	16.7 %
3.	Lake	06	10.0 %
4.	Oil Engine	09	15.0 %
5.	Rented Power Motor	02	3.3 %
6.	Rain water	07	11.7 %
	Total	**60**	**100.0 %**

This table presents the type of irrigation used by the farmers. The maximum percentages 43.3 per cent of the farmers depend on canal irrigation. Some of them 15 per cent have oil engines and still others 16.7 per cent depend on well irrigation. 11.7 per cent of the farmers also depend on rain for irrigation.

TABLE. 19.44: Distribution of Respondents by Type of Labourers they Employ

S. No.	Type of labourers they employ	No. of Respondents	Percentage
1.	Daily Wage	39	65.0 %
2.	Contract and Daily wage	21	35.0 %
	Total	**60**	**100.0 %**

The above table states that 65.0 per cent of the respondents choose labourers for daily wages. They are of the opinion that the NREGS affects them because they do not find labourers for agricultural work whereas 35.0 per cent of the farmers agree that they do not have problem when choosing workers on contract.

TABLE. 19.45: Impact on Agriculture

S. No.	Particulars	No. of Respondents	Percentage
1.	**Duration of Working Hours** Reduced No change	 24 36	 40.0 % 60.0 %
2.	**Involvement of Labourers in** Agricultural Works Reduced Increased	 51 09	 85.0 % 15.0 %
3.	**Impact of Migration on Agriculture** Affected Unaffected	 11 49	 18.3 % 81.7 %
4.	**Use of Machinery in Agriculture** More Less	 41 19	 68.3 % 31.7 %
5.	**Type of Deficiency for labours** Male worker Female worker Male and Female worker	 09 38 13	 15.0 % 63.3 % 21.7 %

The above table shows that 60.0 per cent of the farmers accept that there are no changes in the working hours while 40.0 per cent of them say they the working hours have reduced.

Regarding the involvement of the labourers nearly 85.0 per cent of them agree that the involvement in agricultural works has reduced due to the implementation of NREGS. Labourers shows more interest in the works that give them more wages.

The table shows that migration of labourers has reduced 81.7 per cent of the farmers accept this fact. The farmers 68.3 per cent also agree that agricultural have become machine dependent due to lack of agricultural labourers. The most important opinion of the farmers is that 63.3 per cent of them say that there is deficiency for female workers after the implementation of the scheme. While 21.7 per cent say that there is deficiency of both male and female workers.

Impact of NREGS on Agricultural Works (100 per cent responses from the Farmers)

That all the respondents have their cultivable land and are now cultivating. They agree that they have knowledge about NREGS and it's implementation in their village. All the respondents agree that they had enough labourers for agricultural work before NREGS. They also agree that the labourers expect more wages after the implementation of NREGS. All the farmers are of the opinion that NREGS should be implemented during times of less agricultural work on i.e. during summer when there are no agricultural work.

They also agree that there is deficiency for labourers after the implementation of NREGS. Women get more wages in NREGS when compared to agricultural work. The women opt to join NREGS works only this causes a deficiency of women labourers for some of the agricultural works which could be done only by women labouers.

Cultivation in the Target Area

i. Crops Cultivated

The following crops are cultivated in target area 1. Paddy, 2. Sugarcane, 3. Sunflower, 4. Ground nut, 5. Corn, 6. Gingelly, 7. Red Chilli

ii. Crops Frequently Cultivated

- Paddy – 98 Acre
- Sugarcane – 86 Acre

The farmers of the target area frequently cultivate paddy and sugarcane in a total area of 184 acres.

iii. Crops Seasonally Cultivated

The Farmers of the target area cultivate sunflower, ground nut, corn gingelly and red chilli seasonally in a total area of 60 Acres.

iv. Total Cultivable land

- Wet Land – 184 Acres
- Dry Land – 60 Acres

The target area has a total cultivable land of 244 acres in which 184 acres are wet land and 60 acres are dry land. The cultivation in the wet land mostly depends on agricultural labourers. The implementation of the scheme has created a deficiency of labourers which affects the cultivation in the 244 acres in the target area alone.

Opinions of the Farmers

The data collected from the farmers reveal some of their opinions about the scheme.

- The farmers suggested that NREGS can be implemented during summer, when there are practically no or less agricultural works.
- They suggested that machineries can be used for the most difficult and dangerous works.
- They are of the opinion that age limits should be made compulsory and works should be given to people below poverty line.
- The farmers also said that the works could be finished in particular time. So that there are sufficient labourers for other works especially agricultural works.

❒

20

Discussion

In this chapter the researcher has presented the salient findings of the present study emerging from the survey and interactions. The researcher has also analyzed and compared the findings of the present study in relation to the previous studies conducted by various researchers in the same topic. Subsequently, the researcher has put forth the suggestions based on the study to the various stake holders namely the government, social workers and future researchers.

Salient Findings of the Study

This section, the researcher has attempted to present the salient findings of the study gathered from all the three categories of people namely the beneficiaries, panchayat presidents and farmers.

I. Socio – Demographic Characteristics

- Majority of the respondents 33.6 per cent were in the age group between 41 and 50 years.
- A little more than half of the respondents 51.5 per cent are females.
- A vast majority of the beneficiaries 90.6 per cent were Hindu.
- More than half of the respondents 67.3 per cent belong to the Backward Community.

- Majority of the respondents 35.5 per cent had completed secondary education.
- A Very high majority of 93.5 per cent of the beneficiaries were married.
- Majority 82.2 per cent of the respondents were living in nuclear families.
- A High majority of 84.1 per cent the beneficiary's families had 1 – 4 family members.

II. Aspect Related to NREGS

1. Economic Characteristics;

- Majority of the beneficiaries 70 were involved in agricultural work before the implementation of NREGS while 74 of them joined NREGS after the implementation.
- A Vast majority of 89 among 107 respondents had employment opportunities for 10-15 days per month before the implementation and a majority of 80 among 107 respondents had employment opportunities for 15 – 20 days per month after the implementation.
- Majority of 78 respondents had 12,000-14,000 per year as their annual income before NREGS and majority of 71 respondents had 14,000 – 16,000 per year as their income after the implementation of the scheme.

2. Awareness of NREGS

- All the respondents 100 per cent were aware of the NREGS and its implementation in their villages.
- Majority of the respondents 45 per cent had stated that announcements and bit notices were the methods used to create awareness among the public. Other methods used by and large were advertisement board, news papers, Radio, and Gram Sabha Meetings.
- A vast majority of 86.5 per cent at average respondents were aware of the salient features of the scheme relating to free medical treatment, open administration, compensation, Right To Information Act and Social Audits.

3. Registration and Job Cards

- All the respondents 100 per cent were registered under the scheme and job cards were issued to them. Among those registered 66.4 per cent were writes and 33.6 per cent were oral registrations.
- All the respondents 100 per cent were given job cards and work within 15 days from the date of registration.
- All the respondents 100 per cent were given job cards free of cast and photographs were taken and no charges were collected for it.

- All the respondents 100 per cent had stated that there was no difficulty in registering and getting the job card.

4. Employment and Wages

- All the respondents 100 per cent agreed that wages were given in cash once in a week.
- 100 per cent of the respondents stated that men and women get equal wage under the scheme.
- All the respondents 107 agree that the wage particulars were announced in public and wages were given in a stipulated place.

5. Salient Features

- All the respondents 100 per cent were given 100 days of the work per family.
- 100 per cent of the respondents agree that works under NREGS were not given in contract basis and no machineries were used.
- All the respondents 107 agree that work site facilities like drinking water, shades and crèches were given.
- A vast majority 101 among 107 agreed that first aid was given to them at the worksite.
- All the respondents 100 per cent stated that worksite was chosen within 5 km from their village and when it exceeds the limit they were given 10 per cent of their daily wage for travel expenses.

Findings Related to Assumptions

- The findings of the survey show that women in the NREGS have higher wages than in the agricultural work. Whereas men who were getting Rs.100 in agricultural work are only getting Rs.80 in NREGS.
- The findings shows that 70 among 107 respondents were involved in agricultural work before the NREGS while only 25 among 107 were involved in agricultural work after the implementation of the scheme.
- Assumptions states that the involvement of the women in agricultural work has reduced after the implementation of the scheme. The findings show that 63.3 per cent of the farmers have responded that there was deficiency of women labourers after the NREGS.
- The findings on awareness shows that there is no relationship between the educational level and the awareness on the scheme as 100 per cent of the respondents are aware of the scheme.
- The findings differ from the Assumptions and prove that an average of 23.1 per cent from all age groups participate in the NREGs works.
- The findings prove that there has been a growth in the employment

opportunities for rural people but it has also created deficiency of labourers in agricultural works which is clear from the responses by the farmers.

- The responses from the panchayat presidents 100 per cent proves that the Assumptions that migration has reduced is true.
- The findings show that the annual income of the people has increased from 12,000 – 14,000 per month to 14,000 – 16,000 per month which indicates that the Assumptions is true.

Findings Related to Review of Literature

1. **According to Sharma (2006),** the people were happy about getting the job opportunities in their own villages which the findings prove to be true. The author further states that the participation of women has not been found encouraging. The findings of our survey show that a majority of 51.5 per cent women participate in the NREGS works.
2. **Tamilnadu – A Report (2008),** published in YOJANA and Sudha Narayan (2008) who carried out a survey in Villupuram district conclude that provision of effective childcare facilities like the creaches at worksites should be provided. The findings in the Ariyalur district shows that 100 per cent of the respondents have agreed that water facilities, shed and crèches were provided at the worksite A few 6 among 107 of them have stated that first aid was not given properly.
3. **Mamidipally Rajanna (2009),** who studied the impact of NREGS in Andra Pradeh States that social audits and accurate records are to be concentrated while the findings from the panchayat presidents and beneficiaries more than half 55 per cent have expressed that social audits were done regularly every half year and 100 per cent of them have stated that records were maintained properly.
4. **Singh (2008),** conducted a study in Uttar Pradesh. He came to a conclusion that there is a need for spreading awareness among the people. Rao (2007) who made a study of Karnataka and Andhra Pradesh has also stated the same. The findings in Ariyalur district, Tamilnadu (2009) shows that the awareness on the scheme is better when compared to other states and previous years. 100 per cent of the respondents are aware of the scheme and the benefits they would get from it.
5. **The findings by Rao (2008),** and the findings of this survey conclude that the scheme has reduced migration of rural area to the urban locations.

Suggestions

Based on the researcher's frequent visits to the villages where the data was collected and through observation and interactions with the general people and based on the findings that have emerged from this study a few suggestions for better implementation are here by submitted.

Suggestions to the Government

Men are paid less (Rs. 80/day) in NREGS when compared to other works where they get more (Rs.100 / day) this could be taken into consideration. The scheme has been designed to give equal salary to men and women. The minimum limit can be raised to Rs.100 / day for both men and women. However providing more wages for men would result in better quantity of work.

The survey points out that there are people in the group of workers (20 people) who do not involve whole heartedly in the work but get equal wages as those who do majority of the work. In order that every individual gives equal share of work monitoring based on norms could be strengthened which also leads to completion of work and better quality of work. Self Help Groups could also be used to better monitoring.

The workers under the NREGS were agricultural labourers previously and agriculture has faced deficiency of labourers particularly women, which could be avoided by carefully planning the 100 days work during times of less agricultural work.

NREGS chooses irrigation, rural roads, water conservation etc., as works under the scheme which involves a certain level of danger to the workers initially. Therefore machineries can be used initially to clear out hard surfaces, thorny bushes and for those works that could cause danger to workers.

NREGS provides work for aged people and physically challenged people which is very much welcomed by the public. There could be definite works such as arranging water facilities, shades, looking after crèches etc., can be given to them.

The findings show that there are no limitations as to the number of days and number of workers for completion of a particular work which could be standardized. So that the works can be finished in a particular time limit.

Suggestions to Future Researchers

The future researchers could make a study on the feasibility of bring out standardized norms for the NREGS works on topics related to monitoring, work allotment, registering people and age limit.

The salient features of the scheme have not fully reached the beneficiaries which could separately be taken for study by the future researchers.

The study has excluded those beneficiaries who did not complete 100 days. The future researchers can take up for their study those people so that their problems could be analysed and reasons for non completion could be evaluated.

Suggestion to Social Workers

The social workers who play a vital role in strengthening the government schemes on various levels could help in monitoring and implementation of the scheme so that the aims and objectives of the government are achieved.

The social workers could also take up volunteering work of educating the beneficiaries, implementers and farmers on health and hygiene, saving habits and so on. This could further add value to the scheme.

CONCLUSION

The present study is a humble attempt to describe the important variables such as implementation of NREGS, Awareness on the scheme, salient features of the programme and employment opportunities created by the scheme while considering their socio-demographic characteristics and analyzing the associations among the different key variables. The study has brought out important findings which indicate significant differences between the NREGS works and its relation to the agricultural works, the benefits as against the drawbacks and some valuable suggestions. This study will form a basis for more methodologically sound and rigorous research studies in the broad area of norms related to NREGS works and awareness and reach of the salient features of the scheme.

❐

Bibliography

1. ANANDAKUMAR, N.(1986). A way of life. Catcutta: Vivekananda Kendra yogas publication,
2. ASTRAND AND KEARL RODHAL, A.(1977). Text Book of work physiology. New york: Mc Graw Hill Book Co.,
3. CHANDRASEKARAN, K.(1999). Sound Health Throu7gh yoga. Madurai: Prem Kalyan publication.
4. Danielou, N and Alain, K.(1955). The Method of Reintegration. New york: The Murray printing company.
5. GHAROTE, M.L. (1996). Applied yoga. Lonavala kaivalyadhama, S.M.Y.M Samiti.
6. HOWLEY EDWARD, T AND DOM FRANKS, B.(1997). Health Fitness Instructors Hand Book. Human Kinetics: Illinos.
7. LYENKAR, B.K.S (2001). The path of Holistic Health. Great Britain: Darling Kindersley limited.
8. MAZUMDAR, S.(1956). Yogic Exercise – Calcutta: Trichur Longman limited
9. MC ARDLE, AND WILLIAM, D.(1991). Exercise physiology and energy Nutrition and Human performance. Philadelphia: Lea and Febiger publication.
10. MEHRA, B.K. AND LASHKARI, B.I (1992) High Blood pressure – causes, prevention and Tratment. Delhi: orient paperbacks.
11. MOREHOUSE, AND LAWRENCE, E.(1980). A New Light for Asthmatics. Calcutta : Vivekananda Kendra Yoga publication.

JOURNALS

12. NAYAR, H.S (1975). Effects of yogic Exercises on Human physical Efficienty. India journal of Medical research, 63.
13. POLLOCK, L (1971). Effects of walking on body composition and cardiovascular function of Middle Aged Men. Journal of Applied physiology, 30:1
14. SAHAY, B.K. (1992). Biochemical parameters Normal volunteers Before and After yogic practices. Indian Journal of Medical Research, 76.
4. UDUPA, K.N.(1971). Study on pulse Rate and Metabolic Response to the practice of. Yoga in young Normal volunteers. Journal of Research in Indian Medicine, 75.
15. UPPAL, A.K. (1982). Effect of Endurance, Training of Resting and Exercise Blood pressure of secondary school Boys. SNIPES Journal, 5 No : 1
16. WARIS QIDWAI. K. (2000). Effect of Dietary Garlic on the Blood pressure in Humans. Journal of the Pakistan Medical Association, 50:6.

THESES

17. CHINNASAMY, R.(1992). Effects of Asanas and physical Exercises on selected physiological and biochemical variable among school boys, Bharathidasan University, Trichy.
18. DHANARAJ, A.K. (1995). Effect of selected yogic and physical Exercises on flexibility and cardio respiratory endurance of Madurai Kamarajar university players, M.K. university,
19. KRISHNAN, ARUNAGIRI. (1990). Effect of selected yogic and Bharathiyam Exercises on physiological variables among school Boys, Alagappa university, karaikudi.
20. RADHALAKSHMI, K. (1997). Effect of selected yogic and physical Exercises on physical fitness of school girls in kerala, Alagappa University, Karaikudi.
21. VICTOR RONRCY, R.(1985). Comparative study of the pulse Rate and systolic Blood pressure of college sprinters and long Distance Runners, Alagappa university, Karaikudi.
22. Alysia Y.Blandon, susan D.calkins (2007), The longitudinal associations between maternal parenting behavior and toddler risk with children's emotional and social competence, Development and Psychopathology/ volume22/Issue01/february2007
23. Benally-Herbert-John (1994); Navajo philosophy of learning and pedagogy. Journal-of-Navajo Education; Vol.12 N1 Page no.23-31

24. Bennett,-christene-K,(1991) staff development in light of Maslow's theory. Journal-of-staff-development; V12 N4 Page No.10-14
25. Bertalanffy, L (1960). Problems in life. New York; Harpter torch books.
26. Bhushan.A (1994), Social maturity across sex and family vocations, M.B.BUCH, The Educational Research Volume -2
27. Bynum, Louise. L; Seaman, Michael.A(1993); motivations of third-age students in learning-in retirement institutes. Journal, continuing-Higher Education-Review; Vol 57 N1-2 page no12-22
28. Castejon, Juan Luis (2008), studied on differences Socio-Emotional Competence Profile in University students from different Disciplinary Area, Electronic Journal of Research in Educational Psychology, v6n2p339
29. Desai, Hemant.K (1991); Self help as an adjunct to psychotheraphy; issue of awareness, motivation and self actualization.
30. Friedman Sara R, Rapport lisa J (2003), Social and Emotional competence were evaluated using self-report and behavioral measures in adults with attention deficient hyperactivity disorder (ADHD) and controls, Neuropsychology, vol(1), Jan 2003, 50-58
31. Holeyannavar, P.G.,Itagi, S.K (2011) emotional competence and stressors of primary school teachers, Educational Research and Reviews, Vol 6 n20 p1005.
32. Kathuria.M (1974), "Personality determination of vocational maturity and cancer inductiveness". Dissertation abstracts.
33. Katja Petrowski (2008), studied children's social-emotional competence development
34. Lewis, Joan.D(1995); A study of self actualization and self concept in intellectually gifted students. Journal Psychology in the schools, Vol.32N 1 Page No.52-61
35. Lynn R. Offermann, James R.Baily(2007) studied the relative contributions of emotional competence and cognitive ablity to individual,Child and Adolescent Psychiatry and Mental Health 2007,
36. Malin A.J (1990) A study on the relationship of social maturity with classroom climate and Academic Achievement. Third survey of Research in Education Buch M.B.547-53.
37. Marion. E.young (2009), studied the aspects of emotional competence that protect people from stress, anxiety and depression, and help to promote positive affect, British Journal of Guidance & Counselling, VOL34NO2P231-243

38. Mulia R.D (1991) Journal of education and Psychology, Volume 48 p.145.
39. Parthiban.M(2008), Adjustment behaviour of college students in relation to their self actualization Master of philosophy in University of Madras Chennai.
40. Pattraman Junpangerh (1986) "Social maturity of higher secondary students. Dissertation Abstract International.
41. Pennington, Martha.C(1992). Motivating English language teacher through job enrichment journel language; culture, and curriculum; Vol.5 N3 Page No 199-218
42. Prema.S (2011), Emotional competence, family environment, self concept adolescence in relation to academic achievement M.Phil education, Tamil Nadu Teacher Education University, Chennai.
43. Rogers, C.R.(1963) The actualizing tendency in relation to "motive" and consciousness. In M.Jones (Ed), Nebraska symposium on motivation (pp.1-24) vcf nebrasua press.
44. Saovaluk thongamkhom (1983), study on social maturity as a function of some Psychosocial adjustment factors of higher secondary students fourth survey of research in Education Buch, M.B.Volume 1(p.261)
45. Sarojamma, Y.H. (1990), A comparative study of reaching ability and social maturity of over normal and under achiever of standard VIII, fourth survey of research in education, Buch, volume 2 (p.111)
46. Thiagu.S (2005) Creativity and Social Maturity of secondary grade Teacher Trainees Master of philosophy in University of Madras Chennai.
47. Agarwal, Archana (2000).A study of some educational problems of scheduled caste students. Indian journal of educational research, 19(1), 37-41.
48. Aldwin C.M and Revenson. T.A., (1987). Does coping help? A re-examination of the relation between coping and mental health journal of personality and social psychology, 53:337-348.
49. Alessio, Judith (1996) a study examined retelling in the improvement of reading comprehension scores at urban, lower socio economic fourth grades. Record 2 of search Eric -1996.
50. Anshel M.H and Anderson D.I (2002).Coping with acute stress in sport: linking athletes coping style, coping strategies, affect and motor performance anxiety, stress and coping, 15,193-209.
51. Anshel M.H and Wells B (2000).Source of acute stress and coping styles in competitive sport, stress and coping, 13, 1-26.

52. Anshel M.H, Jamieson J and Raviv.S(2001). Coping behavior acute stress among male and female Israeli athletes, international journal of sports psychology, 32,271-289.
53. AnshelM.H (2001) qualitative validation of a model for coping with acute stress in sports. Jornalof sports behavior, 24,223-246.
54. Bartone, Paul.T (2009).Academic stress and health, Exploring the moderating Role of personality Hardiness, Scandinavian journal of educational research, V53 N5- p421 –429.
55. Baues Ann Leslie (1995) measured the effect of participation in a peer facilitation project on sixth grades self esteem, social maturity and patterns of social choice. Ph.D, kent state university.
56. Bedi (1982) a study on aspirations as related to socio economic status, intelligence and sex, PhD (education) pan U. 1982, third survey of research in education.
57. Best, Abha Remi (1990) vocational stress in relation to socio-economic status and belongingness to weaker sections of society independent study Kurnool university ERIC funded) p. 816 – 817.
58. Blazer (2010).Student stress, information capsule, research services, Miami-dadecountry public schools, Vol 1006.
59. Brickamn, P., Coates D., & Janoff-Bulman. R. (1978), Lottery winners and accident victims: is happiness relative? Journal of personality and social psychology, 36, 917-927.
60. Carver, C.S. Scheier M.F and Weintraub.J.K (1989).Assessing coping strategies: A theoretically based approach, journal of personality and social psychology, 56,267-283.
61. Chanda, Sunanda, (1990). Study on self-concept parental influence of socio economic status and sex in education to career choice attitude among high school students. Dissertation abstract.
62. Chander. Pradhat (1990) " a study of the educational and vocational interest patterns of tribal high school students and their relationship with intelligence, socio-economic status and educational achievement fifth survey of research in education, vol. II p. 1516.
63. Chapaman, Paula L and Ronald L Mullis, (2000)."Racial difference in adolescent coping and self-esteem" journal of genetic psychology vol. 161, pp. 152-160.
64. Chitra, J.Uma, A.P.Thiagarajan and S.Krishna, Santhana (1995). Psycho-socio educational factors of scheduled castes students in higher secondary school. The progress of Education, LXX(4), 87-89.
65. Compass BE, Connor-Smith J.K, Saltzmann H, Thomsen A.H and Wadsworth M.E(2001).Coping with stress during childhood and adolescence: problems, progress and potential in theory and research.

66. Creamer, Don-G (1992). Using a developmental model of maturity. Dissertation abstract from new directions for community colleges, Vol. 20 n3/p. 737-82.

67. Crocker P.R.E and Graham T.R (1995). coping by competitive athletes with performance stress: gender differences and relationships with affect. The sport psychologist, 9:325-338.

68. Daniel F.K (2010).Academic stress and anxiety in children, the role of paternal support, Journal of child and family studies, V19 N1- p90-100.

69. David C (2009). Chinese international students academic stress in the united status. College student journal, V43 N4-p 939-960.

70. Dhami G.S (1974) intelligence, emotional maturity and socio- economic status and factors indicative of success in scholastic achievement buch,

71. Diner, E., and Larson, R.J. (1984). Subjective well being. Psychological bulletin, p. 542-575.

72. Diser, E., Sanwick, E., Scidlitz, L. and Biner. M (1993). The relationship between income and subjective well- being relative or absolute? Social indicators research, 28, 195-223.

73. Doastoor,H.F. (1982). A study of different types of self concept prevalent among nurses, fifth survey of educational research. Dissertation abstract.

74. Dr. Boaz G.D (1971) General Psychology (factors physical and emotional). Board institute of psychological service.

75. Ekusan. A (1994), conducted a study done on the social maturity across sex and family vocations, Buch, MB, the education research, volume II. Cassidy, J.,

76. Farke, R., Buthkobsky, L., & Braungrart, J. (1992). Family- peer connections: the roles of emotional expressiveness within the family and children's understanding of emotions. Child development, 63, 603-618.

77. Fickova E (2000). "Preference of coping strategies in relation to hassles" studia psychological Vol. 42:pp 203-208.

78. Folkman S and Moskowitz J.T (2000).Stress, positive emotion and coping. Current directions in psychological science, 9(4),115-118.

79. Fredrick Millar and ZeitaBeila (1979).studies on emotional maturity buch,1327 IV/V

80. Gerdes and et al (1994).emotional, social and academic adjustment of college students. A longitudinal study of retention journal of counseling and development V 72 n3/p. 281-288.

81. Goardon et al., (1995). Self-concept and motivational patterns of resilient African American high school students. Journal of black psychology; v21 n3, p. 239-255.
82. Gowlnda Reddy (1989) a study of socio economic status and parental education language development in education nov. 1989.
83. GRANDEY, A.A (2000). Emotional regulation in the workplace: a new way to conceptualise emotional labor. Journal of occupational health psychology, 5, 96-110.
84. Grdes et al., (1994). Emotional social and academic adjustment of college students. A longitudinal study of retention. Journal of counseling and development, v. 72 n3/p.281-288
85. Grinert-Wolf et.al (1994) vocational education and socio economic change of the crisis of the dual system of vocational education. Zeits chrift. Fur. Padagogoik. Vol no 3. P. 357 jan. 1994.
86. Gupta, Sceshma (1990) educational as a factor of social adjustment of adolescent girls across different levels of socio economic status PhD (education) Punjab university P.820)
87. Hammer, Allen L. college students, coping counseling services, higher education; individual differences; school counseling; sex differences; stress management, publication date: 1986-04-pages:8Psychological bulletin, 127:87-127.V/II/p-1885.
88. Harnesh. Kaike (1991) a study of anxiety among boys is related to their intelligence and socio economic status. Indian psychological abstracts and views page. 288.
89. Harvkins Denise (993) socio economic family background still a significant influence on SAT scores. Black issues in higher education v.10 n 14 p14-16,. P. 199
90. Hevyer and et al., (1993). The relationship between parental marital status and development of identify and emotional autonomy in college students. Journal of college student development .v. 34, n6, p. 432-436. Nov. 1993.
91. Hunt. T. (1928). The measurement of social intelligence, journal of applied psychology, 12, 317- 334.
92. Kanlukukui, Gay, Hinano (1995). Related emotional maturity in the study of psychology dissertation abstract, 1997.
93. Kellner et al., (1995). A school based anger management programme for developmentally and emotionally disabled high school students; adolescence; p.813-825.
94. Kothi Om Parkash (1989) a study of attitude of students towards religion in relation to personality characteristics intelligence and socio

economic status. PhD education. Punjab university fifth survey of educational research 1988-1992) vol.II.
95. Kumar, Giriesh and R.R.Shankhdhar (1998).Self concept and modes and modes of frustration in urban and rural scheduled castes and non scheduled caste students, Journal of Indian Education ,24(4), 43-48.
96. Lakshmi N(1996). Problem of scheduled castes, Scheduled Tribes and Non Scheduled caste girls of secondary school in Relation to a few social and psychological factors. Unpublished Doctoral Dissertation Education, Bangalore University.
97. Laura.J (2012). Stress and anxiety surrounding forth coming standard assessment tests in English school children, pastoral care in education, V30 N4- p289-302.
98. Leung (2010).A protective factor against the academic stress of school-aged children, Educational psychology, V30 N4- p395-410.
99. Obainkar, Festus (1992) the myth of socio economic dissonance; implications for African- American exceptional students. Contains 34 references record 15 of 15 ERIC 1992-1996.
100. Omoniyi, Tope (1993) price-tagging child bilingualism; an evaluation of policy and the socio-economic and political implications of commercialization of nursery education in Nigeria. Contains 26 references record 14 of 15 – ERIC 1992-1996.
101. Paige D (2009). School Related stress and depression in Adolescents with and without Learning Disabilities, An Exploratory study, Alberta of educational research, V55 N1- p92 – 108.
102. Pomjiyar, Rout et.al (1999) adjustment as a faction of social class and economic status. A social psychological study. Indian journal of psychological issues 1999, 7(2)p.no. 55-58.
103. Revierin, Simard et. al (1992) career paths and socio economic status. Canadian journal of counseling v 26 NL. P15-26. Jan 1992.
104. Richard D(2012). Coping with stress predicts school grades, life safe satisfaction, and feelig about high school, learning and individual difference,V22 N2- p235-241.
105. Robitschek C (1998). Personal Growth Initiative: The construct and its measures. Measurement and Evaluation in Counseling and Development, 30(4), 183-198.
106. Robitschek C (1999).Further validation of the Personal Growth Initiative Scale.Measurement & Evaluation in counseling & Development, 31, 197-210.
107. Robitschek C& Cook S.W(1999).The influence of personal growth initiative and coping styles on career exploration and vocational identity.Journal of Vocational behavior, 54, 127-141.

108. Robitschek, C.(2003).Validity of personal Growth Imitative Scale scores with a Mexican American College Student Population. Journal of Happiness Studies, 9, 13-39.
109. Sarasamma y.h (1990). A comparative study of reading ability and social maturity of over normal and underachievers of standard VII. Ph.D., edu. Bangalore university.
110. Sealdiqui M.M. (1976). Social psychological study of student behaviors wit social reference to indiscipline buch 1327 IV/2
111. Shami, G.S. (1974). Intelligence, emotional maturity and socio-economic status and factors indicative of success in scholastic achievement; buch, V/II/P – 1885.
112. Sharma (1969) influence of socio economic status in the selection of occupations among the boys of higher secondary school in Delhi. Journal of educational research extension 1963. P.No. 30-31.
113. ShoreyH.S , Little T.D, Snyder C.R, Kluck B & Robitschek C(2007). Hope and personal growth initiative: A comparison of positive, future-oriented constructs. Sloan D.M & Marx B.P (2004).Taking pen to hand: Evaluating theories underlying the written disclosure paradigm. Clinical Psychology: Science and Practice, 11,121-137.
114. Shukla S.K and Archana Agarwal (1997).A study of socio-economic status.
115. Smart Reginald (1994) neighborhood socio economic factors in relation to student drug use and programs. Journal of child and adolescent substance. Abuse p. 37-46. 1994.
116. Summons and Pameia (1995) gender, ethnic and socio- economic differences in attainment and progress a longitudinal analysis of student achievement over a years. British educational research. Journal v.21, n4, p. 465-485 September 1995.
117. Talbot J.F and S. Kalpan (1986). Perspectives on wilderness: re-examination the value of extended wilderness experiences. Journal of Environmental Psychology, 6:177-188.
118. Undheim, Johan et.al 91992) socio economic actors and sex differences in an egalitarian educational system. Academic achievement in 16 year old Norwegian students. Scandinavian journal of educational research V36 n 2 p. no. 87-98. 1992.
119. Whitaker A.E &Robitschek C.R (2001). Multidimensional family functioning: Predicting personal growth initiative. Journal of Counseling Psychology,48(4), 420-427.
120. Abzug, Bella., and Davis, Susan. 1998. “India.” Mapping Progress: Assessing Implementation of the Beijing Platform.

121. Budhwar, P. S., Saini, D. S., & Bhatnagar, J. (2005, June). Women in management in the new economic environment: The case of India. Asia Pacific Business Review, 11(2), 179-193.

122. Bunch, Charlotte. "The Intolerable Status Quo: Violence Against Women and Girls." The Progress of Nations 1997 New York: UNICEF

123. Carr, Marilyn., and Chen, Martha., and Jhabvala, Renana. 1996. Speaking Out: Women's Economic Empowerment in South Asia. Southampton Row, London: Intermediate Technology Publications LTD.

124. Differentials by Sex: Evidence from India," Artha Vijnana, Vol. 38, No. 4, pp. 372-386.

125 Gupta, A., Koshal, M., & Koshal R. K. (2006). Women managers in India: Challenges and opportunities. In H. J. Davis, S. R. Chatterjee & M. Heuer (Eds.), Management in India (pp. 285-312). New Delhi: Response Books.

126. Handy, F., Ranade, B., & Kasam, M. (2007, Summer). To profit or not to profit: Women entrepreneurs in India. Nonprofit Management & Leadership, 17(4), 383-401.

105. Heitzman, James and Robert L. Worden, eds., 1996, Area Handbook Series, India–A Country Study, Washington, DC. International Labour Office, 1997, Yearbook of Labour Statistics 1997, Geneva.

127. Khandelwal, P. (2002, April-June). Gender stereotypes at work: Implications for organizations. Indian Journal of Training and Development. XXXII(2), 72-83.

128. National Sample Survey Organization, 1994, Sarvekshana, Vol. 17, No. 3, January-March.

129. Sen, A. (2005). The argumentative Indian: Writings on Indian history, culture and identity. New York: Farrar, Straus and Giroux.

❒